659.2'9'3801

ESSENTIALS OF MARKETING
GENERAL EDITORS: D. W. SMALLBONE AND BERNARD TAYLOR

MARKETING AND PR
MEDIA PLANNING

By the same author

Advertising Today
Dictionary of Marketing and Communication
Press Relations Practice
Planned Public Relations
published by International Textbook Company Ltd

Advertising Made Simple
published by W. H. Allen

Copywriting and its Presentation
Public Relations in World Marketing
by Crosby Lockwood & Son Ltd

Wanted on Holiday
A novel, published by Hodder & Stoughton Ltd

THIS BOOK IS DEDICATED TO MY WIFE, FRANCES

MARKETING AND PR MEDIA PLANNING

by

FRANK JEFKINS
BSc(Econ), BA(Hons), MCAM, MInstM, MIPR, MAIE

PERGAMON PRESS
Oxford · New York · Toronto · Sydney

Pergamon Press Ltd., Headington Hill Hall, Oxford
Pergamon Press Inc., Maxwell House, Fairview Park, Elmsford, New York 10523
Pergamon of Canada Ltd., 207 Queen's Quay West, Toronto 1
Pergamon Press (Aust.) Pty. Ltd., 19a Boundary Street, Rushcutters Bay, N.S.W. 2011, Australia

Copyright © 1974 Frank Jefkins

All Rights Reserved. No part of this publication may be reproduced, stored in a retrieval system, or transmitted, in any form or by any means, electronic, mechanical, photocopying, recording or otherwise, without the prior permission of Pergamon Press Ltd.

First edition 1974

Library of Congress Cataloging in Publication Data

Jefkins, Frank William.
Marketing and PR media planning.

(Essentials of marketing)
Bibliography: p.
1. Public relations. 2. Marketing. I. Title.
HF5415.J44 1974   659.2′9′3801   74–618347
ISBN 0–08–018086–8
ISBN 0–08–018085–X (pbk.)

Printed in Great Britain by A. Wheaton & Co., Exeter

Contents

Acknowledgements		vi
Introduction		vii

PART ONE THE ROLE OF PR IN MARKETING		1
1	*The Marketing Perspectives of Public Relations*	3
2	*PR and the Marketing Mix*	15

PART TWO PUBLIC RELATIONS MEDIA		43
3	*The Nature of the Press*	45
4	*The Nature of Press Relations*	67
5	*Broadcasting*	94
6	*Documentary Films, Video Tapes and Video Discs*	110
7	*Sponsorships*	133
8	*Exhibitions*	152
9	*External House Journals*	164
10	*Seminars and Conferences*	179
11	*Printed Literature and Printing*	187
12	*Metamarketing—A Marketing Myth?*	197

PART THREE PLANNING PR PROGRAMMES		209
13	*Planning PR Programmes*	211
14	*Ten Case Studies*	220
Appendices		
I	*Bibliography*	247
II	*Professional and Vocational Examining Bodies*	249
III	*The Institute of Public Relations Code of Professional Conduct*	250
Index		254

ACKNOWLEDGEMENTS

THE author acknowledges his debt to those scores of students, friends, colleagues and practitioners in the UK and in many parts of the world who responded to his requests for information, case studies, copies of house journals, details of sponsorships. He is especially grateful for the library and research services of the Advertising Association.

INTRODUCTION

"BRITAIN is on the verge of a commercial and industrial revival far larger than any so far seen in the post-war period" said Mr. Peter Walker, the then Secretary for Trade and Industry, when he presented Sir Hugh Fraser with the *Guardian's* Young Businessman of the Year award on 15 March 1973. Mr. Walker went on to say that Britain's growth was coming at a time when the United States, Europe, the Far East, and other parts of the world were presenting massive and fast expanding opportunities. The 1974 crisis did not deny this.

Elsewhere—in both industrial and developing countries—similar prophecies have been made, especially in China, India, Ghana, Malaysia, Nigeria, Singapore, and Tanzania to mention but a few. To promote export trade, Ghana opened four more trade missions in 1973—in Togo, Upper Volta, China and Russia—while Nigeria created an Export Promotion Council and an Export Credit Guarantee Department and is building a permanent trade fair complex near Lagos. And in September 1973 the Duke of Kent opened the British Export Marketing Centre in Tokyo.

If these forecasts and endeavours for the fourth quarter of the twentieth century are meaningful, the message is also that management and marketing needs to become more PR-minded, and public relations needs to become more management- and marketing-minded. This book attempts to show how planned PR, making skilful use of communication media, can aid the many facets of the marketing mix.

There is a mischievous tendency in management and marketing to equate PR with advertising, either as "free publicity" or as a cheap alternative to advertising, and so limit PR to that single though important part of marketing strategy. Those with a broader view see PR as a force which is inevitably associated with most aspects of marketing. And those with real insight recognize PR as being applicable to the total activity of any organization, commercial or otherwise.

Public relations is the business of communicating with every public, internally and externally. This book deals with PR in relation to marketing, a much larger story than mere product publicity, but by no means the whole story. The whole story of PR is, or should be—but seldom is—a major part of management studies. Taken in its larger sense, PR is being superseded by the term public affairs, an equally misleading term. But these are labels, and PR is beset with labels. Finding a new name for PR is like trying to rename the air we breathe.

Sir Hugh Fraser's achievement in rationalizing the House of Fraser group of department stores and taking Harrods into Europe involved a great deal of PR at every level; for to succeed PR must be a management philosophy reaching down from top to bottom of an organization. The marketer who is blessed with a boardroom philosophy that interprets PR as company behaviour will find his efforts enhanced at every stage from product concept right through to after-sales service. PR is not something the marketer can use or reject, for he cannot avoid having relations with other people such as his sales force, distributors, users and customers. What he does about these relationships, how he integrates his communication with them, and employs the techniques and media of communication, is the measure of his use of professional PR. Merely to seek a "free puff" in the press and call that PR is to adopt a kind of idiot amateurism by comparison with the art of planning, budgeting and executing a PR programme that complements the entire marketing strategy.

It is therefore no exaggeration to say that many companies would be spared their losses on new product failures—whether test marketed or not—if those responsible for marketing had, for example, used PR techniques not only to seek market response but especially to educate markets in preparation for a new product launch. Some products are launched with such secrecy that potential customers never do understand them and consequently lack the confidence to make purchases. PR is very much concerned with creating the understanding and confidence without which sales are impossible. The only reason why the circus drum is successful in pulling in the customers is that the customers already know what a circus is. Circuses enjoy marvellous PR.

PART ONE

The Role of PR in Marketing

CHAPTER 1

The Marketing Perspectives of Public Relations

Introduction—PR is Ubiquitous

The practice of public relations is not unlike the ability to drive a car. It is very common. And there are good and bad PR practitioners, like good and bad drivers. However, just as it is obviously wrong to say that only bus companies employ drivers, so is it untrue to confine the use of PR to marketers. In their failure to use PR, some marketing organizations are like bus companies without drivers. But the use of PR techniques is as widespread as the use of driving skills, and there are probably as many people engaged in some form of PR as there are holding driving licences.

That may seem a surprising analogy since PR is so commonly regarded as a rather specialized mystique, and only about ten thousand people in the UK and about one hundred thousand in the USA are gainfully employed in PR. As this author has so frequently said elsewhere, only a hermit has no need for PR. Perhaps "public relations" is a regrettable bit of jargon which invites its critics to search in all sorts of nooks and crannies for supposedly special meanings. So many people—and particularly opinionated television presenters and personalities—invent their own misunderstandings of the subject. Yet all we mean by PR is clearly expressed and clearly understood communication between an organization and all the different kinds of people with whom it is in contact. The object of the communication is to achieve understanding of the organization's policy, activities, services, products and people, according to the particular publics addressed. This also involves understanding how these publics regard the organization.

This rather matter-of-fact statement may be a disappointment to those who imagine PR as gin-swilling press parties, heavy lunches, "conning the press", "twisting editors' arms", having "good Fleet Street contacts", or, as Benny Green, the *Observer*'s TV critic, said on 8 April 1973, "*lying*". It may be true to say that PR is sometimes contorted into what management and marketing people would like it to be. They had better read this book.

But having given that broad description of our subject, it now has to be seen in the particular and limited sense of its relevance to marketing. And right away it is necessary to stress that PR is a more versatile marketing aid than advertising, a point easily misunderstood if we insist on regarding PR as some other form of advertising. PR and advertising are worlds apart, and this distinction should be clearly understood if this book is to be of value to the marketer. Moreover, a mention in the press or on radio or TV is not a "free advertisement" if only that nothing in this world is free, and an item of news is not an advertisement. Doctors have been struck off because their accusers did not know the difference between PR and advertising. It may, of course, be publicity which is not the same thing. An advertisement is a deliberate announcement using paid-for space or time, the message being precisely what the advertiser wishes to say within the limits of the law and voluntary codes. But publicity can result from any announcement made by anyone anywhere, over which the person or organization concerned has no control. As one can see from a quick study of any newspaper, the news is a mixture of good and bad publicity. Some of it may originate from PR sources, but there is no guarantee that the editorial treatment of a story will be favourable to its sponsor. On the other hand, no advertisement manager would dare to change the copy of an advertisement because he disagreed with the claims made.

"Free advertisement" is sometimes applied to PR stories because a rate-card value is placed on them, but this is false for two reasons. Firstly, editorial space is priceless and in reputable journals in most parts of the world it cannot be bought. Hosting does occur on some less reputable European newspapers. Secondly, PR is a costly, labour-intensive business, which is why most advertising agencies that tried to offer press relations as part of the service had to stop doing so before it bankrupted them. It is rare that fortuitous publicity occurs, as when Princess Anne, during her wedding eve TV interview, told 15 million British viewers that her favourite drink was Coke!

PR—Marketing's Extra Dimension

It is a paradox that the affinities between marketing and PR are so great that both tend to claim a monopoly of the same aspects of business communication. In this book it will be assumed that any form of communication between an organization and its many publics must come within the scrutiny of PR. Whatever the purpose of the communication, it is bound to have a PR content for it cannot avoid affecting the attitude or understanding of the recipient. Consequently, although this book concentrates on the marketing function of business, the principles of PR apply to the total organization, all its acts and all its personnel.

Every marketing activity has its PR complement. So does the behaviour of the chief executive, the courtesy of the staff, the appearance of company vehicles, the tone of commercial correspondence, and Stock Exchange quotations. PR is ubiquitous. And it is in the marketing sphere that PR is most omnipresent if only that the marketer has to deal with so many different groups of people in such large numbers and so frequently. The marketer's opportunities for communication are so constant and widespread that PR needs to rank high in his job specification. It is rather like saying that a good motorist is a good map reader.

PR can thus be applied to the entire marketing mix. If the marketer objects to this and retorts that what this author calls PR is what he calls marketing, he is right but only up to a point. That vital point is that PR adds a refinement that is capable of making marketing more effective, just as ability to read a map makes the driver a more effective traveller. To take a simple example: a merchandising scheme can be a powerful marketing device, but it will have PR value if it not only boosts sales but enhances reputation, which in turn may eventually serve as a sales bonus. Conversely, a merchandising scheme that misfires and provokes complaints and sales resistance will be bad PR, ruining reputation and reducing future sales.

In relating PR principles to everything the marketer does, and without meaning to usurp the marketing role, this book aims to give the marketer an extra dimension, like adding rearview and wing mirrors to a car so that the driver can communicate better with other road users. An interesting example of the application of this extra dimension is to be seen in the example on page 27 of the Gillette test-marketing scheme which included press relations even at that early stage.

Advertising and PR Distinguished

Advertising makes known in order to sell, and its message may be as biased as the advertiser wishes, subject to legal and ethical restraints; but PR sets out to foster understanding, and that calls for hard facts that can be evaluated by the editor, producer, reader, listener or viewer. If these facts are biased, they become *propaganda* (if they promote an opinion, cause or belief) or *advertising* (if they promote a commercial product or service).

A very large amount of PR, probably the greater part of it, is to do with voluntary bodies, hospitals, universities, the police, fire services, local and central government, where the non-advertising and informative nature of PR is more obvious. A fire brigade does not advertise for fires.

Since this book specifically relates PR to marketing, it is important to establish its unbiased, factual, informative, and therefore *authoritative* characteristics. For if a PR message is disbelieved, thought to be prejudiced, or seen as a whitewashing operation, the communication is worthless. A distinction is sometimes made between "informative" and "promotional" PR, but this is nonsense and the principles of PR negate this attempted distinction. The best and most elementary form of PR is a conversation between two people who will mutually benefit from what they learn from one another. A rumour-ridden "grapevine" or the "leaking" of stories is the antithesis of PR, both being abuses of straight-forward communication.

Antipathy between Marketing and PR

Some marketers tend to see PR as a doubtful usage of unquantifiable devices (e.g. wining and dining), little short of bribery and corruption, while PR people often see marketing as part of the doubtful persuasive practices of selling and advertising. This means we have two blinkered professions, each accusing the other of being what they are not, a sort of duplicated intellectual snobbery or shortsighted duplicity!

This is partly because marketers do not always appreciate the non-commercial editorial or production side of media and its objectives of pleasing, keeping or gaining readers, viewers or listeners. On the other hand, PR people often have a journalistic or intellectual contempt for business. Perhaps this is part of the British temperament: in the USA there are fewer inhibitions. A welcome start in bringing the two sides together lies in the enlightened syllabus of the CAM Certificate in PR which expects students to study both business organization and marketing. A reciprocal move is vital in the larger field of marketing education where PR is largely ignored or relegated to a quick look at press relations.

Thus, while marketing may be the poor relation of PR it is sometimes the skeleton in the marketing cupboard. This is an idiotic situation, probably caused by marketing buying PR services in a limited way to augment its range of activities instead of management buying PR services for its entire operation. A more sensible situation exists in those companies where management sees the need for corporate and financial PR, has a PR director on the board, and integrates the PR responsibilities of the financial, production and marketing elements of the business. In a firm where PR is a mere whisper in the marketing department the situation can be compared to a firm which permits only its marketing department to have a personnel officer.

The first step towards demolishing marketing's antipathy towards our subject is to admit its existence. Public relations is rather like the weather; good or bad, it exists whether we like it or not. It will not go away. That is why PR is so important to the marketer. He need not advertise or use wholesalers, his vehicles need not be lavishly painted, and there are other ways of selling besides using salesmen, *but he cannot avoid having public relations.*

That is not really as audacious as it sounds.

Whether he suffers from the public relations that occur willy nilly, or whether he makes a conscious effort to adopt a PR philosophy (a mode of behaviour) and integrate communications in a purposeful manner is a question of his mental maturity as a marketer. Otherwise, PR will be regarded as an extra, a luxury, as something to have or not have, like a mistress or an overdraft. Moreover, it is not necessary to employ either a PRO or a PR consultant to engage in PR any more than it is necessary to have a meteorologist to endure a climate. Directly there is a human relationship there is communication and that is all PR is about. Two people talking, social interaction, is PR in practice. It is a sociological phenomenon, not the manipulation of it. That we can leave to propaganda.

At its best, PR is the elementary ability to communicate, which means to be able to talk and listen equally well. Take this a step further and it means the ability to explain, inform, and educate and to monitor the opinions, criticisms and wishes of everyone important to the firm. The listening part is too often overlooked, but it often implies that old-fashioned cliché of the local tradesman "service and satisfaction". The affinities between PR and marketing are very real, for modern marketing produces at a profit what people will buy. The feedback of market intelligence through PR techniques is a valuable part of desk research.

All this means that a PR-minded businessman understands the need to inform other people and to know what they are thinking and saying. It has been said that "advertising is what we say about ourselves but PR is what other people say about us". One of the oddities about some business management—and that includes marketing—is its reticence. More conscious communication between management and men would greatly improve industrial relations. In one of Britain's largest firms, marketing millions of pounds worth of products annually, eighteen out of thirty-five industrial disputes have been through "misunderstanding". Such stoppages are a marketer's nightmare. While this particular company is well staffed with PROs and press officers at marketing level, there is obviously a lack of PR in the boardroom. This was very apparent some years ago when the same company botched a take-over bid. This can be compared with a world famous international company based in Holland which, at the time of writing, has had only a half-day strike since the Second World War.

So, far from needing a press officer in the marketing department, the marketer's efforts can be sabotaged if there is not a strong PR element in the boardroom, preferably in the chief executive's mental make-up.

The Image

What impression, what idea, what *image* is held of the firm, its policy, products, services, staff, distributors? Is it a correct or a mistaken image, a deserved or a cruel one? Is it a deservedly poor impression that can be changed only if the company makes a radical effort to transform itself, and so *earn* a better reputation? Goodwill is another vital area in which PR performs its communication function. How can a firm sell if it lacks the goodwill of the distributive trade or of the buying public or both? Does it bother about trade relations? Some firms are astonishingly lax in this respect, depending solely on their salesmen and disregarding the fact that this eyeball-to-eyeball relationship occurs only once in six weeks. What does the distributor see in the press, hear on radio and TV, learn within his trade or glean from other salesmen during the gap in the journey cycle? What image does the salesman have to contend with?

It is not the job of PR to make excuses for boardroom blunders or production problems. The PRO is not an apologist for irresponsible management, bad design, deficient packaging, poor manufacturing standards, unreliable deliveries, wrong choice of distributors, inefficient after-sales or parts service, slovenly correspondence or irritating account rendering. It is the job of PR to advise that these things be put right, and to proclaim the good news when that advice has been taken. The good PR practitioner is no flatterer. Unlike the advertising agent who butters up the client to keep the account, the PR consultant may need vinegar to justify his fee. And to be worthy of his salary the staff PRO may have to be an unpopular, thick-skinned trouble-shooter.

Through its communication network, PR can often provide management with an early warning system. Reluctance by customers to buy a splendid product because of one of the breakdowns in elementary good relations mentioned above is a direct criticism of marketing skills. This is where the interplay of PR and marketing can be observed, for PR is both the marketer's conscience and his guardian angel. The marketer who fails to comprehend the significance of PR is a liability to his employers.

This liability may exist in the use of packaging or additives that give a sales plus but add to pollution problems. Or claims may be exploited which excite protests from consumer protection societies. Let's face it: if industry adopted a policy of overall public relations in every sphere of its administration, production and distribution there would be no need for consumerism. *Which* magazine would be reduced to reporting the general competition for proof of excellence, Ralph Nader would be playing gramophone records to steady his nerves, the Trade Descriptions Act and the Fair Trading Act could be repealed, and weights and measures inspectors would be grossly underworked, if companies adopted the PR principle of being jealous of their reputations. But how can PR be seen by journalists as anything but lying, how can marketers be encouraged to appreciate PR as something more than "free publicity", when management indulges in or accepts practices which provoke public suspicion and contempt? The classic example is perhaps that of the American car industry where management has reluctantly forsaken its belief that safety is a negative selling proposition, and followed the lead given by Mercedes-Benz of Germany. In other words, marketers need to put considerable pressure on management if their products are to sell under a helpful corporate image. The consumer is on the warpath, and no wonder!

However, it is not always wilful management policy that makes the marketer's life a misery. Neglect of PR by the marketer himself can create a bad company image which works against sales. Here are a few examples.

Example 1. Confectionery Manufacturer

A well-known confectionery manufacturer, whose products are unquestionably among the very best so that there is an excellent *product* image, used such high-pressure sales methods that resentful retailers retaliated by stocking as little of the firm's range as would satisfy minimum customer requests. When this manufacturer ran a heavily advertised merchandising offer it was difficult to find shops which stocked the bar of chocolate from which wrappings were required for the offer. And when this same company advertised a competition on TV, shop assistants had no entry forms—or did not want to distribute them. Here are clashes between over-zealous selling-in and the destruction of good dealer relations, resulting in that marketing crime, inadequate distribution.

Example 2. Shoe Retailer

A girl bought a pair of shoes from a well-known chain of shoe stores. On the first day of wearing, one of the heels snapped off. She took the shoes back to the shop, expecting either a replacement or a cash refund. The manageress retorted: "We're not Marks and Spencer, you know!" and only the persistence of the girl's father secured a cash refund. The management of that multiple shoe dealer had obviously failed to train its staff in customer relations.

Example 3. Unconvinced Stockist

A paint manufacturer produced a new kind of paint and, relying on its good reputation, advertised the product, giving names and addresses of stockists. But when do-it-yourself enthusiasts responded to the advertising and asked for the product in the shops, they found that the sales assistants were derisive about the claims made in the advertising. The trade was so ill-informed about the product that the men behind the counter (whose advice is often asked) actually blocked sales.

Example 4. Uninformed Travel Agents

The travel agent is another retailer whose advice is sought by customers who are naturally unfamiliar with new ideas in foreign holidays, cruises, car ferries and transport. The travel agent is expected to know, and it is not sufficient for him just to thrust a full-colour brochure into the customer's hands. When one of the Continental car ferry services was first introduced, travel agents were hesitant to recommend it because they lacked knowledge of the ports used and their accessibility. That car ferry suffered from poor business in its first year.

Those four examples suggest lack of marketing foresight, which is another very good name for PR. Now let us take some examples where PR-orientated marketing made all the difference.

Example 1. Right Size for the Job

A certain household product was retailed in a range of can sizes, but when a customer asked for the product he was nearly always handed what was mistakenly thought to be the popular size, and the size most generally stocked. Here was a break-down in communication between the manufacturer and the distributor, and again between him and the consumer. Each can size was meant to serve a specific purpose, rather like saying this can of beans is an individual portion, the next size up is sufficient for two, and the third is the family size. A further difficulty was that the customer, not knowing the significance of the different sizes, could suffer a disappointing result which could justify a complaint. This example shows a triple dilemma in marketing communication which is clearly bad PR and lack of trade and consumer education, leading to loss of both customer and dealer confidence.

The problem was solved in two ways which show the interlocking effect of PR, point-of-sale and advertising in a process of total communication.

A "beanstalk" display stand was designed to carry the range of can sizes, each having a panel stating "enough for . . .". The same idea was translated into press advertising. This encouraged the consumer to ask "what size do I need for . . . ?" and for the sales assistant to consult the "beanstalk" display and sell the right quantity for the job.

(*N.B.* The same problem occurs in supermarkets which seldom stock the larger, more economic, sizes of some products, to mention only toothpaste and eye lotion.)

Example 2. The Tourist and Packaged Tours

A glance at a number of packaged tour and cruise brochures will reveal the extent to which the promoters try to understand clients' worries and in so doing create confidence in the offered service. This is mail-order trading where armchair decisions demand credibility. Money has to be deposited months ahead. The geography may mystify the reader. Fears about food, climate, clothes, language, exchange rates, permissible luggage weights have to be met, and some tour operators are to be congratulated on their meticulous and intelligent efforts to dissolve doubts. This is, of course, very different from romantic descriptions of blue skies, perpetual sunshine and glorious views, the accuracy of some having been challenged in the courts under the Trade Descriptions Act, 1968. A good sea view from the bedroom window should not require a periscope. Even so, tour operators complain that getting potential clients to read the carefully-worded advice is a PR problem in itself.

Example 3. Measurements of Concentrates and Dosages

It can be confusing, misleading or dangerous if a chemical or drug has to be measured from a container, and disappointing results may follow the wrong measurement of harmless products. Some instructions refer to "tablespoons" or "5 ml doses (medicinal spoonfuls") and no such spoons may be available. A "heaped lidful" is not very precise either. Measured dose sachets, devices for measuring drops, and bottle caps which accept the equivalent of, say, a tablespoonful, are infinitely better, easing the user's mind and so producing confident application. Once again, we see the affinity between marketing and PR in simple human relations that can spell repeat sales and recommendations. This example also shows how PR enters into early stages of the marketing mix when packaging and labelling are being considered. The PR consequences of marketing start with the product concept, with thoughtfulness and the sensible anticipation of possible disaster.

Example 4. A Teaching Machine

This is an example where the intervention of a PR consultant caused a revolutionary marketing situation. The manufacturer had invested in the design and development of an ingenious teaching machine which had undergone successful tests in a government establishment. Now, the manufacturer wanted to market the machine, recover his investment and make a profit. He appointed a sales manager and engaged a PR consultant, but the latter was doubtful about the acceptability of the machine to teachers. He took the precaution of asking for a survey to be conducted before any marketing action was taken. As a result of the findings of a postal questionnaire submitted to departmental heads in appropriate colleges, the machine was abandoned. If management and boffins had used the PR tactic of communicating with the market in the first instance, the machine would never have got beyond the drawing board. But research and development can often be of a hit-or-miss affair, sometimes through fear of industrial espionage.

The marketer may object that this was a marketing and not a PR responsibility, that market research is the business of marketing. Actually, it was an example of the sensitiveness of a marketing-orientated PR consultancy. Many such consultancies have been created in recent years, two of the best known in Britain being Winkler Marketing Communication Ltd (see James Hayes and Sons case study) and Paul Winner Marketing Communications Ltd whose very business names speak for themselves. Another, of international repute, is Lippincott & Marguilles of New York, Toronto and London who are consultants in marketing, communications and design. Increasingly, PR consultants are becoming marketing-orientated. They cannot exist in a press relations vacuum. That is why the ex-journalist PRO who thinks selling is a dirty word is becoming more and more a liability in PR.

Example 5. Franchise for an Imported Service

A company with servicing teams strategically placed throughout the country was suffering from severe peaks and troughs owing to the seasonal appeals of its work. The technical director read of a compatible service which could be operated throughout the year, but there were two snags. First, an unsuccessful venture of a similar kind had produced a warning from a government research station while the successful application was patented in a foreign country. The UK rights were obtained, but it was still necessary to overcome the scepticism aroused by the official warning. For some eighteen months a PR programme was mounted, consisting of free applications in places which produced excellent press coverage, especially in the trade and technical press. Once the value of the service had been proved beyond all dispute it was nationally advertised. Resulting business was so good that a separate division was formed in the company to handle this service alone. But had the service been advertised *before* the market had been educated, the venture would probably have flopped unless it had been supported by such a weight of advertising that the selling price would have been much higher. As it was, a comparatively small outlay on PR made it possible for eventual advertising to produce profitable business at a reasonable price.

From these examples, and from what has been said earlier in this chapter, it should be clear that PR is simply good business.

CHAPTER 2

PR and the Marketing Mix

THE previous chapter will have demonstrated that PR, in relation to marketing, can be independent of advertising, and may well precede and anticipate it. In fact, advertising may not work without preliminary PR. More important still, PR may concern every part of the marketing mix. By analysing the marketing mix we can now see how PR is or can be useful to each element. Not all these applications may be regarded by the marketer as PR, either because he gives them other labels or because he does not label them at all. An analogy may be taken from the modern health service where the variety of treatments has increased with identification of conditions never previously classified.

Public Relations Defined

A simple definition, and a slight variation on that of the Institute of Public Relations, is that PR consists of all forms of planned communication, outwards and inwards, between an organization and its publics for the purpose of achieving specific objectives concerning mutual understanding.

That is a deliberately broad definition, but unlike the IPR definition it includes *objectives*. The tangibility of PR depends on its success in achieving predetermined results, for the cost-effectiveness of PR can only be measured against set targets. This will be discussed more fully in Chapter 13, but from now on the reader should try to think of PR as a marketing aid which can be used quite deliberately, not something haphazard like hoping that a good story will "break". Moreover, we shall be discussing the use of numerous media, not only the news media and press cuttings. The definition may therefore be taken to embrace each and every communication aspect of the marketing mix. These individual aspects are best considered in the following more or less chronological sequence.

1. Conception, including Research and Development

Despite the growing tendency to rationalize and impose certain restrictions on consumer choice—a trait of economic marketing in the seventies when it became necessary to compromise consumer sovereignty with rising costs—the birth of a modern product or service remains customer-orientated. And despite the strictures of certain marketing theorists, the more successful firms still test-market before launching new products. Gillette are even wise enough to incorporate PR in their test-marketing. So, there is still no point in attempting to thrust something new on the market: it is more economical to produce and sell at a profit what the market will buy. The exception may be the product ahead of its time or subject to market conservatism as in our case study of the Hope Anti-Jack-Knife device.

New product development may require field research, but inexpensive desk research can include feedback from the market as part of the normal monitoring work of the PR department or consultancy. As the "eyes and ears" of the organization, the PR staff can collate, interpret and report on what distributors, users, consumers and critics are saying. True, this is not statistically representative, but complaints, misconceptions, and suggestions do not have to be. After all, one complaint can be one too many, and it may be foolish to say "We haven't had *many* complaints." The marketer should be grateful for complaints which provide the opportunity for eradicating faults. Some firms are shy of inviting complaints as if looking for trouble is negative and needless. The firm that welcomes complaints will always create confidence and invite more business, for the establishment of consumer communication is something to cherish. A firm that is remote from its millions of customers can insert a packer's number in the goods, while a retail firm with immediate customer contact can exchange goods or make cash refunds on the premises.

The Necchi Lydia automatic sewing machine was marketed at its comparatively low price by discovering how many of the sophisticated embroidery stitches were actually sewn by users of more expensive machines. They were then able to market a machine that offered what most people wanted at a price which a larger number of people were likely to pay. This was excellent PR-orientated research and development to which, for good measure, the Padua designers added extremely simple operation.

Conventional research techniques can organize group discussions or obtain answers to questionnaires. They can sample the universe to discover preferences, opinions or motives. But none of this will reveal, for instance, that the entire women's press is prejudicing the market against a product, that motoring correspondents are condemning an accessory, or that evening newspapers throughout the country are scaring house-holders about this or that fuel or chemical. Such information has to be amassed, interpreted and then acted upon. It may lead to an improved product which can be launched with explanatory PR exercises as important marketing aids.

Consumer organizations, MPs, anti-pollution propagandists, doctors, teachers, TV commentators, government officials, and other opinion leaders like Elizabeth Dunn of the *Guardian* Check Out feature can be monitored by PR staff. The role of PR is thus one of two-way communication, detecting as well as disseminating. It can be an excellent form of market intelligence that reveals the hostilities and prejudices of the market in which a company is trying to conduct business. Sometimes, when a product is handled by wholesalers, specifiers or supermarkets the original manufacturer is divorced from the end-consumer. Even a consumer panel survey will not have enough open-ended questions to provoke voluntary criticisms. But if a link can be established with the customer (such as a questionnaire on the guarantee card that appliance purchasers return), information can be obtained as a result of direct customer communication. This is cheaper than independent market research and it has the advantage of being frank, personal and committed.

When a company is preparing against the day when the current model has to be replaced—as discussed below under "Product Life Cycles"— or when the marketing policy is to give the product a periodic face-lift— more aptly called "induced obsolescence"—the flow of information from PR sources can be useful. Changing fashions, trends, buying patterns and new demands, new buyers or lost interests can be reflected in this information that may come by way of salesmen's reports, suggestion boxes, incentive schemes for new ideas, customers' letters and editorial comments.

Here are three examples: A well-known menswear retailer, normally advertising in the weekend colour supplements with upper middle class readerships, learned from its sales staff that customers of a lower than usual social grade were now patronizing branches. As a result, advertising was placed in a popular weekly in addition to the three weekend colour supplements. The manufacturer of an industrial dishwasher showed a prototype at Hotelympia, invited the reactions of visitors to the stand, and as a result incorporated modifications in the final model so that it was more marketable. The third example is of a women's hygiene product which owed its introduction to the action taken by the editor of a women's magazine who thought something should be done about a feminine problem which was repeatedly the subject of readers' letters. As a result of talks with a hospital specialist and a manufacturer a new product was created which that editor helped to launch with a whole-page article.

2. *Product Life Cycle*

To talk of product life cycles is fashionable, and some marketing theorists make rather strained attempts to fit products into life cycle models that the manufacturers had never previously suspected. What sort of life cycle has tea, branded or otherwise, or a branded beer like Guinness? Life cycles are convenient for comparatively short-lived products for which past experience has shown a predictable lifetime, or because a successor, rival or otherwise, is inevitable due to inventiveness or new ideas. But how is a life cycle to be predicted for sophisticated products like transistor radios, record and cassette players and Hi-fi equipment capable of replacement by technical developments, new spending power, different uses and the impact of imports from, say, Japan, Taiwan and Hong Kong? In recent years, Philips underestimated the possible demand for small cassette tape recorders, in spite of intense competition. There are therefore both vertical and horizontal marketing considerations. Moreover, we have to decide whether we are talking about the duration and capacity of a product group or of an individual brand or model: marketing theorists are seldom clear about this.

It is in this conflicting world, where there are no convenient bell-shaped life cycle patterns, that PR techniques can aid the marketer in his need to convince distributors and consumers about a new product or an improved model. An expensive innovation cannot creep hopefully upon a competitive market as firms like IBM know. They have to overcome market lethargy through customer education, an excellent and practical form of PR. Pharmaceutical companies have to educate the medical world if new products are to sell quickly and research costs are to be recovered. Roche launched their controversial Librium and Valium with one of the most imaginative of sponsored films, aimed at doctors.

Even where the product has a fairly short life cycle, because it is subject to fads and fashion, PR techniques may be applied to prolong sales life if it is still profitable to do so. Many conventional foods will, for instance, continue to sell alongside convenience foods, but they may need to be seen to justify their existence. Even potato scraping still has its advantages, if only that it's cheaper.

But if we take examples like the gas fire and the bicycle we can see how PR can play a big part in a product life cycle trend which is shaped more like a friendly Loch Ness monster.

3. *Naming*

Consideration of successful products with strange names like Swarfega, Cuprinol, *Woman's Realm*, Oxo or Swan Vestas may imply that a meaningful name is irrelevant. Swarfega was derived from the Derbyshire word swarf meaning clean (not metal waste), while oxo was used to denote "ditto" by a company clerk! But there is a lot to be said for an instantly comprehensible and easily remembered name, and with product (or company) naming we are in the province of PR. The simple reason for this is that the name helps to communicate the image. The more apt, descriptive, characteristic, realistic and convincing the name, the more quickly can the corporate or the product image be established.

Short names, making strong use of vowels, are evocative and powerful persuaders to mention only Omo, Fiat and Daf (what lucky initials), Volvo and Aspro, while descriptive names like Tide, Rinso and Brasso are simple and effective. So, too, are strikingly memorable names like Mr. Kipling, Dr. Pepper and Quaker Oats, Hygena and Easiclene. Along with these must be reckoned those names that have the enviable personal appeal of the original proprietor's name, e.g. Boots, Ford, Gillette, Guinness, Marks and Spencer and Woolworth. In the advertising agency and PR-consultancy world—where personal and professional services are being offered—names of founders and partners are preferable to invented names, although some American-owned agencies with a string of foreign-sounding names (mostly ex-European!) are so incomprehensible that initials such as BBDO are necessary.

Names can be communicative or confusing. How right to change S. Smith & Sons (England) Ltd to Smiths Industries, or for British Ratin Co Ltd with a string of impossible-sounding names like Disinfestation Ltd, Fumigation Services Ltd, Insecta Laboratories and Scientex Ltd and so on to adopt the name of its small retail product company, Rentokil, as the name for the world's largest pest control organization. Less happily, perhaps, well-known names like Rank, Hovis and McDougall have been submerged in the meaningless initials RHM, while the initials AA can mean Advertising Association, Automobile Association or Alcoholics Anonymous. Names and initials must be meaningful. Initials such as IBM and KLM are meaningful even if their origin is unknown, but others like BOC and BOCM can be confusing. The decision to drop the "Son" from W. H. Smith & Son has helped to give the company name greater impact.

Unmistakably, naming is an act of such basic communication importance that it demonstrates perhaps more than anything else that PR belongs to the early stages of the marketing strategy.

The product or service that is instantly understood by its word picture name needs far less selling effort than one that has to be painstakingly explained. Instant communication cuts selling effort as can be seen by comparing product names such as fish fingers, rice crispies, washing-up liquid or soap powder with transistor, stereophonic, detergent, deodorant, or heriditament. Thousands of people still have no idea what a transistor actually is: in fact, the name has come to mean a complete small radio receiver and not a component.

In a competitive marketing situation time and money can be wasted on securing conviction about a product's merits if it is not immediately comprehensible, credible and acceptable. Sheer weight of advertising—there was a three months' preliminary campaign to launch *Woman's Realm*—may help to establish a new product (which must then justify the claims made), but fish fingers (five or ten to the packet!) were the sheerest instant communication compared with such possible descriptions as fish pieces, fish tasters, or fish portions. While fish sticks is mentally pictorial, it lacks the alliterative appeal of fish fingers.

Naming is often the responsibility of copywriters, understandably because they are literary communicators or "wordsmiths". They are also sales-orientated, which is very good. However, since there are other implications bound up in corporate as distinct from product description or market segment imagery, naming of all kinds requires either the co-operation or the full responsibility of the PR practitioner. In this, it also helps if there are PR-orientated management and marketing personnel, and also PR-minded agency copywriters (which is perhaps asking rather a lot since advertising and PR people so seldom work on sympathetic wavelengths) because PR is much more a philosophy of communication than the private preserve of PR specialists.

Consider the forgettable Meraklon furnishing fabric, with its American equivalent trade name Herculon which is memorable.

4. *Market Segment and Pricing*

Market segmentation has become one of the major subtleties of modern marketing since it helps to eliminate wasteful effort and concentrates the selling on more precise areas of sales certainty. Here again, PR techniques can assist because of its familiarity with the segregation of people into numerous publics. The PR practitioner is not concerned with broad publics, with "housewives" or "motorists", but with categories of housewife or motorist. Nor are PR publics limited to the social grades as adopted for market research purposes. This facility of grouping people can be valuable to the marketer who seeks to fill a gap in the market or to operate in the price range of a certain section of the market. It means that the PRO can use the right medium (and not just the press) most capable of communicating with the market segment.

For example, it may be pointless to advertise to tomorrow's market, yet good PR to run children's competitions or exhibitions. The Philips Evoluon exhibition in Eindhoven is a perfect example, together with its project awards for young scientists.

There are also PR implications in pricing. One of the worst marketing mistakes ever made was the underpricing of British watches made by Smiths Industries: they failed to sell largely because the public took their low prices to mean cheap British watches in comparison with more expensive and presumably better foreign ones. On the other hand we all know of products which make very fine gifts and prizes because everyone knows how costly they are! The psychology of pricing is so vital that some mail-order traders do sample mailings to learn which is the most popular price, a matter of pence making all the difference to the eventual total volume of sales. And as drapery stores found out many years ago, £1.00 sounds ominous compared with 99p, although it sounded even better when it was possible to say 19s 11¾d! This is the pricing policy with "budget" records selling at 87p, 99p and £1.99. Nothing could be more antagonistic to price psychology than the destruction of resale price maintenance by one Conservative government and the grey world of double pricing and recommended prices, followed by the imposition of VAT by another Conservative government. What could be more inhibiting than a price complicated by odd amounts of VAT? And this creates yet another PR problem—how to overcome the apparently inflationary appearance of prices. The public resent ever-reducing chocolate bars, but appreciates the jar that contains a pound of jam.

5. *Range, Styling, Colours*

Definition of the range of products, and their sizes, styles and colours —sometimes denigrated as product proliferation but also rationalized as the minimum economic number, as with milk bottles which used to include half pints and quarts—may have PR implications. There may be a service angle, as when different sizes are recommended for specific purposes. Aspro did well when they brought out sealed packs of aspirin that were handy for carrying in the handbag. Carry-home packs are a convenience offered by brewers and soft drink manufacturers. Paint manufacturers offer a multitude of shades by equipping retailers with mixing machines. There is a lot of marketing thoughtfulness or PR-mindedness in these ideas.

Mentioned above are factors of customer relations, often linked with dealer and customer–dealer relations, which invite the attention of the marketing-orientated PR practitioner. They are aspects of communication likely to be quite foreign to ex-journalist PROs, and yet these are the very people who sometimes refuse to undertake any training in PR, let alone in marketing.

Typical PR-marketing questions may be: which choices of size, shape or colour will result in the most satisfactory relations? Will, for instance, the exotic colours offered by Ford maintain the popularity of Ford with its rather special segment of the car-buying market? This is a joint PR–marketing customer relations commitment, one which was seemingly overlooked in the luckless Edsel episode of American Ford. To take another case, Dunn & Co (once "Dunn the Hatter") has the reputation for being able to fit anyone with an off-the-peg suit. To draw attention to their range of flavours, Corona ran a flavour-naming contest one year and linked a free-film merchandising offer with their slower selling flavours. Apart from the merchandising angle, these promotions helped to familiarize the less popular drinks with those who had not tried them. Tree Top soft drinks were launched with the three most popular flavours, according to research, and then year by year a new flavour was added so that the range was extended in a way acceptable to the market.

Styling tends to follow the dictates of the market rather than lead it, except where production can be geared to a brief life cycle as with fashion goods. The Japanese have been accused rather unfairly of being copyists: very sensibly they try to export what is acceptable in overseas markets. When Datsun cars were first imported into Britain they looked remarkably like Ford Cortinas, but with all the optional extras as standard equipment. Yet a criticism of the quite beautiful looking Necchi Lydia sewing machine was that, without all the conventional knobs and spindles, it looked like a toy.

6. *Packaging*

The preservation and presentation of products—from shirts to frozen peas, soups to hair sprays, indoor plants to musicassettes—has been a revolution of the mid-twentieth-century decades. The extra services of hygiene, freshness, impeccable condition, convenience and availability all enhance external relations including those between distributors and their customers. Customers patronize a shop for its own sake as well as for the merchandise and the prices. Modern packaging, bulk buying, and multiples go together. The day of the untidy little grocer's shop where tea, sugar, rice and other commodities were bagged in the back shop largely disappeared in the fifties.

True, new materials have assisted the packaging industry, but demand and purchasing power was also the inspiration of innovation. Sometimes, consumerism gives little credit to these advances which show respect for customer interests. Again, it is unfortunate that less dangerous, lighter and generally much handier containers (e.g. plastic bottles) have had their attributes obscured by failure to pursue their advantages to the point of destruction or conversion. Here, marketers were only partially PR-orientated and incurred the boomerang effect of pollution and its critics. The PR repercussions of the non-returnable bottle are as vital as the more obvious initial advantages, both economic and social.

With £1000 million a year being spent on packaging in Britain in 1972, and up to ten times that sum in the USA, this is a vast subject with incredible PR implications that have been merely touched on by Barry Commoner in his book *The Closing Circle*. If one-trip plastic sachets replace the traditional 30–50-trip glass milk bottle, they will provide enough waste plastic in two months to reach the moon, according to a report, *Packaging In Britain*, published by the Friends of the Earth in 1973. Soft drink manufacturers and milk suppliers have already had a taste of public resentment about non-returnable plastic containers: the problem can be resolved only on a PR basis, for no company can afford to achieve a bad corporate image as the price of more economic packaging.

7. *Distribution*

The choice of channels of distribution, and of the treatment of distributors, or of public attitudes towards various outlets, also have their PR considerations. Will a product be judged by where and by whom it is sold?

Is the image of a Necchi sewing machine enhanced by its availability at Harrods? Does a Brother typewriter have a lesser image because it is retailed in stores not normally associated with office machines? Do we favour Heinz beans or Stork margarine because it is obtainable anywhere? What do we think of an apparently excellent product like Close-up toothpaste which Tesco's, to the irritation of some customers, did not stock in the larger, more economical sizes although larger sizes of older brands were on display? Are potential car buyers impressed by the number and accessibility of dealers? (Distribution has been the bane of British car exports in countries as different as the USA and Nigeria. Significantly, the Japanese—or their British concessionaires—have worked hard at gaining good distribution. Volkswagen have an international reputation for good dealer relations.)

But when Haywards (Brooke Bond Oxo) offered free paperbacks for labels from three jars of pickles, was it not disappointing that some shops stocked only two or three items, while sizes of jar varied from shop to shop? This exercise hinted at that old-fashioned marketing idea of gaining distribution by creating demand at the cost of customer frustration. Presumably, however, the firm had failed to win adequate distribution before taking expensive colour pages in mass media like *TV Times*. There was a breakdown in the marketing–PR–advertising relationship, so that the advertising did not marry up with the sales effort.

Choice of distributors and adequate distribution are important factors in PR-orientated marketing. It may be that the best distribution is through one's own shops as with shoes, bespoke tailoring and special products like Singer sewing machines, Dennis and Robinson kitchen and bedroom furniture, or Plumbs chair covers.

A product may well be judged by whether it is stocked by a retailer recognized for certain standards of merchandise, the best example being whether electrical goods are stocked by electricity board showrooms. The status of the store lends the product status. It has a halo effect. Conversely, some firms dislike having their products offered as loss-leaders, while others revel in the extra publicity resulting from a store promotion. A decision has to be taken as to whether special offers cheapen a product or secure wider acceptance, and repeat sales, through bargain sales. Harveys are perhaps the most price-cut of sherries—and the brand leader! Similarly, some confusion may be caused when a cut-price dealer advertises a special offer of an obsolete model: this may be an excellent way of clearing old stocks from the factory warehouse, or does it belittle the status of the firm's products as a whole? Calculated risks occur here.

A few years ago some manufacturers hesitated to sell their products to gift houses (e.g. cigarette manufacturers who give coupons, and trading stamp operators) or as premium offers because of representations from retail traders who, rather narrow-mindedly, saw these gifts as alternatives to shop sales. Few if any of these manufacturers hesitate today, and are pleased to see their goods pictured in mass distributed catalogues. The extra publicity may even help to promote retail sales! Nor do they refuse to supply the giant warehouses of discount firms like Comet, or the great hypermarkets now to be found in Europe and the USA. Failure to be represented in gift catalogues or discount price lists (which often fill a whole page in an evening or Sunday newspaper) could infer that the items are not deemed good enough by these huge distributors.

In fact, acceptance by the supermarket chains, with their hundreds of branches, can determine whether or not a new product gets off the ground at all. To quote two actual instances, because supermarkets refused to take yet another furniture polish one brand was a failure; because a new soft drink was taken up by supermarkets, it did exceedingly well when test marketed, and became a leading national and eventually international brand. There were, of course, other factors such as advertising support, but both products were promoted on television.

8. *Test Marketing*

A test marketing operation will not simulate full marketing conditions if it does not include the PR activities which would accompany the national launch. With regional evening and weekly newspapers, regional TV and local radio it is not difficult to miniaturize a news media PR exercise, just as the advertising campaign can be miniaturized. There can be problems of timing as there can be no guarantee when a story will be used, but if the product is one that interests, say, the women's page it is possible to gain reasonably simultaneous coverage as journalists will wish to print the story while it still has news value.

A. R. M. Sedgwick, European Director of Corporate Public Affairs to The Gillette Company, described use of PR in the test-marketing of Feel Free anti-perspirant/deodorant in the January/February 1973 issue of *Marketing Forum*. He wrote:

> "The PR plan was so devised as to give specific support to the test area in which the product was initially to be launched. For this reason the national press was not canvassed and the operation was confined to 200 weekly and daily local newspapers. Each paper received a copy of the release accompanied by a product sample. It was considered advisable that the heading of the release should not identify Gillette so as to enhance the product's feminine image, which at this moment in time is not considered by the consumer to be a particular attribute of the Gillette name, a name still strongly masculine, although in our corporate public relations we are working to change this.
>
> "A second phase of the PR operation was concerned with propagating a success story to the trade and consumer press based on factual evidence gathered from those retailers who had had notable success in selling the product to their customers."

The test marketing took place in the Spring of 1971. The news release projected the "one-spray-a-day-girl" appeal of the product, was concise and precise, admitted at the foot of the sheet that it came from "a Division of Gillette Industries Limited", and issued on 22 April it achieved coverage in newspapers published in April, May and June.

9. *Selling*

The sales operation, whether of technical representative to user, field salesman to distributor, direct salesman to customer, mail order trader to customer, or retailer to consumer, involves a mixture of human contacts in which information, education, understanding and confidence are PR responsibilities. Two sets of relations are to be considered here, those between the manufacturer or supplier and all types of salesman, and those between the user or consumer and the immediate source of supply. This is further complicated since a salesman, even a shop assistant, may be the consumer's only link with the manufacturer so that the retailer acts as a substitute for the producer. The distributor can therefore occupy an unenviable position as when the car dealer is abused by dissatisfied buyers, or the showroom salesman has to bear criticisms of the performance of an appliance. Bulky goods such as cookers and refrigerators are a good example, the order being taken by a gas or electricity showroom salesman and the appliance being shipped direct from manufacturer to customer. But if, through poor packing or a mishap in transport, the item arrives damaged it is the *supplier* who receives the complaint, *not* the manufacturer. Thus, the manufacturer has a PR responsibility to pack and convey goods so that the salesman does not suffer unwarranted complaints.

The extent to which the manufacturer accepts the burden of customer dissatisfaction is the measure of his understanding of his PR responsibilities to both distributors and customers, and sweet are the rare words "Don't worry, this firm is very good about complaints. They won't let you down."

The motor-car industry is notorious for its bad relations with distributors, largely because it expects dealers to put right defects yet allows the customer only a six-months guarantee. On average it takes eighteen months, if the owner is sufficiently persistent, to get almost any make of car into a condition worthy of putting it on sale in the first place. Car manufacturers seem to work on the fatalistic basis that the car will probably be traded in within two or three years. But it is the dealer who receives the irate telephone calls, the rude letters and the refusals to pay accounts for putting right things that should have been right at factory inspection stage. It is therefore shameful that it takes a Ralph Nader to make the car industry PR-conscious. On the other hand, after four failures to repair a gearbox, an irate customer of British Leyland got instant satisfaction by sending a telegram to Lord Stokes.

Coming nearer home are the good relations with the company sales force which is really only another branch of staff relations. Nevertheless, it is part of marketing's recognition of PR to the extent of appreciating that the field sales force is not particularly interested in the company newspaper circulated among factory workers, and deserves the privilege of its own journal. Such consideration is incredibly rare. Because travelling salesmen are the company's ambassadors at large, job satisfaction is a primary PR responsibility.

10. *Educating the Market*

A company with new products or services that are unknown, liable to be misunderstood, capable of creating prejudice and hostility, or of being underrated, cannot expect super salesmen and heavy advertising or special promotions to pulverize the market into purchasing. The market will respond only when its desires are active and its confidence is high. And until the market has been educated to the point when sales occur it will be a long battle to win even the "early adopters".

For example, the Chrysler 180 car (a Simca product) was slow to achieve acceptance in Britain although popular in France, and yet the motoring correspondent of the *Observer* was able to describe it as an "underrated car". There was plenty of goodwill among motoring correspondents who genuinely liked the car, but it was still a comparative rarity on British roads even when two years later the 2000 version was launched. The more expensive Audi NSU and Toyota cars did not suffer from such peculiar lack of market education.

The shorter the initial take-up period, the quicker development costs can be regained, and profitability achieved. It may mean, as some car manufacturers have discovered, allowing a number of typical drivers to test-drive a new car for six months under normal conditions so that teething troubles can be eliminated *before* the car is generally distributed. Or a technical appliance (e.g. Staines Rotascrub pan washer) may be installed for a test period (as the Rotascrub was for a year in the London Hospital kitchen) on a work-or-bust basis. The success story of the Rotascrub made an ideal press room release at Hotelympia 1972.

Again, a food product may first have to be introduced through industrial catering, a fertilizer through agriculture, an insecticide through horticulture, or a paint through commercial painting and decorating, before it can be sold on the mass consumer market. Then it can be presented to the layman with the proof of commercial usage. The durability of a floor covering was proved by laying an area of carpet on the much-trodden forecourt of a railway terminus, while a floor-tile was tried out for a season on the floor of the coffee lounge of a holiday camp. Given such physical evidence, the market can be educated by PR techniques using facts, photographs, statistics, exhibits and films.

11. *Advertising*

While advertising is a very different animal from PR, it does have a PR content which cannot be ignored. Will the advertising enhance the reputation of the company, does it reflect the true image of company or product, does it obey codes of practice and so show the company as one that acknowledges its social responsibility, is the house style followed? These are a few of the PR questions applicable to advertising, ones which need to be raised at agency plans board meetings, and at campaign presentations by the agency.

Was the Stork Challenge demolished by the refutation by *Which* magazine and the criticisms made by Elizabeth Dunn in the *Guardian* on 5 January 1973? Van den Berghs thought not.

The motor-car industry has for years indulged in knocking copy, attempting to justify its actions because of the sheer competitiveness of the business. A typical example is Opel's claim to have crushed the Beetle. Yet this is contrary to the British Code of Advertising Practice and to the advice of America's Better Business Bureau. Such behaviour may tend to provoke contempt for these manufacturers, especially when without knocking copy other international competitors seem able to offer better value for money. Denigration of others is a mark of desperation, but regrettably some advertisers are not sufficiently PR-conscious to realize the self-damaging effect of unfair comparisons.

Being PR-conscious does mean putting one's own house in order first, and that is a matter of industrial relations too. Perhaps, so far as the British car industry is concerned, there is no answer short of either worker participation in management or industrial trade unionism or both. At present the end-product of chaotic management–labour relations is knocking copy so that the car industry's PR is bad at every level. It is especially bad when a motoring correspondent can present a TV programme in which PR is condemned on the evidence of the bribery offered by this industry.

The use of house symbols and house styling by way of standard colour schemes and especially typography can introduce a powerful PR element into advertising. A bonus publicity effect can be obtained if there is a recognizable link between the diverse interests of a large group of companies. Typical examples are those of Tube Investments, Monsanto Chemicals, ICI, British Oxygen and, more recently, a very deliberate attempt by Sterling Products to bring together a great many family remedies under one umbrella. Mention was made under "Naming" of the way in which Rentokil Ltd gained its name. It can also be said that as a result of the decision to name the group "Rentokil" it then became possible to give hundreds of vehicles the same livery. The company thus gained an impression of size and nation-wide organization by the emergence of a large fleet of vehicles which had previously existed in different colours and bearing different names. Later, when a symbol and a slogan were adopted, they helped to link together press advertisements, similar slogans such as "Rentokil Guards Your Property" creating the impression that the company's products and services preserved customer's possessions. The company's ability to advertise in this fashion was enhanced by PR-orientated management decisions.

The PR eye needs to study proposed advertising for possible risks of contra-suggestion. Will implausible claims harm the corporate image? Does the copy need extra information to be convincing? Is it wise to promote a product without identifying the maker's name—an annoying feature of some TV commercials? Does the address remain on the advertisement after the coupon has been clipped? Is the coupon large enough for enquirers to write legible names and addresses? Does the coupon follow out the CAP requirement that no salesman will call unless requested? Very few do. Is there absolutely no chance of infringeing the Trade Descriptions Act or the consumer protection legislation of other countries? A court case can be the worst possible PR, and a good many prosecutions would not have succeeded if there had been vigilant PR scrutiny of advertisements and sales literature.

There is a long-standing argument as to whether or not advertising should be controlled by the PRO. Many years ago Hubert Oughton, in his capacity of president of the Institute of Practitioners in Advertising, made the startling remark "Public relations, of which advertising is a part." Advertising is, of course, a part of a company's total communication or PR. However, while PR is journalist-dominated, it is unlikely to assume the full role of commanding total communication, but when the PRO of the future is proficient in his knowledge of management, marketing and communication techniques, then he should be responsible for advertising.

12. *Sales Promotion and Merchandising*

The multiplicity of below-the-line promotional schemes (that may delight the cherry picker housewife) may boost sales, stave off declining sales, challenge competition, keep products in the supermarkets and sometimes prove more effective than traditional above-the-line advertising. Breakfast cereal manufacturers maintain brand loyalty by follow-on schemes that require collecting and therefore regular purchase.

But too many promotions have produced public criticism of advertising itself—which has been unfair to advertising—and scores of complaints have been received in recent years by the Advertising Standards Authority, mostly arising from inefficient organization and delayed deliveries of merchandise offers. In other words, an inexperienced brand manager who fails to collate a realistic anticipation of demand with a practical guarantee of ability to supply in a very short time has damaged customer relations and encouraged disbelief in the reliability of advertised claims. "Allow 21 days for delivery" seems to be the brand manager's current insurance policy, and while it staves off complaints for two or three weeks it still does not say much for the efficiency of an organization that needs that length of time to turn round applications. An efficient organization should be able to do the job in seven days, and a really efficient mail order or package tour operator makes sure he beats competition by turning round enquiries or orders in twenty-four hours.

Here we have a supreme example of over-zealous or ill-organized but all-too-typical marketing producing a bad customer relations situation, simply because the marketer did not stop to analyse the disastrous PR effect of careless planning.

However, it is necessary to distinguish between the PR content or liability of a sales promotion exercise and distinct PR activities, for while a premium offer is not in itself a PR activity it can have PR overtones and consequences. In far too many cases the PR effect of merchandising and premium schemes is overlooked, possibly because these promotional devices are quite wrongly thought to be PR efforts in themselves. We have only to observe how the large Anglo-American advertising agencies pass sales promotional tasks to their PR department or PR subsidiary to realize why this misunderstanding exists. In one respect it is an abuse of PR, but it is also indicative of the slightly different and more persuasive nature of American PR which undertakes the publicity stunts abhored by British PR.

Perhaps this is a good moment to reflect on the different interpretations given to our subject in different countries, especially when so many American companies have interests in Britain and Europe, and when the Common Market is throwing up fresh international PR problems.

In the USA, PR is more allied to publicity, more akin to press agency, seeking to persuade and influence in a way which the British PRO would regard as propaganda. There are questions of semantics, as for example when Ernest Bernays speaks of "engineering consent". That type of thing would not serve in Britain if only because the press editorial and TV programme staff will kill any story that does not merit publication on the strength of its news value. Moreover, our media intelligentsia resolutely refuse to believe that Vance Packard's book, *The Hidden Persuaders*, was about advertising and motivation research in particular, and have borrowed this American expression for their permanent curse on British PR.

On the Continent, other standards apply. North European media apply similar standards to our own, while South European media (especially French and Italian) are venal to the extent of selling editorial space or accepting bribes for editorial mentions. European attitudes to PR also derive from the small circulations of numerous peripheral journals which have little advertisement revenue and welcome income of any kind.

Reverting to sales promotion, time after time the premium offer goes sour and induces contra-suggestion. The PR content of these schemes can be very bad indeed when customers are disappointed by inferior goods or uselessly late delivery of a seasonal product. Picture frames from one firm arrived broken in the post because of stupid packing, colour films and prints were long-delayed in one offer, and there was an almost non-existent supply of leg-halves in the matching pictures of footballers issued by one oil company. The latter exasperated both petrol station attendants and motorists to such an extent that attendants were prising open the "halves" to appease customers. The amazing thoughtlessness of so many premium offers reveals yet again the don't-interfere-with-us attitude to PR which some marketers and brand managers adopt. It does not occur to them that PR is a matter of business management behaviour, not merely the despatch of news releases.

Sometimes the package turns up so late that the source is forgotten! Why do senders of offers so seldom identify themselves? A simple compliment slip is all that is needed. Here is a good example:

From
The Bisto Promotions Service
We enclose
your free Bisto Roasting Tin
with our compliments
and hope that it gives you good service over the years

Merchandising is surely the most slovenly of marketing undertakings, and this is entirely due to three weaknesses: (1) lack of training; (2) lack of thoughtfulness and organizing ability; (3) lack of PR understanding.

On the other hand, when Buitoni refunded 5p for every label submitted in 25p multiples, or when HP Sauce gave away an extra 4 oz in an enlarged can of beans, the housewife had good reason to feel well disposed towards the sponsors. Price-conscious housewives may well remember a cash benefit, but who recalls the sponsor of the premium offer beach ball, bath towel, art reproduction, sun-bed or pair of tights? The goodwill benefits of many premium offers are nil or negligible, however valuable the short-term selling-out result.

However, when Golden Wonder offered sets of tea and coffee spoons for 50p and six potato crisp bags, Golden Wonder were not bothered with posterity but with gaining six quick repeat purchases which certainly helped the dealer to sell out and want to re-order. Good dealer relations and the possible bonus of brand loyalty through acquired taste were the advantages of this offer. On the whole, the immediate sales boost is bound to be the marketer's *first* thought, but he should reconcile sales gains with *either* the risk of provoking ill-will or the chance to inspire goodwill. Thus, marketing can take one more step and accept or exploit the PR possibilities of an offer.

A splendid example of attention to customer relations occurred in the Crosse & Blackwell (Nestlés) Maggi Soups knife offer. First, the various knives could be purchased or they were available as a gift for a number of empty soup packets. But the following letter—produced as a miniature and tucked in with the knife in the package—is worth quoting in the hope that other marketers will copy:

Dear Customer,
MAGGI SOUPS KNIFE OFFER
We thank you for your interest and your recent application in connection with the above offer.

If upon arrival the item should be damaged in any way, kindly return it, within 7 days, to the offer address in BURTON LATIMER shown above, when a replacement will be sent to you and your postage refunded.

Please note that each knife is despatched separately and if your complete order has not arrived kindly allow a further 7–10 days in case the parcels have become separated in transit.
Yours faithfully,
Crosse & Blackwell Ltd.,
Quality Control Department
(Signed) Mrs. J. GOACHER

That is a model of thoughtfulness, pure and perfect marketing PR written by a PR-minded person. Such consideration is rare with marketing offers, most of which arrive without any sort of enclosure or identification of the sender. A PRO has to be a good organizer, and if that can be interpreted as anticipating mishaps, the Maggi Soups letter is a good example of good organization. Someone took the trouble to sit down and think what could possibly go wrong—and then did something simple and practical about it.

That this is a consistent marketing communication policy was seen a year later when sets of colour pens were despatched in response to a Crosse & Blackwell Alphabetti spaghetti offer. This time, the letter—produced rather larger—was signed by G. M. Holmes, senior executive, marketing department.

Finally, sameness spoils some offers, and motorists must have become bemused by the plethora of competitive drinking glass offers. But which is best: a scheme which ties the purchaser to one petrol station (BP) or which allows the motorist to collect vouchers at any station selling the brand (Mobil)? This is a tricky one, the first pleasing the station proprietor, the second pleasing the motorist who can take advantage of the offer wherever he may be. Perhaps the first is a good idea in the winter, the second in the summer.

13. *Corporate PR*

The company image, and financial PR, may not be marketing matters if we take marketing to be but one of three sectors of a business, the other two being finance and production. Even so, corporate and financial PR affect the status of the organization in the eyes of an increasing variety of people, the High Street shopkeeper no less than the investment analyst. Every popular newspaper has its city page, and city editors are frequently seen on television. Stock Exchange prices are becoming as commonplace as football results. Perhaps the amusing corollary of this is that when the *Financial Times* conducted a reading and noting survey it found that one of its least-read features was the share information service, which was actually a tribute to the paper's general news and subject coverage.

So, while the marketing division will not engage the services of a specialist financial PR consultant, and his fees will not appear in the marketing budget, the selling of products may well be influenced by the opinions of financial journalists. The High Street shopkeeper may read the city page of the *Daily Express* as closely as the stockbroker belt commuter reads *The Times, Financial Times* or *Daily Telegraph*. And Mrs. Jones, with her Unit Trust savings, may follow the fortunes of combines and conglomerates in her evening paper, with possible effect upon her choice of brands at the supermarket. Even if these effects of financial news seem improbable, the morale of the field sales force can suffer from depressed share prices, with their possible threat of a take-over bid. Conversely, successful marketing, excellent trading figures, good interim and final dividends, full order books, export developments, and maybe a national award all make first-class financial PR.

Corporate PR plays an important role in marketing in the EEC, for the securing of a foothold in the Common Market means at best one of two things: the acquisition of European production or distribution facilities, or the familiarization of the company in the minds of people to whom it is utterly strange. So insular have been the British in the past that thousands of company and brand names, which have been household names for generations in the UK, are totally unknown—totally *foreign*—beyond only twenty miles of sea. Moreover, corporate PR has had to pave the way for marketing by harmonizing many practices, not least of which has been legislation hostile to British (and American) ingredients or formulations. In one case, a foodstuff commonly used in Britain and the USA was banned in Europe simply because it was wrongly listed as a chemical, and it took an Anglo-American corporation three years to disentangle and harmonize the legislation so that the product could be sold in the EEC. The harmonizing process—that is, trying to get identical laws and agreements throughout the Common Market—will doubtless last for decades of costly frustration.

In some spheres there can also be resistance to harmonization and Lord Bowden, Principal of the University of Manchester Institute of Science and Technology, condemned the Brussels efforts to standardize professional qualifications in such a way that they could be awarded only by universities and not by such professional bodies as the Institute of Marketing and the CAM Education Foundation.

In large developing countries, with all their problems of geographical size, paucity of communications, diversity of peoples, religions, languages and dialects, and their anxiety to be independent of expatriate companies, corporate PR is required to establish confidence in comparatively new organizations with indigenous owners. Not surprisingly, in countries like Ghana, Nigeria and Tanzania there is enthusiastic interest in training and qualifications in marketing and public relations. Ironically, there are more people willing to study public relations in Nigeria than there are in Britain! The subject is even taught in Lagos University where there is an Institute of Mass Communication, whereas it is taught in no British university, except as a minor aspect of marketing.

A basic problem of corporate PR in developing countries is that frequently the native people have no confidence in their own countrymen's abilities. It is to their credit that expatriate companies like the United Africa Company and the Bata Shoe Company have organized training for Nigerians in management techniques, including marketing and public relations.

14. *After-Sales Service*

Whether it be a "twenty-year guarantee", a first-class spare-part service for mechanical goods, or the 24-hour service operated by hirers of TV receivers and computers, what happens after the product is sold is a serious claimant for the buyer's trust and confidence.

Compare the following situations: ask most British stockists of electronic goods which brand they recommend and more often than not they will say Bush. Asked why, the stockist will say there is less servicing, which means less trouble for him as well as for the customer. That dealer attitude has been consistent throughout the sixties and seventies. By comparison, Potterton—whose boilers once had a "Rolls-Royce" reputation—found it necessary to set up a servicing network, and that can be read to mean either that their boilers need servicing more often or can be serviced more quickly. Crane rely on the installers to carry out any necessary servicing, and fall between the two stools of having no servicing network and believing that their equipment is too reliable to need one!

Sewing machines are often made abroad and a priority consideration of a potential buyer is the efficiency of the spare parts and repair service. That usually means "Is the product widely distributed on a national basis?"

Foreign cars, meaning any make of car sold outside its country of origin, may be novel, but they are a nuisance if there is a poor spare parts service. British manufacturers have still not overcome their bad reputation in this respect in overseas markets. In developing countries, where road and weather conditions are gruelling, British cars are more likely to need spares and repairs than French, German and Swedish makes. Largely because they combined swift recognition that right-hand driving was going to be introduced (and so shipped cars with the steering wheel on the correct side) with a good parts service and marketing zeal, Japanese Datsun, Toyota and Mazda cars swept the Nigerian market so that in less than a year they had dominated the roads and won the taxi market. Peugeot, Mercedes-Benz and Volvo remained popular, but the Japanese picked up the market which the Morris Marina had toyed with a year earlier. The Nigerian car buyer had to decide between a six months wait for a British spare part or quick delivery of a more expensive Japanese replacement.

In Britain, foreign cars—and especially the Japanese whose Datsun, Toyota and Mazda models were eating into the home market—earned unfortunate publicity because cautious British insurance companies were placing foreign cars in higher groups that rated higher insurance premiums. This was grossly unfair, and stirred foreign car concessionaires to advertise the excellence of their after-sales service.

After-sales service is therefore the ultimate in more ways than one. Goodwill towards a company, its products and its distributors can be ruined at the point-of-initial-purchase if there are doubts about or known bad experience of the servicing side. Here, then, is an essential, area of PR and the PR adviser's first question about a new product, export market or import could well be "How good is your after-sales service? Have you set up distribution of spares? How explicit is the servicing manual? Are service engineers thoroughly trained? How does the customer go about getting service?" These can be devastating questions, and woe betide the marketer who cannot respond with unchallengeable answers.

There are cases where the repair service is appalling, as when the retail supplier is unwilling to handle the repair and advises the customer to make direct return of the goods to the manufacturer. By contrast, there is the equally serious PR situation where the customer is unwilling to admit that the product has worn out and that it would be cheaper to buy a new one. Alarm clocks cost very little, yet buyers expect them to last a lifetime, and clockmakers' servicing departments look like museums! Part of market education should include understanding of the life-expectancy of a product. For example, one dreads to think how many domestic cupboards are stuffed with bottles, jars and tubes of pharmaceutical products which have deteriorated, yet this risk is not stated on the label or pack. The practice of declaring product life has long been adopted by makers of photographic films, while packaged foodstuffs are now given a shelf-life, after which they are removed from sale.

After-sales services are not free gifts; they have to be covered by the retail price or extra charges when guarantees have expired. One of the big arguments in favour of resale price maintenance (one of the greatest protections the customer ever had) was that it allowed a price to be charged which would cover the cost of training distributors to provide after-sale service. Obviously, this applied to consumer durables rather than small-unit goods. The question is: is the customer so price-conscious that he will prefer a lower price to one that includes a guarantee of service? This can be a dilemma for the marketer until he recognizes the PR implications of confidence versus complaints. The moth-proofing of carpets must incur a cost which is carried by the price, yet it offers tremendous peace of mind to the customer.

A criticism of discount houses—mostly from traditional retailers but taken up by the press—has been that they merely sell goods and take no responsibility for their performance. But reputable discount houses have taken care of this worry, appreciating that no customer can buy with confidence (and some of the items cost a lot of money) unless assured of servicing. Confidence is what PR is all about. It is not the job of PR to make apologies when things go wrong, but to act as an early warning system capable of preventing things from going wrong.

15. *Maintenance of Consumer Interest and Trust*

Advertising may be seasonal. It is likely to be more intense during the launch of a product. But PR is a constant activity, and because of this characteristic it can be a continuous marketing aid. If advertising can be likened to a dripping tap or a rolling snowball, PR resembles the essential air we need to breathe.

For example, the common cold is a perennial topic, and it is not confined to the winter since summer colds seem to be fairly prevalent. In 1971 a well-known pharmaceutical firm marketed a lemon and paracetamol preparation with a measure and dosage scheme. It was advertised on TV and displayed in drug stores. But next winter it had disappeared and chemists had forgotten it, unless they still had old stocks to sell. Was this just another case of a new product that had failed? If the product was still available, the retailer's interest should have been maintained, irrespective of consumer advertising. This was a job for PR. Enquiries showed that retailers had actually forgotten the existence of the cold remedy—it was only twelve months old!—and were prominently displaying two rival brands. Was lack of sustained retailer knowledge the reason for this product's demise? (It could have been a packaging problem, rival lines being in handy sachets, the vanished brand having a bottle and a plastic measure. Marketers can be too clever!)

The continuous nature of PR also results from the peculiarities of media. A story may be released to a press consisting of evening, morning and weekly newspapers and weekly, fortnightly, monthly and quarterly magazines so that considerable intervals of time may elapse between issue and publication of stories. Thus press coverage may introduce a wide time-spread of information. Advertising can be controlled to secure simultaneous publication of announcements, or they can be restricted to a shorter time span. Generally speaking, once several stories have been released over a matter of weeks it is likely that they will produce coverage over a period of months. This tends to give PR activity a more continuous nature than advertising. When advertising is of a continuous or permanent nature it is not very informative, serving only to remind and to plug a name as with posters, signs and newscasters.

These sixteen points may represent a sophisticated analysis of the marketing mix, but it admits that PR can extend beyond the marketing function of a company since we have brought in corporate and financial PR as it impinges on marketing. But it is also exclusive because large and important areas of PR are not touched on at all, these being community, potential and actual staff, and supplier PR. In this larger format, PR is taken as serving the three primary functions of a business; finance, production and distribution or marketing.

Ideally, complete company PR is best integrated by a PR director serving on the board who can allocate his resources to all three functions. Not surprisingly, in so doing he tends to gain a different title (e.g. public affairs director), although this is an unsatisfactory title because it excludes internal relations. Even so, it is in marketing that there can be the most regular, complex and exacting use of PR techniques if only that we are dealing with a very large number of people in a kaleidoscope of relations with the company.

Staff relations are not solely the preserve of Personnel, and this was brought out by the communication requirements of the Industrial Relations Act. One may dare to point out that there is a marketing content in the sometimes separated PR function of personnel management. Industrial strife does not help the corporate or the product image. Doubts about delivery are a form of ill-will derived from strikes. When a film was shown on ITV showing the voluntary group system operating in the Volvo car works at Gothenburg the inference was that of a strike-free manufacturer who could supply reliable vehicles on time. It was superb PR, especially when the comment was made that Leylands were studying Volvo's methods! Similarly, when another TV film showed how redundant Dutch miners had been absorbed into the Daf car factory it made one wonder about the conservatism of redundant British workers. The PR responsibilities of both government and employers can effect marketing and the economy as a whole.

The underlying message of this Part is that PR is a function of management throughout an organization, a philosophy of company behaviour from top to bottom, from managing director to operator, van driver, telephone receptionist or office boy. The PR consultant, the PR manager and the press officer are not the only exponents of communication resulting in communication and understanding. Consequently, all those who belong to the marketing team should be conscious PROs.

Here are the contrasting attitudes towards clients by two companies, one in central heating and the other in computers. The central heating salesmen consider that taking their clients out to lunch is excellent PR. But expense-account lunches are frowned on by the computer company. Both are American firms with factories in Britain. Which is the better exponent of PR? In this author's view the central heating salesmen do not have the slightest idea what PR is all about.

PART TWO

Public Relations Media

CHAPTER 3

The Nature of the Press

IN the UK the press predominates, despite broadcast media, as the chief means of communication with large numbers of people. Yet it is perhaps more mercenary than the American press which, despite Supreme Court rulings on the sanctity of a journalist's sources of information, enjoys a constitutional role known as the "fourth estate". The British press is also free of the over-emphasis on profit which is common in some sections of the Common Market, while the press in most Third World countries resents the attitude of some European PROs that their press must be as mercenary as the European.

The role and significance of the press varies enormously from country to country. In some countries the press, or a large part of it, is state-controlled (e.g. Nigeria), or capable of being bought by sectional interests (e.g. Italy), or can be most authoritative (e.g. Germany), is free subject to "D" notices, law of libel, and the Official Secrets Act (e.g. United Kingdom), or is totally state-owned (e.g. USSR and China). In a country where there are some state-owned and some privately-owned publications, as in Nigeria, there can be an undeclared form of censorship when it is possible for an editor to offend the government and suffer imprisonment, so that no editor is quite sure of the extent to which he can be critical. However, on a subject like the deficiencies of the Lagos bus service, all papers are permitted to be as critical as they wish. And as we have seen in the USA, where there are ten-thousand newspaper editors, the American press is jealous of its right to print official documents if it deems this to be in the public interest, no matter how "secret" they may be. No British newspaper would dare do this. When a comparatively minor official report on transport plans was published, it resulted in a police raid on some trade press offices.

When one sees how a 3½ million circulation can be bought at pounds per reader for a newspaper in which contests, features and gimmicks show the British reader's contempt for news e.g. the *Sun*, while *The Times* must be a costly hobby for the Thomson organization; and the *Daily Mirror* and the *Daily Express* (both having lost more than a million circulation each in recent years) tried to resort to door-step canvassing in 1972 to urge home delivery sales, the UK press is something of a media curiosity. The *Guardian* and the *Financial Times* represent respectively intelligent and informative journalism. The *Daily Telegraph* remains the best labour market place.

Nevertheless, this medium predominates among literate people, and in PR the practice of press relations predominates among PR functions. The paradox in Britain is that because so many publications have failed in the last two decades, British PR has recruited mainly from the redundant or available labour force of ex-journalists or working journalists. This has been a good and a bad thing, forgetting for the moment that there are as many different grades and categories of journalists as there are "engineers" who can range from boiler maintenance staff to designers of bridges and tunnels. Obviously, a very experienced journalist is an asset to PR because of his wide knowledge of the world. However, the journalist is a mixed blessing in PR for two reasons: a first-class journalist (not a cub reporter from the *Bisley Bugle*) has experience, knowledge and ability which is *adaptable* to PR, but unfortunately this earlier career tends to inhibit the journalist from undertaking training in PR techniques which are by no means confined to press relations. It is perfectly true that some journalist applicants for PR jobs think that attendance at press receptions is all they need to know about PR. The result is a PR labour force enjoying nothing like the training undertaken by marketing personnel. A marketer may be forgiven if he takes lightly the advice of a PRO or PR consultant whose only training is that of having been a journalist. Many eminent journalists have failed to market newspapers and magazines successfully.

The importance of the UK press rests more on its nature than on its practitioners. Britain has a long history of literature, as witness the eighteenth-century novel, and coffee house newspaper, the more professionally produced nineteenth-century novel, the lending library and novels published in weekly or monthly parts, the newspapers published to proclaim political causes, and the evolution of the popular daily newspaper culminating in Northcliffe's ha'penny *Daily Mail* in 1896.

The compactness of the British Isles, the rapid spread of railways, urbanization and industrialization, the Forster Education Act of 1870, mass production and mass consumption—all these dramatic forces of the mid to late nineteenth century helped to create the twentieth century British press. A glance at directories such as *Advertiser's Annual* or the *Newspaper Press Directory* will instantly reveal the thousands of titles that exist, no matter how many failures there may have been.

Urbanization, industrialization, transportation and education are the keys to the nature of the UK press. A compact land, densely populated, enjoying a high standard of living, educated and literate, encourages a diversity of interests and tastes. The result is a press that aims to satisfy far-ranging demands; rival publications covering topics which would be no more than single features in general magazines in most other countries; and a set of national morning and Sunday newspapers completely unlike each other. In most countries of the world the only available periodical on the great majority of technical subjects is one imported from either the UK or the USA.

There is one even more important distinction. While it is true that England, Scotland, Wales and Northern Ireland each has its own national press, it is also true that when we speak of the "national press" we mean that which radiates from the principal UK press centre of London's Fleet Street. (Fleet Street has become a somewhat mythical expression since many publishers are now operating up to fifteen miles from the former Grub Street.) Even so, the bulk of the UK national press is "London" based. As will be explained, this is not so in many other countries which have neither a single press centre nor nationally circulating newspapers.

Couple this centralization of the British press with the rail, road and air communication network of the UK—which has made distribution possible despite transportation breakdowns and strikes—and the immediacy, complexity and volume of publications makes the press a medium of major importance to the British PR practitioner. The centrality of the British press is not likely to be disturbed but rather enhanced when it becomes possible to print late edition national newspapers from regional centres, copy being received electronically from London editorial offices.

An Analysis of the UK Press

The following is a breakdown of the main groups of publications that exist in the UK:

National mornings	Regional mornings
London evenings	Regional evenings
National sundays	Regional sundays
National magazines covering class and specialized interests	Town, surburban, regional weeklies
	Free sheets—usually weekly
National trade, technical and professional magazines	Regional magazines—city, county, Chamber of Commerce, trade journals
Directories, Year Books	Local directories, guide books, maps

This analysis is peculiar to the British press whose structure owes much to compact geography, heavy urbanization, and good road, rail and air transportation. Different structures occur in other countries. In France some of the largest circulation dailies are found outside the capital in cities such as Marseilles. In Western Germany the press tends to range from regional papers like the *Frankfurter Allgemeine Zeitung* to provincial dailies such as the *Trierische Landeszeitung*, with the *Bild Zeitung* having local editions. Large land masses such as the USA have many large-circulation local dailies (often with syndicated national material), and famous American titles are the *New York Times, Baltimore Sun, Chicago Tribune, Washington Post, Los Angeles Times* and the *San Francisco Chronicle*. Italy has its big circulation press centred on cities such as Rome, Genoa, Milan, Naples and Turin. The Japanese press is almost wholly centred on Tokyo. In Nigeria, where newspapers tend to be based on states, the *Daily Times* of Lagos (itself located in a far corner of a vast land) has sought to penetrate the country as a whole and circulates a thousand miles away from base. India, where numerous languages justify regional dailies, has the English language *Times of India* published simultaneously in Bombay, Delhi and Ahmedabad. In Singapore and Malaysia the *Straits Times* enjoys a dual national coverage with simultaneous publication in Kuala Lumpur and Singapore. Australia and Canada follow the US pattern with major city newspapers to name only the *Sydney Morning Herald*, *Melbourne Age*, *Toronto Globe and Mail* and the *Montreal Gazette*, Canada's oldest newspaper.

With so many thousands of journals published daily, weekly, fortnightly, monthly, quarterly or annually, the scope for press relations is clearly enormous, provided skill is applied in the choice of media, the preparation of suitable material for particular classes of journal, and the correct timing of its despatch. But as we shall see in the next chapter, poverty of press relations skills results in 70 per cent of PR material being useless and therefore rejected. The principal unlearned skill in press relations is the ability to despatch the fewest possible necessary stories to the right editors at the right time. The PRO who boasts of the number of stories he sends out is a menace to his employers, the PR profession and the press. The PRO who can be congratulated on having achieved maximum coverage with the minimum number of releases containing the minimum number of words and sent to the minimum number of editors is a model for all to copy. He hardly exists.

Requirements of the Press

To succeed with press relations it is essential to understand for each individual publication:

1. Editorial policy
2. Frequency of publication
3. Copy date
4. Printing process
5. Circulation area
6. Readership profile
7. Method of distribution

To have a fair working knowledge of these seven points is to understand something of newspaper and magazine publishing. Not many journalists know this much about the individual paper they work on, let alone about the vast British press as a whole. It is an anomaly of the press world that journalists seldom know much about the publishing business, and journalists are therefore often nonplussed when they enter

PR and need to have an intimate knowledge of these seven factors which are often common knowledge to advertising personnel. Marketing people may know even less about publishing than journalists, and their slight knowledge of the advertising side is likely to be irrelevant. The PRO should know more about press media than either the journalist or the marketer. More than that, the PRO needs comparative knowledge, so that he can be selective when making mailings or sending out invitations. In effect he must market releases and press events. So let us now examine each of these seven factors in turn. It will also help the marketer to appreciate the specialized knowledge that he may expect in a proficient PR practitioner.

1. *Editorial Policy*

Obviously, no-one can read every newspaper and magazine. Even if one did, quite a few would change in the course of time. Titles change, merge, come and go. Some new magazines succeed—like *Cosmopolitan*—yet others fail as did *Candida*. The *Daily Telegraph* succeeded with a colour magazine, but the *Daily Mirror* was unlucky. *Woman's Weekly*, with a change of printing process, succeeded with a format hardly different from that employed forty years ago, but *Woman's Day* never had a birthday.

The PRO has to be familiar with this battleground of the press, in which each publication is utterly individual. The mass mailing of the same story to scores, even hundreds, of journals seldom makes sense, although one need not go to the extreme of writing exclusives. But editors do complain with justification that they are sent far too many stories of no possible relevance to them.

How does the PRO find out what editors want? There are published guides such as *British Rate and Data*, the *Newspaper Press Directory* or the *PR Planner*. Overseas press directories are listed at the end of this chapter. Newspapers and magazines are displayed on bookstalls and in libraries of various kinds, and may be found in reception rooms, offices and other people's homes. It pays to study publications at every opportunity—there are plenty of opportunities for the inquisitive traveller—and it should be no hardship to make oneself thoroughly familiar with the twenty or thirty journals which are of direct day-to-day relevance to one's trade or industry. Then it will be seen that there is no such thing as "the press" or the "mass media", but that journals have distinct characteristics like all the people one deals with individually. On top of that, each is produced by an editor with a mind of his own, with his own likes and dislikes, with an identity, not merely "the editor".

Understanding editorial policies is fascinating, time-consuming, important and it distinguishes the professional PRO from the hack bulk-mailer of useless news releases. This is very different from the false idea that a good PRO is one with "Fleet Street contacts". A "good" PRO needs no contacts if he has a publishable story and knows how, when and where to place it. There is no substitute for skill and knowledge and above all hard work. These skills can be studied, learned, acquired and applied by anyone, man or woman, who has three basic qualities: ability to communicate, organize and get on with other people.

This is because, in order to survive in a desperately competitive world, an editor must first of all please his readers. If the PRO can help the editor to please readers and sell papers, his story will be welcome.

2. *Frequency of Publication and Copy Date*

As a general rule, the more frequently a journal is published the more topical will be its contents. A newspaper tends to carry hundreds of small items, the magazine a smaller number of longer features. Again, the fewer issues per year the less opportunity there is to carry over material to the following issue without it becoming stale news. Moreover, while a monthly magazine may go to the printers weeks, perhaps months, before publication, the lead time is days with a weekly and hours with a daily. Consequently, it is necessary to know how often journals are published, and the last dates for copy. This knowledge can require the elimination of certain otherwise interested journals from the mailing list, for no editor is pleased to receive a good story if only he had received it a week ago. Such a lesson would seem to be obvious, yet the common practice is to mail stories to standard lists irrespective of what has been said above. It is like sending a load of bricks to a builder after he has built the house.

3. *Printing Process*

Closely related to frequency and copy date is knowledge of the printing process. Is it letterpress, photogravure or offset-litho? This information is given in *BRAD*, but general assumptions may be that national daily and Sunday newspapers are printed by letterpress, regional evening papers by either letterpress or web-offset-litho, big circulation magazines like the women's weeklies and weekly television magazines by photogravure, and trade journals by either letterpress or offset-litho. That still calls for more perfect knowledge, either from published details of mechanical data (e.g. on rate cards or in *BRAD*), or by the ability to recognize how a journal is printed.

Also, certain printing processes predominate in certain countries.

A simple recognition process is to look at the type. With letterpress there is liable to be an indentation of the paper, with photogravure the characters will be made irregular by the grid-like resist, while with offset-litho the characters will be perfect and seem to sit on the paper. Again, cruder papers like newsprint are used for newspaper printing by letterpress; women's magazines printed by photogravure use a cheap but polished supercalendered paper (they are *not* glossies), the illustrations are ill-defined, flat and velvety, and the smell of the ink is usually noticeable. With offset-litho, detail of pictures is very good and the inks are glossy and rich, and well-finished papers are replacing the hard, cartridge papers that used to typify offset-litho.

It is necessary to be familiar with printing processes for two reasons: (1) the type of illustration required, and (2) the lead time between editorial production and print production. While letterpress plates can be changed for different editions of the paper, litho plates take rather longer to produce, and photogravure sleeves take very much longer. Moreover, with a photogravure job it is likely that there will be four colours so the platemaking time is quadrupled. This is important when timing the distribution of news stories and pictures, holding press receptions and organizing press visits. A really big story could be given to a national morning during the previous afternoon and printed overnight, but a story for a women's magazine is likely to be required three months in advance. It would be useless to mail the same news release simultaneously.

In fact, understanding of printing processes could result in a Christmas gift story being issued in January for the trade press, July for women's magazines, November for regionals and December for nationals.

Again, this is vital to the marketer who, aware of the mechanical restraints on the PRO's ability to publish, can keep him briefed as early as possible, not thrust a press relations task upon him when action is no longer feasible. Press officers frequently try to excuse themselves by saying that the timing of a release was bad because of the lateness of authority to issue it: quite frankly, such a story should be spiked by the press officer, not by scores of irritated editors. This is yet another instance of how marketers and PROs need to learn from one another.

4. *Circulation Area*

In a large town it may be found that one weekly concentrates on a particular circulation area, while another paper circulates elsewhere. Similarly, one national daily may tend to sell more copies in the north than in the south while another has a more generally national distribution. Some trade, technical and professional journals may have either mainly UK or largely international circulations. The circulation areas of regional newspapers are described in the *Newspaper Press Directory*, but one may have to be wary of the implied overseas distribution of a journal with *International* in its title. The extent of overseas circulation might be wishful thinking or be based on uninvited postal distribution to foreign addresses. In some large countries, specialised journals are often confined to geographical areas, or several publishing centres publish similar journals, and so these publications lack national coverage.

A typical example of the importance of circulation area occurs in the mailing of a product story to regional newspapers, say to home page editors of local dailies. What is to be done if the product is not available in every large town covered by an evening newspaper? The PRO has two options: he can do a blanket mailing or a selective one to papers covering the towns where there are stockists.

The temptation may be to cover the lot in the hope that reader enquiries will spur retailers into ordering stocks. But most journals (especially nationals) will not print a product story unless assured about availability of goods. This can be difficult where the manufacturer has a range of lines and does not know precisely what any stockist holds, and it becomes even more tricky when distribution is through wholesalers.

A solution is for a salesman with buffer stocks to stock up a shop whose address has been given to a local newspaper that is publishing a story about the product.

Sometimes a national advertiser may have virtually national distribution, yet not have a stockist in every town covered by the regional press. It is therefore embarrassing if the local daily runs a story about a product which is unobtainable in local shops. This is just as bad as the marketing mistake of advertising a product which has inadequate distribution. The annoyance of readers can recoil on the journalist concerned. This in turn is bad PR for the newspaper, and can set up bad press relations for the future between the PRO and the journalist who has been let down.

To play fair with journalists, and so encourage acceptance of press material, the news release mailing list should be matched against the stockist's list. The release can then be accompanied by either a note assuring the editor that there are stockists in the paper's circulation or, better still, a list of actual stockists' names and addresses can be added to or attached to the release. This is even more helpful than sending the editor a complete national list which requires searching through for relevant addresses. The onus is on the PRO to save the editor the trouble.

Precisely this operation was carried out when a new Necchi sewing machine was introduced, and journalists were also invited to visit a dealer and accept a demonstration of the machine. That is a practical instance of marketing a story by appreciating the circulation areas of the newspapers involved, and deleting those which were not relevant. Moreover, it shows the PRO's understanding of his client's marketing strategy, and includes the bonus client service of helping to create or maintain good dealer relations. It also indicates how marketer and PRO need to co-operate, the marketer making available stockists' lists and PRO taking the initiative in making use of them. But from the purely PR point of view, it is an example of the thoughtfulness that cements press relations. It is to such a PRO that the local journalist bothers to send a change of address when moving to another newspaper!

5. *Readership Profile*

Who reads each journal? Sex, age, income, social status, employment, interests—all this statistical information is available in the JICNARS readership survey, and in individual survey reports issued by publishers, of which the *Woman* and *Financial Times* studies are particularly well known. Publishers of controlled circulation magazines will also supply breakdowns showing classes of reader and proportions of these classes to whom the journal is sent. From the *Newspaper Press Directory* one can learn the readerships aimed at by each magazine. There is no dearth of such information, and once again the message is that PR properly executed is hard work and time-consuming.

Perhaps this is a good point to admit that in employing PR the marketer can expect only what he is prepared to pay for. If he wants PR on the cheap, then it may well be less expensive in time and labour costs to blanket mail all and sundry and maintain the contempt of editors.

But armed with the vital statistics that are available, it does become possible—and sensible—to select for a mailing list (and each story deserves its own) only those journals which are read by prospects, and therefore by readers likely to be interested in the story. This will then be apparent to the editor who will be encouraged to find space for the story. It is not so much a case of not sending a story about a motor hearse to a sports car magazine as restricting stories to sports car magazines to those of interest to sports car enthusiasts.

One final warning: titles may not indicate the true readership profile. Consider, for example, the titles *Marketing* and *Marketing Forum*. How would one expect the average twenty-year-old account executive in a PR consultancy to know the difference in readership, unless he or she took the trouble to find out? The chances are that the same story would be sent to both, yet neither prints many PR stories, and their readerships are quite different.

6. *Method of Distribution*

How the journal reaches the reader can be a measure of its impact and influence, determining whether it should be placed on a mailing or invitation list. Often, it will also distinguish the kind of content and therefore whether it is suitable for the supply of news item, picture, feature article, or interview material. Methods of distribution are:

(i) Bookstall or retail/counter sales.
(ii) Bookstall or retail/home and business delivery.
(iii) Postal subscription.
(iv) Postal controlled circulation—membership.
(v) Postal controlled circulation—request/selected.
(vi) Free sheet—door-to-door.
(vii) Free customer distribution—various (external house journal).

To explain the difference between (i) and (ii), reference may be made to the controversy over canvassing by the *Daily Mirror* and *Daily Express*, in 1972, the object being to increase home delivery sales. Papers like the *Daily Mirror* and *Sun*, having largely working-class readerships, have fewer home delivery sales than, say, the *Daily Telegraph*, because their readers usually start work earlier and so leave home before newspapers are delivered. Home delivery is a better guarantee of regular purchase, and it may also secure some family readership before the paper is taken out of the house and perhaps discarded during the day.

The class and quality of readership of a journal is as valuable in PR as in advertising except that in PR the tendency is to appeal to a broader spectrum of people, or to people not addressed by the advertising. While a firm may not advertise its mass market products in the *Financial Times*, this will be the medium for corporate news. Although the circulation may be less than 200,000, the average readership of four persons per copy plus its influential overseas circulation makes the *FT* more valuable than a multi-million circulation daily like the *Daily Mirror* or *Daily Mail* for the appearance of a corporate or a financial story. It is even worth remembering that while most newspapers suffer a drop in circulation on Saturdays, the *FT* enjoys a rise, and its home delivery sales are consequently of great importance.

Postal subscription sales may or may not be indicative of a journal's power. In the case of a trade or technical magazine, copies posted to subscribers may represent meagre penetration of the market. Far greater penetration is usually gained by controlled circulation journals.

On the other hand, a specialist magazine like the internationally famous *National Geographic* depends on postal subscriptions for such a large, scattered, international circulation.

Membership of a professional body such as the Institute of Marketing or Institute of Public Relations entails receipt of a regular journal, and its value can be judged to some extent by the membership figures and the calibre of membership. *Marketing* has a monthly circulation in excess of 18,000, *Public Relations*, also monthly, is just over 3000. Appropriate conclusions can be drawn from these revealing figures. *Campaign* sells about 14,000 copies weekly. *Adweek* 5000, partly bookstall, partly postal subscription. The *Financial Times* runs its Marketing Scene feature every Thursday, and its sale of nearly 200,000 copies is mostly retail.

Thus, a story equally suitable for all five might be published in a daily, two weeklies and two monthlies over a period of probably two months. Time-scale, probability of acceptance, influence of journal have all to be considered. On a considered evaluation of the media mentioned it may be decided that only certain of the five editors will be interested, or that only certain of the five readerships matter (they are by no means identical), or that the time-scale is too protracted for the story to retain its newsworthiness.

In other words, as we have said before, the story has to be marketed even when we can narrow down the mailing list to only five titles. According to the substance of the story, we may reduce the list to one or even decide that it is of no interest to any of them, however much we would like to see publication. Such care reduces the volume of stories distributed, as well as the number of copies sent out of any one story, and so enhances the welcome of those that are received.

However, the point to be emphasized in the above exercise is that the mode of distribution can be a useful guide to the inclusion of a title in a mailing list. For example, privately circulated professional magazines seldom have space for material other than domestic news, conference reports and possibly commissioned features, and have no space for PR material that is not of direct member interest. Yet they are frequently mailed by PROs with no knowledge of their content and purpose just because they have a promising title.

Free sheet publications seldom have a generous editorial content, but the circulation may be enormous, perhaps 100,000 copies in a single residential area. A strong community interest story may find the free sheet an ideal medium, but so too may it be a good medium for product stories of seasonal, household or gardening interest. Free sheets are a modern publishing phenomenon not to be ignored. They can have massive penetration with great reader interest as response to advertising proves.

The last form of free distribution concerns the external house magazine on which a special chapter is devoted, as this is an exceptionally interesting PR development that has yet to be fully exploited.

Nature of the International Press

The above examples, taken from the UK press, may be applicable to the press in other parts of the world, but the nature of newspapers and magazines elsewhere is bound to differ according to local conditions such as size of country, communications, literacy, multi-language problems, cultural influences and so on. Marketing/PR practitioners will therefore have to adapt their tactics, and the following are some of the differences and special characteristics which may be encountered.

Small Circulation

When one realizes that many countries—for example some members of the EEC—have territories and populations no larger than English counties, while the capitals of huge countries like Australia are no larger than English provincial cities, it is possible to view the circulations of their newspapers—and the parochial nature of their contents—with proper understanding. It may be, for example, that they will report nothing not directly concerning their readers. Save during the 1965-6 civil war, the British daily press is almost completely silent about affairs in Nigeria while, save, for English football results, the Nigerian daily press is similarly disinterested in news about Britain. But excellent reports about Nigeria (and other African countries) can be read in the *Standard Bank Review*, *West Africa*, *African Development* or the Third World magazine *New Internationalist* which probably published more in its May 1973 issue about Tanzania than had appeared in the British press for years. So, when the temptation is to send a news release to the press of other countries the question must be asked, "Is it likely to interest the people out there?" The chances are that the sender is the victim of wishful thinking, and he has not even bothered to try to relate the story to the needs of the distant reader. Even seemingly relevant stories may be rejected simply because the assumed relevance is not obvious in another country. It is hard, perhaps, for a foreign company (i.e. any exporter) to realize how alien, how unknown, how uninteresting that company is to people beyond its own frontier or shore. Interest develops only when there is a local subsidiary employing nationals, or when the product or service is put to actual use in the overseas country. People are interested in their own, and in many countries this is on a religious, provincial, regional, state, village or tribal basis. More than that, when papers are small they are too full of their own affairs to have space to spare for outside topics. As a further on-the-spot example, it is only necessary to look at a regional daily in Britain to see how little of its space is devoted to national British news let alone foreign news.

Thus small circulation and emphasis on local news go together.

Languages and Literacy

A great problem in some countries is the multiplicity of languages so that a single mass circulation newspaper is impossible, and several different language newspapers are required. This situation occurred in the USA when immigrant communities could read and speak only their own home tongues, and German language newspapers persisted in the mid-West for a long time. Often, radio is the natural mass medium and it is interesting that native workers on the Tan-Zam railway were mostly recruited by announcements on Tanzania radio.

Language is a problem not only of developing lands but of Belgium (French and Flemish), Canada (English and French), Switzerland (German, French, Italian and Romansh), Israel (Hebrew, Arabic, English and French), Arab Republic of Egypt (Arabic, French and English) and South Africa (English, Afrikaans, Zulu, Xhosa and Sotho).

Among developing countries the problem of numerous languages may be seen by these examples: India (14), Ghana (8), Pakistan (7), Malaysia (6), and Nigeria (10), although there is generally an official language such as English, Hindi, Urdu or Malay. In addition, there is the tragedy of *lost literacy* when the language learned at school, say English, is lost when the young person finds non-commercial employment and reverts to the local tongue of farm and village, or loses ability to read and write but retains speech on the learned language. In both cases, radio becomes the only broadscale medium.

Antipathy to PR

If one is used to the press relations situation that exists in the USA and the UK it may be hard to appreciate why the press in some other countries is reluctant to accept PR material. The reasons are varied and may differ from country to country and between classes of journal. Some reference has been made above to small circulations and multi-lingual problems, and these are at the root of certain attitudes.

Specialized journals may rely much more seriously on advertisement revenue than UK journals with similar titles, and with smaller incomes from cover prices owing to smaller sales their editors are more inclined to see PR stories as "puffs". With fewer pages to fill, they do not have to seek material from PR sources, and when PROs offer them material that they do not really need they will invite the sponsor to pay for the privilege of publication. It is an ironic twist on the anxiety of the British PRO to maintain the integrity of the press and help it to do its job. The struggling publisher of a small journal sees the PRO as someone with a company or a client that has something to sell and money to pay for its promotion. The larger and probably more frequently issued British or American journal will have a greater demand for all sorts of editorial material compared with a journal confined by territorial and language barriers. People the world over may read a journal printed in English, and to some extent in German or French, but less so in Dutch, Swedish or Portuguese.

There is still another dilemma facing foreign publishers for in the countries of the EEC circulations are falling and for economic reasons the PR story will be welcomed only as a source of revenue. The lineage system of charging by-the-line for product stories is common in Europe, especially among German technical journals, while hosting is typical of French newspapers, editorial space being as much for sale as the advertisement columns, and journalists writing PR features at rates fixed by the editors. In Mediterranean countries, bribery may be the accepted way of achieving publication, but we have to realize that the newspapers concerned have circulations often smaller than British regional evenings. There are also French women's magazines where all the editorial-looking features are paid for by advertisers. Nevertheless, there are bigger circulation, successful and reputable publications which accept legitimate news material from PR sources. The main trouble is that in Europe there are too many struggling, peripheral publications which will accept income one way or another.

When the author talked to the news editor of the Nigerian *Daily Times*, it was emphasized how Nigerian journalists resented "the envelope" containing banknotes which sometimes accompanied news releases handed out a press conferences. It was also chastening to see how an expatriate oil company, seeking coverage of a story about the award of two scholarships, had been obliged to insert the story and pictures in the advertisement column. The editor had taken the view that it was paltry of such a big organization to award only two scholarships and then to expect press coverage. But the same issue of the newspaper contained a picture story about a piece of British mining machinery which merited space because of its reader interest in a country anxious to expand its indigenous extractive industry.

These observations are made because while it is true that PR is a universal practice, press relations can be a sophistication enjoyed in Britain and the USA but perhaps in diminishing degrees in many other parts of the world, including Europe, where journals are smaller, in less need of editorial material but in great need of financial support. A plea is made in Chapter 9 for the privately published external house magazine as an answer to the dearth of technical journals in developing countries.

Decentralized Publishing Centres

Another difference between the UK press and that of other countries, including the USA, is that a national press centre like Fleet Street is rare. Mostly, this is because of the greater size of other countries. Sometimes it is because of regional languages, and it may be bound up with delineations of states or former independent kingdoms. While this is true of very large countries like the USA and India, it is equally true of Germany which is well known for its important regional press centres. The much-vaunted so-called "national" *Frankfurter Allgemeine Zeitung* sells fewer copies than the *Guardian*, and although the popular picture paper *Bild Zeitung* does win 90 per cent of street sales with a circulation of 3½ million, it is printed in eight different cities with localized editions.

Decentralized press centres tend to operate against big circulation national journals, and result in numerous city newspapers, often with much syndicated material common to all of them, which would be amalgamated as one national daily or Sunday newspaper in the UK. However, cities like New York, Chicago and Los Angeles are so far apart that their city dailies have a status superior to the regional city mornings in the UK which have to compete with the London giants.

Distance and Transportation

The excellent road, rail and air communications found in industrialized countries, whether compact like Britain or huge like the USA and Australia, and the technological wonders of facsimile and teletypesetting processes, make possible the production of mass circulation newspapers containing up-to-date news. These urbanized communities are also literate, so that there is a demand for cheap, regular publications. But in developing countries, of which fast-developing Nigeria is a good example (being a vast country that contains a quarter of the black population of Africa), big distances, modest transportation, illiteracy (and lost literacy), and many languages deter the building of large circulations and the provision of up-to-date news. The biggest circulation Nigerian daily, the *Daily Times* (230,000 circulation), is worked up forty-eight hours in advance, printed at midday, and sent on sixteen-hour road journeys to far-off cities like Kano (900 miles away) where it is sold next day as the morning paper. This means that news releases are required three days in advance of possible publication! In contrast, British morning papers are just as available in Amsterdam or Cologne as they are in Plymouth or Huddersfield, and they can be bought in Lagos (3000 miles away) the day after publication. No doubt the rapidly expanding domestic airlines will bring about improvements in the distribution of Nigerian newspapers, and while the *Daily Times* seeks to be national, there are regional dailies throughout the country.

British Publications Overseas

For a great many years the British trade, technical and professional press has vied only with the American as producers of authoritative journals of international repute. The *Financial Times* has an important overseas circulation which makes it one of the great newspapers of the world and, as we shall see in Chapter 7 on Sponsorships, its "Clipper" yacht race is partly aimed at enhancing this international reputation. With such a good name already well established, entry into Europe has given the British press a well-deserved opportunity to become leading European publishers, crossing frontiers with a continental instead of national press.

Among British publishers, IPC have pioneered ventures of value to British marketers and PR practitioners, one of the most striking being *Electronic Product News*, which was launched in Belgium in September 1972. It is edited in Brussels and printed in Doetinchem, Holland. The controlled circulation exceeds 50,000 copies, and the requested circulation was 43,000 in 1974. It is circulated free of charge throughout Europe and Israel, but readers outside *EPN*'s control requirement may subscribe, and paid subscriptions outside Europe are sent air mail. The circulation is split between technician, management and purchasing personnel. The publishers are now Elsevier IPC Europe BV.

This is a new kind of export journal in more ways than one. First, it is printed in *English*. (It is interesting how English is becoming the accepted journalistic language in Europe, while European firms issue international PR material in English, especially the Dutch and the Scandinavians.) Second, the applied for reader is given a number rather like that on a credit card, and he uses this to seek reader enquiry information. If he changes his address or job function he is given a fresh number. Third, the reader enquiry card (with English, French or

German versions) permits the reader to state whether he wishes to receive a telephone call, literature, a salesman's visit or a stockist's address. The editorial columns consist of typical cc journal illustrated product stories with reader enquiry reference numbers. The items are not solely European and include reports from Israel, Japan and the USA.

Another innovation from IPC is International Business Press Associates which links together leading national trade and technical journals so that they have integrated editorial policies. They are also closely linked with international exhibitions. Thus both advertising and PR coverage can be obtained in groups of similar journals covering electronics, plastics, packaging, mechanical handling, chemicals and traffic management. The packaging group includes *Emballages* (France), *Imballaggio* (Italy), *Industrial Verpakken* (Holland), *Neue Verpacking* (Germany), *Pack* (Sweden), *Package Engineering* (USA) and *Packaging Review* (UK). Using such groups of magazines, a producer can promote his goods simultaneously in reputable foreign language journals whose editorial and advertisement content is subject to policy discussions in which IPC has a powerful voice. There are nine member publishers in the IBPA organization representative of the USA, Spain, France, Italy, Sweden, Hong Kong, Germany, Holland and the UK and a total of 320 titles.

Yet a third IPC enterprise has been the purchase of shareholdings in European publishing companies and the extension of British editorial expertise to found new journals. In 1962 Koradin-Verlag of Stuttgart published magazines about interior design, jewellery and textiles, but with IPC's association the first German-language electronics journal was launched. Moreover, it was a cc tabloid, something quite new in Germany. Other titles followed covering chemical processing, design engineering, traffic management, computer operations, data processing, packaging, oil and coal, machine management and paints, varnishes and lacquers.

In these ways British traditions and experience in trade and technical journalism have been taken to other parts of the world, principally Europe, so that the wealth of press relations long experienced by editors in Britain and the USA can now be enjoyed by editors heading journals of similar calibre elsewhere.

Sources of Press Information

Advertiser's Annual, Mercury House, Waterloo Road, London SE1 8UL
British Rate and Data, 35–39 Maddox Street, London W1R 9LD
Newspaper Press Directory, Lyon Tower, 125 High Street, Colliers Wood, London SW19 2JN.
PR Planner, Morgan's PR Systems Ltd., 1, Lily Place, Saffron Hill, London EC1 8YJ.
Willings Press Guide, James Willing Ltd, 3–4 Holborn Circus, London EC1.

Overseas

USA	*Standard Rate and Data Service Catalogs*, Standard Rate and Data Service Inc., 5201 Old Orchard Road, Skokie, Illinois 60076.
AUSTRALIA	Thomson Publications (Aust) Pty Ltd, 47 Chippen Street, Chippendale, New South Wales.
CANADA	*Canadian Advertising Rates & Data*, Maclean-Hunter Ltd, 481 University Avenue, Toronto 2.
FRANCE	*Societe d'Edition de l'Annvaire de la Presse*, 24 Place Malesherbes, 75017 Paris.
HUNGARY	*Magyar Hirdeto*, PO Box 367, 1 Felszabadu Terrace, Budapest 3.
ITALY	*Dati e Tariffe Pubblicitarie, SpA*, Via Meravigli 3, Milano 20123.
JAPAN	Dentsu's Japan Marketing/Advertising, Dentsu Advertising Ltd, 1–11 Tsukiji, Tokyo.

MEXICO	*Medios Publicitarios Mexicanos,* Av. Mexico 99–501, Mexico 11 DF.
SCANDINAVIA	*Media Scandinavia,* Dankse Reklamebureauers Brancheforening, 7 Frederiksgade, Copenhagen K.
SPAIN	*Guia de los Medios Publicitarios Espanoles,* Maria de Molina 68, Madrid.

CHAPTER 4

The Nature of Press Relations

'UNIQUE" is one of the cliché words of bad news release writing, and the surest way to kill a story is to claim that a subject is unique. Along with "breakthrough", "wide range", "this point in time", "facilitates" and "invalidates", it belongs to every editor's collection of PR clichés.

All the same, in cultured industrial countries which enjoy a sophisticated press that serves countless specialist interests, there is inevitably an unsatisfied demand for original material. Rivalry between journals, frequency of issue, size of issue and range of topic all contribute to this demand. In this surely unique situation the press officer serves the press first and his master last. His master—maybe a marketer—may protest that he pays the piper, not the press. But consider, there is no sense in paying a piper whose pipe is muted before he blows a note. Pleasing his master last may be the only way the press officer is likely to please him at all.

It is therefore fair to say that it is a unique situation, when editors and journalists are unable to produce their journals without the help of PROs and press officers. Without this help they would never know of the majority of topics which fill their columns, and they would never know where to turn for information.

Addressing the World PR Congress in Geneva in April 1973, Professor Cutlip, the American PR consultant, claimed that recent studies had shown that "35% of the news content of the American press came from PR typewriters."

Not for nothing do journalists, when changing jobs, plead to be kept on PR mailing lists. When new publications come out, editors and feature writers regularly circularize PR sources asking to be kept informed. And most editorial offices have a well-used copy of the

Hollis Press and Public Relations Annual which lists thousands of PR addresses. In countries with fewer, smaller journals the situation is different, but in the UK, USA, Canada, Australia and other countries with a considerable press, even front-page political stories have usually been serviced by PROs. No organization can now afford to be without its own press relations service, whether it employs its own in-house staff or uses an outside PR unit.

Incidentally, when American politics and elections are being criticized it is usual to imply that candidates and politicians are "manipulated" by PR men. But it is curious that we learn time and time again that the people employed to promote parties and presidential candidates are *advertising agents*, not public relations consultants. Some people simply do not know the difference; others do not want to. It would be difficult to imagine a British politician being "manipulated" by his civil servant chief information officer, while the PR consultants employed by British prime ministers in their election campaigns seem to have been inept rather than evil! Their advertising agents have been comedians compared with those who have tried to "make the President."

Reverting to press relations in this situation where information is welcomed, the point to be taken into account by the marketer is that it is the PRO who does the favours, not the press. No longer are we talking about gin and tonics and "good Fleet Street contacts", the fairyland of management playing at PR. The hard facts are that the press want to publish information of interest to their readers, otherwise circulation will slide and journals will fold. Any attempt to "con the press", or any failure to supply publishable reliable facts, technically well presented and correctly timed, will create bad press relations and rejection.

This is a lesson that suppliers of news releases and pictures seem astonishingly unwilling to learn, and as a result the press regard much of the British PR business with contempt. Conversely, their praise and respect for truly professional PROs is generous to the point of their entertaining PROs instead of the traditional opposite!

It is not at all difficult to satisfy the press, always accepting the little gamesmanship played when reporters harry VIPs for revelations they know they cannot possibly get! The rules of good press relations are remarkably simple. The biggest single problem is that far too many news releases are sent out, the next that the subject of the story is very seldom obvious at first glance, while the majority of PR pictures are not only bad but uncaptioned. We shall refer to PR pictures later in this chapter.

News editors of nationals claim that they have about one second flat in which to make a first assessment of each of the hundreds of news releases that confront them every day. What chance, then, has the typical three-page news release, which refers to the subject at the foot of page one or the middle of page two, or which has been rewritten to please the managing director, or in which the brand name is repeated at every opportunity and written in capital letters—if not underlined—to please the advertising or marketing manager? These are the monstrosities and absurdities of press relations served up in Fleet Street every day by some of the biggest firms the reader has ever heard of. This is no exaggeration, and any editor on any journal can prove it. Public relations is the profession of untrained amateurs. But for how much longer?

Once upon a time a bad story was "spiked", but the flood of PR material has instituted the giant editorial plastic dustbin. So here we have a ridiculous paradox: a sincere demand for original information exceeded by a supply that is 70 per cent rubbish. The only beneficiaries are the Post Office and the paper industry, the waste paper industry especially!

The editor of *Marketing* went further in the issue of February 1973 when he wrote: "We throw away something like 95 per cent of the releases received, and more than half of what we receive could not possibly be of the slightest interest to us. Indeed a good proportion could not be of interest to anyone."

The remarks made so far have not been intended as an attack on PR because quite clearly those deserving of this criticism know nothing about PR. The point is that in using PR services it is necessary for the marketer (a) to understand PR himself and (b) to employ personnel who beyond any shadow of doubt also understand PR.

It is also necessary to discover why editor after editor goes on record to condemn the standard of press relations. The bulk of obtuse non-stories rejected by editors are produced by ex-journalists, many of whom hold membership of the IPR. This author's own study of the problem reveals one stark, startling fact: bad news releases result from press officers having such lowly status in their organizations that they have no control over what is sent out in their names. Management, marketers and advertising agents are largely responsible for this prostitution of PR and for giving PR its undeservedly bad name.

This author's experience during the past fifteen years is that status has to be snatched by ignoring authority, and maintained by arguing from a position of strength because one's professionalism has succeeded when the wishes of authority would have failed. To maximize press coverage, the press officer cannot afford to be a "yes man".

To emphasize the need to apply marketing techniques to PR, here are a round dozen of the major faults that bedevil press relations. They can be righted by the application of simple marketing rules, the most obvious one being study of the market. It will be apparent that with a discard of 70 per cent very few news release writers and distributors have much knowledge of the market, that is the needs of the media. Couple that with the really destructive fact that most news release writers are primarily concerned to satisfy the wishes of their client or employer and it becomes perfectly plain why the PR game of postman's knock earns very few embraces from editors.

Twelve Reasons why 70 per cent of News Releases Fail

1. *Sent to the Wrong Publication*

Through lack of knowledge of the readership and editorial content of publications, mailing lists contain irrelevant titles. This occurs because it is not realized that a news release mailing list needs to be compiled as painstakingly as a media schedule for an advertising campaign. There is no sense in "taking a chance" because it involves just one more stamp: the cost of mismailing is an editor's spleen. Why dissipate his time and your welcome? Two faults lie here: media ignorance and careless compilation of the media list. Each story deserves its own list, for reasons which will be spelt out in these twelve reasons for rejection. There are some stories that suit only one editor, others which need different versions.

A really good PRO is a media expert, but how many know the difference between *Export* and *Export Times*, *Chemical Age* and

Chemist and Druggist, Sunday Post and *Sunday Independent, Midland Industrialist* and *Midlands Industry and Commerce, Electrical and Radio Trading* and *Electrical Review*? Similar titles, perhaps copied from a directory, can be very misleading to the uninitiated. Not surprisingly, if the special requirements of these journals with disarmingly similar titles are not known, they are likely to be sent useless releases.

Let us take two prime examples: The *Newspaper Press Directory* index lists some 150 titles under Agriculture and a similar number under Education, but very few stories (except perhaps those from government departments) are likely to be relative to more than between six and twenty titles. That might seem terribly obvious, but blanket mailings of every journal are indicated by the large number of editors (like the *Marketing* editor quoted above) who receive stories of no possible interest to them.

It is quite easy to find out what editors want, and it is set out very clearly in the *PR Planner* (see page 79). With regular up-datings of the information, the *Planner* and media service costs about £20 a year.

2. Sent to the Right Journal Too Late

In the previous chapter reference was made to the importance of knowing whether a journal is printed by letterpress, photogravure or offset litho, web-offset meaning that the work is printed from reels instead of single sheets of paper. Failure to appreciate the significance of the printing process can result in mistiming of distribution, like selling fireworks to the trade in mid-November. Yet it happens all the time because standardized, omnibus mailing lists are used unthinkingly.

Even if the printing process is understood, it is still important to know just how late one dare send out stories to certain newspapers and periodicals. It may be impossible to record every copy date, but at least one knows that most weekly newspapers come out towards the end of the week; that Monday is about the last date for uncommissioned copy so that to be really safe the release ought to be delivered by the previous Friday, that is the day after or the day on which the last issue was published. But—unless it is an extremely important story, about which the editor may have been telephoned—it is useless to deliver on Wednesday a story for a local weekly which is printed on Thursday for sale on Friday.

To follow this example further, a local weekly, a Sunday, a morning and an evening newspaper may all be printed letterpress, but their copy dates vary by hours to days, and it would be quite wrong to send them all the same story on the same day.

According to the type of story, or the kind and frequency of journal, it is wise to stagger mailings. Because of this time factor it may be found necessary to eliminate titles. Very urgent stories may need simultaneous despatch by a wire service such as the Press Association (if they will take it) or Universal News Service (if the sender is a subscriber), hand delivery or right-up-to-the-minute despatch by telephone. Mass mailings to all and sundry belong to inefficient PR departments of consultancies manned by untrained, inexperienced underpaid juveniles, a fault to be expected with consultancies that attempt to operate on uneconomically low fees. There are some 600 PR consultancies in the UK, far too many for efficiency. Most of them sell cheap services to clients who do not understand what they are buying.

This is a management problem, for if management wants to buy "on the cheap" it can expect only what it pays for, and PR is labour-intensive with man-hours the chief servicing cost. The kindest thing that can be said about some 400 of these so-called PR consultancies is that they know not what they do do and do not know the harm they do to PR. But the day will come when the Public Relations Consultants Association will have the status of the Institute of Practitioners in Advertising which should also mean that principals of PR consultancies will also have to be members of the CAM Society, not merely members of the Institute of Public Relations.

3. *Stale or Premature News*

News may be defined as fresh and original information. Immediacy is the keynote of the news media, and is made all the more essential by the advent first of radio and then television, and again with local radio. Many a good story is killed because management has been tardy about giving approval, but the PRO cannot get away with vague terms like "recent" or "last week". How recent is recent? Equally, prophetic news can be just as bad: no editor wants to mention a product which his readers cannot yet buy. So, just as it is bad to advertise before adequate distribution has been achieved, so is it vital to withhold posting of a story until national distribution (preferably with stockists' lists available) can be guaranteed. A marketing dilemma may be that in order to maintain security the marketer does not want to release information too early, but the decision has to be made whether he wants coverage in say the women's press or the trade press and is content with the national and regional dailies that can be reached at shorter notice. Inevitably, we are back to timing again!

The point to be noted here is that while delayed dispatch may suit the vagaries of managerial in and out trays. or the convenience of those who wish to play God, editors will not publish stories which they should have had yesterday, last week, last month or three months ago. Stale news is dead news. In contrast to this there are the timeless stories which editors set up, keep in galley proof, and use as "fillers" when empty spaces occur.

4. *The Story is a Puff*

Although the result of publication of a news release will be publicity of some sort—it *could* be unfavourable!—the story should contain unadorned facts free of comment. This is a hard lesson for marketers to learn, and press officers frequently complain that marketing, advertising and sales colleagues ruin news releases by trying to convert them into advertisements. Press coverage is not free advertising. It has nothing to do with advertising, and the marketer who misunderstands this is guilty of puffery. By putting company and brand names in capital letters, underlining them or repeating them, and by the use of unsubstantiated claims, generalities, self-praise and superlatives, a news story can become an advertisement or puff worthy only of the editor's spike or waste bin, or a paid-for insertion in the advertisement columns. There are even those on the marketing side who approach advertisement managers with requests to publish write-ups, again showing that they do not know the difference between advertising and public relations.

Such is the fear of giving free advertisements in the editorial columns that many editors—the bigger the journal the truer this is—delete all brand and often company names from stories, unless the reference is bad publicity for the brand or company. In the *Daily Express*, for instance, product names are usually eliminated from the product stories in Mary Collins's women's feature, while in criticizing products in the

Guardian Elisabeth Dunn names them. This obeys the Fleet Street precept that bad news is good news, good news is no news. But to be serious, the rule to follow is that a brand or company name should only appear in a sentence because no other word will fit, not because it is another chance to work in a plug.

5. *The Release is Too Long*

This is a good place to describe the four types of release:
1. The story that is publishable as it stands.
2. The background story.
3. The technical story preceded by a summary.
4. The extended caption story attached to a picture.

Clearly, these can be of varying length, but if every word counts, the length will range between the change of address amounting to a mere sentence and the explanation of a complicated piece of equipment which might run to two or three pages. However, it is not uncommon for some writers' ideas of a change of address story also to run to three pages!

Few press stories warrant more than a single A4 sheet, and it is not always necessary to fill it. *A golden rule is to try to get a news release onto one piece of paper.* Surprisingly, perhaps, this is nearly always possible. Most releases can be kept within 200–300 words. Unfortunately, when a perfectly reasonable story is being "approved" it is liable to suffer additions, as if other people seem to think that the mailing of a simple story is too good a chance to miss of saying extra things that really have nothing to do with the original story. A responsible press officer will discard these irrelevancies before running off copies, but, as we have said earlier, the lowly status of too many press officers precludes their ability to behave professionally. Instead, they behave like doctors in a hospital run by the patients.

6. *No Obvious Subject*

This major fault is both laughable and tragic. When pointed out, the fault is funny; but the tragedy lies in that one second editorial appraisal when the subject must be obvious in headline and opening words. This author has sat in editorial offices, news agencies and exhibition press offices and seen release after release without any obvious subject on the first page. These non-stories were on the printed headings of famous businesses, government departments and well-known PR consultancies. These were not, as might be expected, the ham-fisted efforts of people who would not be eligible for membership of the IPR.

In fact, some news release writers adopt a school essay style of "beginning, middle and end", or, quite deliberately, try to tease the editor into trying to guess what the story is all about. The correct technique—an extraordinarily easy one—can be learned simply by reading and analysing the opening paragraph of any newspaper story. Here are the opening words of reports from the front page of an issue of the London *Evening News:*

"Gasmen's leaders are prepared to talk . . .".
"Shock price increases . . .".
"Ten lions will set sail . . .".
"Former Beatle George Harrison . . .".
"Battling Joe Bugner flew . . .".
"Labour would double rates . . .".

The subject in each case is clear at first glance. Yet a typical news release starts: "H. G. Forman and Sons Limited, a member of the international group World Concentrates Incorporated of Boston, Mass., USA, have introduced, after extensive tests in their Hawaii research laboratories, a new jam jar that is square shaped and so more easily packed for bulk distribution." Far too many stories are written exactly like this when editors would be pleased to read something like "Forman's new jam jar is square-shaped and therefore easier to pack for bulk distribution." Who cares about Boston, Mass., except the company secretary? From these remarks the reader may gather why news releases should not be distributed internally. The patient's record sheet is not put under his pillow for him to read. What matters is the result of the treatment, or the resultant press clippings.

7. *No Identifiable Source*

Some releases do not state the sender's name and address and telephone number. The editor does not know on whose authority the story has been issued—it could be a hoax—and he is unable to ring back to query a point or seek extra information. All stories should carry the author's name, and also his home telephone (as well as his daytime) number, since many editors are working during the evening or at the weekend. A night editor may well want to check a proofed story before running it. When companies have several divisions or addresses, the one responsible for the story should be clearly stated. Even when there is a printed news release heading it pays to sign off the story with the writer's name and telephone number, especially if there is a continuation sheet. The writer may not be a PRO or press officer but on this occasion he should wear the hat of "press officer" because he is operating in that capacity. Editors are apt to be suspicious of stories from marketing, sales or advertising personnel.

8. *Incomplete Information*

There are two ways of making sure that the story does not invite requests for missing information: have a checklist of essential details required before writing, and then check what has been written. The editor should not have to beg for basic information which would have been included if only the writer had taken more trouble. News release composition is a painstaking job. Too many stories state "in three pastel shades," "in four popular sizes" or "at reasonable prices". Such naïve vagueness deserves the waste bin. What are the shades, the sizes, the prices? There is no secrecy about them.

A Seven-point Formula* can be applied which follows the following sequence: Subject—Organization—Location—Advantages—Applications—Details—Source. This makes an excellent drill for researching, composing and checking a publishable news release. While the subject should be in the first three words, the first paragraph should be a summary of the whole story. This elementary journalistic technique can, again, be seen in any press report.

9. *Cliché Ridden*

Everyone uses some clichés, and we all tend to create our own habit expressions, but as stated in the opening paragraph of this chapter there are some which are the favourites of news release writers.

* See F. Jefkins, *Press Relations Practice*, Intertext, London, 1968.

10. Too Literary

An article, short story or novel can and should be written with style and personal feeling for words, but a news release should be utterly utilitarian, factual and impersonal. The writer's personality and views should not obtrude. Releases should be written with the monotonous similarity of *Daily Express* reports. It is up to the editor to introduce editorial comment and house style, just as the stories on the *Financial Times* technical page, although mostly based on news releases, are carefully rewritten. But first the editor must have the bare facts. If they are presented much as he would have written them he may do no subbing, hence the ideal news release is one that is publishable, that is, acceptable as the editor's own work. That is the highest compliment a press officer can have, especially when a PR story is printed intact over a staff writer's byline. One way to avoid clichés is to keep a *Roget's Thesaurus* as a desk book.

Incidentally, we have so far recommended a useful miniature library which any PRO—or marketer, for that matter—should have. These have included the *Newspaper Press Directory, Hollis Press and Public Relations Annual, PR Planner, Press Relations Practice*, and *Roget's Thesaurus*, to which we would now add *Printing Reproduction Pocket Pal, Advertiser's Annual*, and the author's *Dictionary of Marketing and Communication*. And although this is an expensive monthly publication to which the marketer or PRO is unlikely to subscribe, it is useful to have a recent back number of or access to *British Rate and Data (BRAD)*. The bibliography at the end of Chapter 3 and at the end of this book gives fuller details of these and other references and textbooks.

11. Unsubstantiated Claims

While advertisement copy may use generalized or bombastic expressions such as "the fastest ship afloat" or "the strongest binding material", the news release must state the top speed of the ship or the degree of strength of the binding material. A news release is a factual report, and anything which cannot be substantiated is best left out. Claims such as first, last, shortest, longest, and so forth are usually impossible to guarantee, and editors detest having to apologize to those who protest that they have a better claim. There are other vague claims which are almost clichés, three of the worst being "ultramodern factory", "exhaustive trials" and "extensive research".

12. *Too Many Releases*

Frequent despatch of stories is not the best way of proving that consultant or PRO is working hard and earning his fee or salary. There are a great many times when it would be more professional if the release fell in the PR practitioner's own solitary wastebin instead of in scores of editors'. "Little and seldom" is a good rule and one bound to create good press relations, unless one's organization is so continuously newsworthy that a constant flow of news is justified, expected and welcomed. Press attachés of embassies send out daily to weekly bulletins of news according to the size and importance of their countries, but a country is a large complex "organization". Unhappily, there are companies of modest size which send out at least two stories a week and so tend to wear out their welcome. That is psychologically bad press relations.

One eminent PR consultant told the author "Nothing pleases me more than to walk round my office and see people pushing out stories for my clients." He was a menace to both PR and the press.

However, the mass of PR mail that hits editorial desks every day can be restrained and reduced in other ways, and these have been spelt out under subsections 1, 2, 3 and 4 of this chapter. Selection and evaluation of story and media are equally important.

Processing News Releases

The day of the grubby-looking release crudely duplicated on soggy paper is thankfully only a bad memory of older PROs. Most releases are clearly reproduced on office litho machines. But the greatest advance in legible news release production, coupled with efficient distribution, has been the setting up of specialist houses of which PRADS, Greencoat House, Francis Street, London SW1P 1DH is the pioneer and the best organized. PRADS offer a UK, North American and continental Europe service for the complete handling of release (and pictures) once the client has finalized the copy and chosen the media. The media list is maintained on a monthly basis and is more up-to-date and comprehensive than anything the individual PR department or consultancy has time to produce. The production and distribution of releases is a chore (and often an uneconomic cost) which the more efficient PR units now hand over to PRADS to service. PRADS will not, of course, select media, but the way in which their ring-binder catalogue is organized makes it very easy to pick journals title by title, instead of by whole subjects, because they are classified and numbered.

On an even more international scale, EIBIS, 3, Johnson's Court, London EC4A 3EA, translate, produce and distribute news releases to overseas journals. Their excellent work over many years has established their reputation with thousands of overseas editors who welcome material that has been carefully prepared for them. Again, the service not only opens doors but leaves the PRO to concentrate on the story, and leave the mechanics of export PR to the professionals.

Alternatively—and this may suit the PRO operating in a specialized field—UK and overseas mailing lists (subject to some inevitable dating) can be compiled from the 1000-page *Newspaper Press Directory* which is also very informative about the circulation areas of regional newspapers and the readership and contents of magazines.

The *PR Planner* lists newspapers, magazines, trade and technical journals that take PR material. Editorial requirements are given under twelve headings of new products, personal news, coming events, financial, by-lined articles, letters, photographs, trade literature, contracts, industrial films, entertainment and book reviews. An especially useful section identifies twenty-five different categories of correspondents and specialized writers. Subscribers receive a media service bulletin every three weeks which updates information, while revision pages for the *PR Planner* are supplied every six weeks, the newspaper and correspondents lists being re-issued every twelve weeks. See also Chapter 3, page 65. A mailing service is also available.

PR Photographs

We promised to return to this topic. If editors are hostile to PR because of the twelve points mentioned earlier in this chapter, they are even more hostile because of the poor quality of photographs they receive from PR sources, and the unprofessional manner in which the majority of pictures are supplied.

The typical grim industrial record shot, the super salon managing director portrait, and the dolly girl and product picture are seldom of any value to most editors. They only help to cause an overspill of editorial plastic dustbins. In fact, Mike Colmer, former Picture Editor of the *Financial Times*, has made up a slide presentation of just this sort of nonsense.

The *Financial Times Industrial Photography Awards* are made for pictures which ought to be commonplace. Even so, the 1973 Awards were accompanied by the following wry words from John Chittock, industrial film correspondent, in the *FT* on 16 February:

"The Assessors this year repeat an annual complaint that creative standards still leave room for improvement . . . the entries for the Export Category . . . leave doubts as to whether Export Managers ever communicate with the photographers they commission. The absence of well-thought out marketing strategies . . . a patchy sense of values at the top . . . the difference between paying £100 for a top photographer and £10 for a rush job by the local newspaper stringer. The difference shows with embarrassing impact in the results, and ultimately can reflect on the company . . . all the way round the world."

More money is wasted on useless PR photography than is alleged to be spent on PR expense accounts. The composition of pictures, the application of pictures to stories, and the ability to buy photographic services is but one more unknown skill of the average PRO, in the opinion of Fleet Street picture editors.

Once again it needs to be stressed that the PR practitioner has to be proficient in many arts and crafts, very much a Jack-of-all-trades compared with the more specialist personnel found in advertising. Above all, the PR practitioner needs to be able to compose a good photograph, understand what a picture can show, know when and how it can be used, and appreciate especially what it will suffer from the printing process. He then needs to be able to communicate all this knowledge and desire to the photographer so that the best possible picture can be taken. Poor pictures result from two errors: use of the wrong photographer and inadequate instructions and supervision. Good photographers are specialists: mindreading is not one of their specialities.

That photographers are specialists in various classes of work such as studio portraiture, table-top, action, animals, architecture, interiors aerial views, and so on is not generally understood. But photographers are like most artistic people, they are not general practitioners. Before booking a photographer it pays to study a file of his work. There are of course photographers of no great skill who pretend to be general practitioners, the people referred to above by John Chittock who take on cheap rush jobs. News picture agencies which offer to photograph any PR subject are not merely ignorant of PR needs but are taking money under false pretences, however, leading PR practitioners use them and editors tear their work up.

Common Faults in PR Photography

1. Pure record shots are taken which have no pictorial, dramatic or news interest to make them publishable. Typically, a vehicle is taken up a lane beside the factory and photographed against a hedge, or the photographer stands at one end of a factory and takes a long shot so that benches converge into the distance like railway lines.

2. Promotion and appointment portraits are usually the hackneyed salon portrait which the subject's wife keeps on her dressing table. Worse still, he is seated at his desk with a battery of telephones. He is never seen to be doing anything interesting.

3. Pictures are lighted badly, making the subject look unshaven or giving him two black eyes. He has a "wanted" look.

4. The picture shows too much (like the factory shot mentioned above), or the scene is too "busy" with extraneous objects or people, all of which will reproduce very small and indistinctly. Remember, the nice big glossy whole-plate picture may be reproduced no larger than a bus ticket.

5. Side-on views of vehicles, vessels, aircraft, machines and buildings so that they appear to have no dimension. For good photography of this kind, note the superb shots of BEA aircraft in TV commercials, taken head-on, from above and so on.

6. Cheese-cake, dolly girl, bikini clad (or unclad) models are used in the most unlikely situations such as mowing the lawn, driving farm tractors, fixing wallpaper, using domestic appliances and even doing

factory assembly work. An example of this was a business exhibition at Olympia when pictures of children of all nations welcoming the official opener appeared in the business press, and an airline's use of a pin-up secured coverage in papers like the *Daily Mirror*. Children and animals continue to have greater reader interest than bosoms and bottoms, except in the women's press where the majority of nudes will be found. Obviously, such pictures are excellent to illustrate a story about deodorants or the removal of body hair.

7. Blatant displays of company or product names, which are best shown partially or obliquely if at all.

8. A common fault with, say, window contest pictures is reflection, and this can also be a fault in pictures of products with polished surfaces such as steel or aluminium. Care should be taken with lighting, but retouching is probably necessary.

9. Wrongly dressed subjects are another common fault, such as a subject with extended shirt cuffs doing a dirty job for which sleeves are usually rolled up or overalls worn, or a person smoking when this would be slovenly, improper or unhygienic. One also has to be careful of jewellery: would the girl in the picture be wearing all those rings or bangles while doing that job?

10. Finally, interior shots should not be taken which reveal untidy or old-fashioned premises which are no credit to the organization. Sometimes, factory backgrounds are irrelevant to the picture and no-one has thought of taking the picture elsewhere, or of obscuring the unnecessary background by using a neutral backcloth such as a sheet or a roll of white paper.

Listed like this, most of these faults are absurd, and even people guilty of such errors must laugh ashamedly at what they so often do. Yet a picture is often more important than the news release, and a good picture and caption can produce more interest and publicity than a couple of paragraphs tucked away in an editorial column. On the other hand, pictures can be a waste of money when the story will rate no more than two or three lines. This is true of the typical promotion or appointment story in *The Times* or *Financial Times* when it is best for the picture editor to ask for a picture if he can use one. This can be prompted by a telephone call. But most of these personal stories, often written up as three-page biographies, are accompanied by whole-plate prints that no-one wants. They merely add to the PR bill, a form of PR unproductivity.

The way to overcome these mistakes so that publishable pictures are supplied to the press is to follow these simple rules:

1. Be aware of how and where the picture is likely to be reproduced, meaning printing process and quality of paper.

2. Seek a picture that exemplifies the story, not accept one that has been taken for some other or no other purpose.

3. If possible, try to compose the picture in a rough sketch so that the photographer knows what you have in mind. This alone can avoid wasted time and money, but unfortunately it is too often left to the photographer to guess what is required. Ninety-nine times out of a hundred, he will guess wrongly.

4. Be present when the picture is taken. Have a pleasant working relationship with the photographer so that he invites you to look in the viewfinder and see what he has got.

5. Make sure that the interest or news value of the picture is fully brought out. For instance, when photographing a Staines dishwasher it is essential to show that it has nylon brushes that scrub the plates clean. To obtain the best possible picture the photographer needs to be higher than the machine, no crockery must obscure the action, the machine must be run to produce suds and then stopped to allow the suds to subside so that they do not obscure the brushes. It is not easy to give such instructions, in a letter or over the telephone, perfectly simple to do so on the spot where the positioning of the operator, and her appearance, can also be stage-managed.

6. Introduce some element into the picture to give an impression of size, a small object being held by hand or a person operating or standing beside a large object. The introduction of such an element may also indicate the right way up! Matchboxes and coins are devices that have been overdone in the past.

7. If people are working, make sure that they are concentrating on their job and not grinning into the camera.

8. Don't take colour pictures unless an editor has asked for them, or slides are required. Never make black-and-white prints from colour pictures. If black-and-white pictures are to be issued, take them on black-and-white film.

9. Work close up to subjects so that a big-subject negative is produced, and if the composition is done in the viewfinder cropping becomes virtually unnecessary except regarding shape of picture when finally reproduced in the journal.

10. Make sure that prints are glossy but unglazed. The supplied prints should be neither matt nor glazed. The latter are liable to crack and attract fingerprints, and are therefore useless for plate-making. One of the mysteries of PR photography has been the emergence of glazed prints: no editor wants them.

Photo Captions

No marketer would put unlabelled products in the shops, yet remarkably few PR pictures have captions. The usual excuse from consultancies is that captioning pictures takes up too much time, and quite truthfully time to fix captions may depend on whether the fee permits this expenditure of man-hours. Meanwhile those who do not understand what goes on in editorial offices blithely imagine that because story and picture go out together they will stay together.

An uncaptioned photograph is a liability to its sender and a nuisance to its recipient. Why should the editor have to guess what the picture is all about? Why take the risk that the editor will guess wrongly?

Fixing Captions

The manner in which captions should be fixed is a controversial topic, the two principle methods being to flap captions so that they fall below the picture and can be read while looking at the print, or to fix the caption to the back of the print by adhesive or Sellotape. Either way, the caption should be secure, not dangle precariously so that it is apt to get ripped off and lost, nor be so heavily glued that it crimps the picture. Large quantities of prints are sometimes captioned directly on the backs with a spirit duplicator. One of the best methods is the double caption, which permits one perforated copy to be removed while leaving the other permanently fixed to the back of the picture. The important thing is that the picture has a caption.

Content of Captions

Unless the following two rules are obeyed, captions will be useless:

1. *The caption should explain what the picture is about.* It is pointless having a set of pictures with identical captions, say a bald reference to the product. Captions should explain what each picture shows, what is going on in it, and so provide information otherwise unavailable by looking at the picture. If there are people in the picture, they should be correctly named from left to right, standing, sitting, kneeling and so on. Attention to initials, spellings, ranks, positions and marital status must be meticulous especially when this information can alter, in the course of time, from picture to picture as when people are promoted or marry. The PRO is still often at the mercy of the old, filed picture which is pulled out and used long after it was sent to the press.

2. *The caption should identify the source of the picture.* Incredible though it may seem, very few captions do identify the sender, but the really efficient PRO uses a printed caption heading which sets out the name and address *and* telephone number of the organization. Unless the source is identified in this way—and the telephone number (usually missing) is imperative—the editor has no means of seeking another or a different print, or of being certain who the sender is, that the sender owns the copyright, and that the picture may be reproduced without fee. The sender should *not* state that it is a copyright picture which must not be printed without permission (since that makes the picture unpublishable!), nor should editors be asked to print acknowledgements (which they probably won't), and they should never be asked to supply free press cuttings.

Exclusive Signed Feature Articles

Very different from the news release sent out to a list of editors who may discard, cut, rewrite or print it in its entirety today, tomorrow, next week or next month is the exclusive signed feature article. In contrast to the short, precise, factual news release that makes no comment, the article can be more creative and bring out the author's literary talents. It has the advantages of being a substantial indexed feature, perhaps offering authoritative information of permanent reference value. Reprints may be obtained for other purposes such as direct mail shots, give away leaflets, enclosures to accompany letters and information material for showrooms. A good feature article can therefore serve as an excellent marketing aid, and may well do so for many years.

PR articles can be published in one of three ways: (1) by giving an editor an idea and providing facilities for him to obtain material for an article; (2) by offering similar facilities to a contributor; and (3) by agreeing with an editor to provide an article. In the third case the piece will be supplied without fee, and it may be written by a member of the organization, by the PRO or PR consultant, or by a freelance writer commissioned for the purpose.

Such articles should not be written speculatively. The best plan is to put a clear proposal on paper and ask the editor of a carefully selected journal whether he is interested and if so how many words he requires, whether he wants pictures, which issue the article will appear in, and the deadline for copy. The editor must also be assured that permission will be obtained to write the article which will then be approved for accuracy before submission, and that commercial references will be kept to a minimum.

The last proviso and promise is vitally important, for no editor wants to print a publicity blurb with company or product brand name plugged indiscriminately. The article should be worth publishing on its merits, the sort of piece that the editor would have written himself or commissioned on a fee basis from a professional author. The fact that it has come from a PR source should not detract from its ability to stand comparison with non-PR material. This is another tough lesson that the marketer may have to learn: articles are not free platforms, a kind of soft sell. Article writing is another press relations service, giving the editor material he could not have known about nor written himself. Once again, we have the criterion of reader interest first and resultant publicity second. So, the article becomes a compromise between what the PRO wishes to say and what the editor wishes to publish, the two culminating in what the reader is willing to read.

The opposite of this is the newspaper or magazine feature, produced not by the editor but by a special editorial section of the advertisement department, which prints articles very few people bother to read as bait to sell advertisement space. Articles discussed in this chapter have nothing to do with advertising or blackmail to buy advertisement space. Anyone who buys space because an article is being published about them is really negating the merits of the article, unless there is genuine additional value in taking space to offer, say, sales literature or some other sales aspect which cannot be mentioned in the text. Moreover, articles do not always appear in publications which suit the advertising schedule. It is best to keep PR and advertising apart, for each has its job to do in its own way. When PR editorial and advertisement appear in juxtaposition there is the danger that one will devalue the other. Media advertisement managers, anxious to sell space, are unlikely to understand this for it is not in their interests to do so. Similarly, they may be jealous of editorial mentions and features, feeling quite wrongly that bread is being stolen out of their mouths. There is a difference between providing a market place for advertisements of a certain kind (e.g. holiday advertising at the turn of the year) which are accompanied by appropriate editorial, and the idea that because the editorial deals with a commercial organization that organization should pay for the privilege by purchasing advertisement space in the same issue.

Article writing is time-consuming, and in PR time costs money. Exactly what time is involved may be seen from this sequence of activities: Permission must be obtained to write the article; the right journal must be selected and negotiations undertaken with the editor; research, interviews and photography have to be conducted wherever the location may be; the first draft is then written, and approval and amendments sought which are then incorporated in the final version for submission to the editor to meet the agreed deadline. All this may cost between £50 and £250 according to the time and expenses involved.

This can be a PR-marketing tool of great value, a single well-documented, well-placed article being a major thrust in a marketing campaign, especially when a new market has to be educated. The reader of such an article can see his problem solved in the real-life experience of someone else, for the case study approach is the style often adopted. Thus, some PR programmes include regular and frequent publication of articles that pose a customer problem and show how the company's products or services have solved this problem and resulted in worthwhile rewards. Such articles are welcomed by the trade, technical and specialised press, whether they be about a new piece of equipment, a new device for the home handyman, a new transport service or a health and beauty aid. Moreover, the article lends itself to the planned and initiated press relations programme aimed at achieving definite objectives. There is nothing intangible about such an organized effort.

Syndicated Articles

The kind of article described above—and there are other treatments apart from the case study method—is an exclusive one that cannot be published elsewhere. It is offered on the basis of its exclusivity. It cannot be distributed like a news release, or offered to another editor at a later date, except with the first editor's permission. Any subsequent publication would be in another country or possibly in the same country provided that the second journal had a non-competing circulation and due acknowledgement was made. This is stressed because it is sometimes thought that once an organization possesses an article it can distribute it at will. It depends whether first publication was on the basis of exclusive or syndicated publication.

The syndicated article, in PR terms, is one that is offered, usually simultaneously, to journals which—once again—have non-competing circulations. For example, it could not be offered at the same time to two rival newspapers published in the same city, but it could be offered without objection to newspapers published in cities many miles apart, where there is no rivalry of readership.

This can be an excellent marketing aid and is used in the holiday and travel business. P & O offer articles on cruising, written by well-known writers, together with a sheet of miniature photographs, larger prints being available on request.

Where rival publications do exist (e.g. weekly newspapers) the first-refusal offer makes possible a later offer to a second choice journal. This also means that articles are not distributed until offers have been accepted, a method which, in the author's opinion, places greater value on the article than if it is sent out like a news release. It is better to supply an article because an editor has asked for it, having first received a synopsis, than to expect him to publish something uninvited. The psychology is obvious. The offer method also allows the editor to take more interest, as when he requests a longer, shorter or slightly different article to suit his particular paper. The mailed article is a rather take it or leave it affair that eliminates the normal negotiation and commissioning that occurs between editors and writers.

Syndicated articles may also be offered to similar journals in different countries and again it is better to make an offer rather than send an article, partly so that in the event of refusal another journal can be approached, but also because a translated version is likely to be wanted. It would be wasteful to prepare translations in several languages before it was known which versions were wanted beyond, say, French, German and Italian.

With an organization such as International Business Press Associates, representing international groups of magazines and having regular policy discussions, it may be possible for a **PRO** to project an idea for an article, or an actual article, throughout a set of titles on one subject published in half a dozen major countries.

Other well-organized and respected services exist for the distribution of syndicated feature articles. The Central Office of Information, Hercules Road, London SE1, includes in its world-wide distribution of information about British activities and achievements original articles which it has commissioned and also published articles for which permission to circulate abroad had been obtained from both publisher and author.

Then there is the EIBIS service (see page 79) which can distribute translated news releases to 23,000 overseas journals but will also offer feature articles to overseas editors. A 1500-word exclusive article offered in twenty countries, with five translations, costs just over £500—to which must be added the sponsor's expenses in producing the original article. For another £100 the same feature article can be offered to editors in an additional twenty countries.

Paraphrased Articles

This third method combines the merits of the exclusive and the syndicated article, the same basic material being used for original articles slanted to please the readerships of journals in different fields. For example, a manufacturer of burglar alarms has certain basic information about this equipment, but the needs and problems of different users from say golf clubs to three-star hotels, fishmongers to department stores, could suggest from a dozen to twenty different articles on the same subject in different circumstances. Each circumstance would need to be researched. A number of computer manufacturers publish this kind of article. Press officers of exhibitions publish similar articles in advance of the event.

Press Cutting Services

Cutting agencies tend to be criticized for not producing a large enough proportion of possible cuttings. Much depends on the instructions given—does the topic allow a sufficiently wide search?—and on whether the agency is sent a mailing list. Cutting agency fees are not high for the work involved, and it has to be remembered that a cutting can be missed because the story did not appear in every edition of a newspaper.

In the UK, well-known agencies include International, Duttons, Pressclip and Romeike & Curtice. PRADS offer a service covering 14 European countries and other parts of the world, while Euroscan Press Information Ltd, 15-17 City Road, London EC1Y 1AL read and clip business newspapers and trade and technical journals from the Common Market. The latter offers a special reading service with translations useful for corporate and financial PR purposes. Press cutting services in some thirty countries are listed in the services and supplies section of the *Hollis Press and Public Relations Annual*.

American press cutting services include Allen's Press Clipping Bureau of Los Angeles (mainly west coast publications), and Luce Press Clippings of Mesa, Arizona and Burrelles Clip Service of Livingston, New Jersey which cover the entire US press.

Press Kits and Packs

A fetish with some PROs is to produce needlessly elaborate press kits stuffed with irrelevant material. At press receptions, or on press visits, it is thoughtful to supply a convenient wallet in which loose items such as photographs and news release can be carried, collected or supplied on leaving. But that is too simple and sensible for those who mistakenly exploit the occasion with publicity-mad ornate kits which convert a courtesy into an advertising nightmare. Some wallets are multi-coloured, embossed, cut-out cardboard or heavy ring-binder affairs, and their typically useless contents include calendars, blotters, company histories, staff journals, sales leaflets and price lists, not forgetting the inevitable and unwanted very large portrait of the chairman placed prominently as item number one. Some kits even have an index to all this rubbish.

Perhaps the classic example of this sort of nonsense—unforgivable in the minds of journalists—occurred during the threat of a paper famine at the end of 1973. The Swedish papermaking industry invited a party of British journalists to come and see what was being done to cope with the world shortage of paper. During this press trip the guests received company reports, digests, news releases and other material weighing no less than 21 lb.

At press receptions it is polite and obliging for the receptionist to offer guests a press kit on leaving. On visits it may be useful to give guests a wallet in which to place items collected during the visit. There is no point at all in placing press kits in exhibition press rooms, and they are banned by sensible press officers who do not relish the job of dustman at the close of the show. In other words most press kits (other than simple plastic wallets containing the bare essentials) are a costly nuisance. Their only possible value would seem to be as a means of impressing an ignorant client, and they belong to the black list of bad PR practices such as wining and dining, asking editors for cuttings, and pretending to have editorial contacts. In most cases all a journalist wants when visiting an exhibition press room is a piece of paper, with the facts clearly set out, which he can put in his pocket. He does not carry a suitcase.

Press Events

The principal press events are the conference, reception, facility visit and exhibition press room, and a few notes on each will define their characteristics.

The *press conference* is called to make an announcement, perhaps at short notice, and journalists are usually seated to receive the message and ask questions. Hospitality will suit the time of day, but the event will not be a cocktail party.

The *press reception* is a more elaborate affair at which a product or service may be demonstrated or explained. It should not be a stand-around occasion, although hospitality will be cocktail party style with maybe a finger or fork buffet, possibly a lunch. There should be a well-timed programme of activity such as reception, talk, demonstration, film, buffet, coffee, and it is a good idea to put a timetable of events on the back of the invitation ticket or in the letter of invitation. If a form of reply is included with the invitation, and it is a worthwhile event, the majority of acceptances and refusals should be known within forty eight hours. Yes, even a press reception has to be marketed!

Three things are essential to the success of a press reception: the importance of the story to the press, the accessibility of the venue, and the quality of the food, and in that order. One's own host party (especially sales staff) are liable to inflate the cost of drinks unless the PRO agrees a limit with the barman. The best way to close a bar, and end a reception, is to serve coffee. It is quite untrue that the press are only there for the beer, but it does pay to know whether any guest has a favourite but unusual drink like the famous but retired science correspondent who was unhappy if his brandy had been overlooked.

A *facility visit*, whether for a single journalist or a press party, involves transport, meals, possibly overnight accommodation, but certainly very careful planning, timing, rehearsal, control and hosting. The visit may be to an installation or a site, premises or a vehicle of transport. Nearly always, there is a numerical controlling factor on visits (apart from budget) which must be predetermined. It may be the number of seats on coach or aircraft, the number of people who can be physically shown round, or the seating capacity of the lunchtime venue. To encourage guests to make an early start, breakfast can be offered on the train. Guests should never be encumbered with heavy press kits at the beginning of a journey, although itineraries and basic information should be supplied, sometimes in advance if that is helpful. Other material can be offered when suitable, or on the return journey.

An *exhibition press room* is the place where one can undergo an education in the idiocies of PR, for here on display can be seen how not to write news releases, how not to take photographs, and why captions are essential while press kits are not. Ideally, the PRO for an exhibitor should make himself known to the press officer some months before the event, and find out what PR services are being provided, and how he can exploit them to the fullest possible extent. Hundreds of pressmen visit exhibition press rooms in search of stories, but few are to be found, and magnificent opportunities to secure press coverage are sacrificed.

CHAPTER 5

Broadcasting

RADIO and television are combined in this chapter because the broadcasting media are often controlled by one authority to mention only the British Broadcasting Corporation, the Independent Broadcasting Authority, Radio Telefis Eireann, the Nigerian Broadcasting Corporation, All India Radio and Voice of Kenya. Separate radio and television companies operate where there are independent programme companies, either local or regional, but usually they are licensed by a state authority like the IBA in Britain which licenses operators such as Thames TV and Capitol Radio. Other electronic media are discussed in the chapter on industrial films and again under seminars and conferences, these being closed circuit TV (narrowcasting) and various forms of cartridge, cassette and video disc playback and recording devices.

Confining ourselves in this chapter to the publicly broadcast sound and vision media, there are certain distinctions to be made. Public service broadcasting provides programmes subject to a government-sponsored authority and financed by license fees, taxation or, in the case of the IBA, by advertisement revenue. Throughout the world there are two kinds of radio and TV financed by advertising, commercial and sponsored. Under commercial broadcasting the advertiser buys time as he would buy space in the press and the programmes are put on by the station, whereas under sponsored broadcasting the advertiser supplies complete programmes which include his "commercials". Thus in the USA the Ford Motor Company will produce and present a detective series, but in the UK the same series, without commercial references, will be presented by different programme companies according to their programme planning, and the six-minutes-to-the-hour of natural break time will be sold to a variety of advertisers who present approved commercials of 15-, 30- or 45-second duration. On Nigerian television, the mid-evening sports programme is sponsored by an advertiser, as when the Nigerian bottlers of Coco-Cola sponsored the programme for about ten days to show highlights of the Munich Olympics, interspersed with commercials of the "Real Thing" and "I'd Like to Teach the World to Sing" kind familiar to British viewers.

However, largely because of production costs, the tendency with sponsored broadcasting has been for full sponsorship to give way to spots and commercials, as in the case of Radio Luxembourg during the past decade, while in Ireland commercial radio is broadcast around breakfast and lunch time with commercial TV taking over in the evening.

Another distinction should be noted. The expression "sponsored" has different connotions in different countries, for in a country with a one-party or military government all broadcasting may be said to be sponsored by the state.

Facilities also differ from country to country according to political influences, legislation or commercial demands. Gaullist influence in France made French TV very state-dominated and biased, while in Germany viewing hours are restricted by law. In Nigeria, items in the same TV magazine programme may be charged air-time because they are rated as advertising while others will be shown free of charge because they are considered of news value or educational. This is very different from the British experience where a commercial topic of genuine news interest would be treated as such. The finer distinction made by the Nigerians is largely one of economics: income is scarce and opportunities for earning revenue must not be overlooked! But in Britain it must never be so much as suspected that a commercial interest has bought its way into legitimate programme material. And while Nigeria has had TV for a number of years, there is no TV in Tanzania at the time of writing and its possibility is still under discussion in South Africa, the only industrialized country without it.

The country with the largest number of receivers is said to be Russia. But up to September 1972, India had only one TV station—New Delhi —with All India Radio opening up a second station in Bombay in October 1972 and developing a national network between 1973 and 1980. Mainly in the cities of Nairobi and Mombasa, there are some 20,000 receivers of Voice of Kenya TV. Pakistan and Bangladesh have

TV, and the expansion of All India TV seeks to recapture audiences from foreign transmitters such as Lahore. As would be expected in the country more advanced than any other in audio-visual electronics, Japanese TV has been established nearly as long as American. In the fifties, the New Zealand Meat Producers Board bought time on Japanese TV and televised cookery demonstrations to teach Japanese women how to cook that then unknown foodstuff, New Zealand mutton. Since December 1967, colour television has been spreading through the TV regions and entering an increasing number of British homes so that it had reached 20 per cent of viewers' homes in 1973 and is expected to reach 60 per cent by 1976.

Radio is, of course, by far the older medium, the BBC radio celebrating its 50th anniversary in 1972. While British TV began in the thirties with the rival systems of Baird and EMI (shown on alternate nights!), it did not become a popular medium until the 50s when it was greatly popularized by the televising of the coronation of Elizabeth II. Independent TV was created in 1955, followed by commercial radio being legalized in 1972. The first British commercial radio licences were awarded in 1973.

This background review is given because although there is a reasonable similarity between a daily newspaper in most countries of the world —*Pravda*, with its meagre advertising, being an exception—the kind of radio or TV is likely to vary strikingly between one country and another. The PRO, operating in this or that country, among the countries of the Common Market, or throughout the export markets of the world, must study and evaluate broadcasting facilities nation by nation. The only way in which he can adopt anything like a blanket approach is if he distributes his material initially through either the external services of the BBC or those of the Central Office of Information.

But it is quite useless to expect that the conditions and facilities that exist in one's home country are likely to be repeated elsewhere. Even in places as near to one another as Britain, Ireland, France and Germany the broadcasting systems are completely different. This is unlike the ability to distribute a news release or a picture on an international scale and achieve world-wide publication. If anything, broadcasting media are more concerned with internal, domestic and local matters than the press, and they also have the advantage of being multi-lingual.

With the exception of certain news and documentary programmes, they concentrate on material of direct interest to their audiences, supporting this on radio with national style music in developing countries and pop music in Europe, and on TV with British, American, Indian or other films according to the particular part of the world.

BBC External Services, Bush House, London WC2B 4PH. From its headquarters in the Aldwych, London, the BBC External Services broadcast in English and 39 other languages 24 hours a day and within the total of 745 broadcasting hours a week are programmes of direct interest to British exporters. It tells the world about industry, new products, export orders, visits abroad, sales missions and participation in exhibitions and trade fairs in programmes such as *News Ideas* (mainly consumer products), *Science in Action*, *Business and Industry*, *Money and Markets*, *Discovery*, *Farming World* and *Outlook*.

The World Service goes out in English to Europe, Asia, Africa, The Americas and Australasia. Then appropriate language services are broadcast to South Europe, Central Europe, East Europe, Germany, France, together with Arabic, Far Eastern, Eastern, African, North African, French-speaking African, Latin American, and Caribbean services.

Some examples of the value of these services can be quoted from the *Reader's Digest* which said in an article by Geoffrey Lucy that:

> "The BBC is probably Britain's best export salesman, for some of its prestige rubs off on the products it features in such programmes as 'New Ideas', and thousands of enquiries flow into Bush House, whence they are passed on to manufacturers. In this way the makers of an anti-theft car-locking device won a £100,000 order from the United States; a firm which had never exported previously found itself with dozens of orders for a new type of stretcher, and a manufacturer of portable cement mixers, writing to tell Bush House of enquiries from 43 countries, added 'Help! And thank you'."

BBC External Services are described in the annual *BBC Handbook*, while an eight-page illustrated brochure *Exporters and Broadcasting* can be obtained from the address given above. Items or ideas should be addressed to the Export Liaison Officer, PO Box 76, at the same address, or telephoned to him at 01-240 3456 Ext. 2393/2039. There are also BBC External Services producers offices at the Broadcasting Houses in Belfast, Cardiff and Glasgow.

Information submitted should be fully detailed. For example, news about an export order should state the value, quantity, identity of goods, name and address of manufacturer or supplier, name and address of overseas customer, details of its likely use, method of shipment together with date and details of aircraft or vessel. The more precise, factual and topical the story the greater are its chances of being used. If advance information about despatch can be given, so much the better because this gives the producer and scriptwriter time to prepare a story that reads something like "Leaving London Docks today is a consignment of...".

Central Office of Information, Hercules Road, London SE1 7DU. Television and cinema newsreel services are combined since the same material may be used by either medium, and more than 1000 industrial stories are used by the COI every year. The London Television Service supplies broadcasting stations throughout the world with short filmed items for inclusion in local news bulletins, and collaborates with TV correspondents in London and with visiting producers from overseas TV. (The latter can be particularly useful in connection with the Common Market, and stations like North German TV frequently film news and documentary material in Britain.) The COI also produces TV series, including a science and technology series, for international distribution, a special programme for Africa, and weekly TV reports. Exhibitions are popular subjects with the COI and it will pay exhibitors to ask the exhibition press officer whether there will be COI (or any other TV, newsreel or radio) coverage if a new and newsworthy British product is going to be shown on the stand.

As stated in the COI booklet *Worldwide Export Publicity* (available from the above address), "These services need a constant flow of news stories suitable for export publicity, as well as advance information about events in the export world."

The COI also records several thousand radio programme items a year, taking as its chief themes economic, industrial and scientific subjects. Overseas trade activities are high-lighted, such as British trade missions, trade fairs and Joint Venture exhibitions. Programmes in

English are heard in forty different countries, and there is co-operation with the BBC External Services mentioned above in the supply of stories broadcast direct from London in English and foreign language versions. The *Newsline* service by cable transmits urgent stories to the world's radio centres.

The simplest way to interest the COI is to put them on the mailing list for all new British product, export order, overseas trade visit and similar stories. Better still, such stories should be tailor made with all details likely to be of interest to overseas audiences, as suggested above when sending news to the BBC External Services. The same story can be sent to both, and each may use it in different ways, especially since the COI has many departments dealing with different media. With a major story, whether it be an exhibition or the launch of a new tanker, a conference of COI departmental heads may be warranted, at which the PRO can present the story as it may appeal to those dealing with news stories, feature articles, photographs, newsreels, TV and radio.

British Broadcasting Corporation, Broadcasting House, London, W1A 1AA, is the public service authority for non-commercial radio, and the *British Broadcasting Corporation*, Television Centre, Wood Lane, London W12 is similarly responsible for providing non-commercial TV. The main difference between the BBC and the IBA (described below) is that the BBC produces and transmits programmes but ITV programmes are the responsibility of the fifteen regional programme and advertisement time-selling companies. In addition to the two BBC television channels and four radio stations, there are nineteen local radio stations in Birmingham, Blackburn, Brighton, Bristol, Derby, Humberside (Hull), Leeds, Leicester, London, Manchester, Medway (Chatham), Merseyside (Liverpool), Newcastle, Nottingham, Oxford, Sheffield, Solent (Southampton), Stoke-on-Trent and Teeside (Middlesbrough). These local non-advertising stations are not to be confused with the independent local radio (ILR) stations operated by the Independent Broadcasting Corporation.

Addresses of regional radio and TV stations, and much more information about the BBC, will be found in the annual *BBC Handbook*.

Independent Broadcasting Authority, 70 Brompton Road, London SW3 1EY controls commercial television and radio. Unlike BBC1 and 2, commercial TV is not nationally networked (except for ITN programmes like *News at Ten*) but is regionalized, licences being awarded to fifteen companies with two operating in the London area, Thames (Monday–Friday) and London Weekend. This is not to say that some, most or all of the fifteen companies could not agree to show the same programme produced by one of them, and a form of networking will take place, but the same programme may not necessarily be transmitted at the same time or on the same day by each region. Each company does its own independent programme planning but obviously an outside event of national interest, such as a sports event, will usually appear simultaneously on all stations. (Similarly, commercial TV is a regional advertising medium and only the very largest advertisers use all regions while one such "national" TV advertiser, Guinness, does not use Ulster.)

The more recently introduced commercial radio aims, according to the White Paper, at providing "a truly public service . . . combining popular programming with fostering a greater awareness of local affairs and involvement in the community." Difficulties in finding sites for transmitters slowed down the introduction of the five stations announced by Christopher Chataway in 1971, and the ten plus eleven subsequent stations announced by Sir John Eden in 1972, although sixty stations were mentioned in the original proposals.

Of these twenty-six stations, the first two to be awarded to contractors were the London specialist news station (London Broadcasting Company) and the London general radio station (Capitol Radio) in February 1973. No programme sponsorship or advertising magazines are permitted, advertising being restricted to spots. But the emphasis on involvement in the community is clearly of interest and importance to the enterprising PRO.

On ITV (meaning independent television, there is no organization bearing those initials) news is provided by Independent Television News which is jointly owned by the fifteen regional programme companies.

BBC radio and television, and ITN, have facility units which act as central filters for incoming news, such as that from PR sources, to which six copies of stories should be sent.

Cable Television consists of companies which receive programmes from several stations (usually more than can be received by viewers in the area served) and diffuses chosen programmes to viewers by cable so that they enjoy perfect vision free of any interference they might suffer with direct reception. The cable companies also offer their own programmes. There is also communal aerial TV (e.g. Rediffusion) when programmes are re-transmitted by cable to private houses, hotels and other centres of the service, but without the extra programmes of the cable companies mentioned above.

TV in the USA

At a time when Britain is at long last accepting radio as well as TV advertising from British transmitters, America has set up the Corporation for Public Broadcasting, a federal government sponsored body to support non-commercial broadcasting. The largest and best organized non-commercial network in the USA is the Pacifica Foundation.

In Britain there is therefore a very complex network of radio and TV services, complete with national, regional and local stations, studios and transmitters. Happily it is free of state interference beyond the maintenance of standards in the public interest. Indeed, Mr. Wilson had his differences with the BBC and Mr. Heath wisely avoided too many TV appearances. It has also been shown in the courts (e.g. the Warhol episode) that individuals cannot succeed in preventing programmes from being shown. But while the British Code of Advertising Practice is a voluntary code where press advertising is concerned, it is written into the Television Act and places legal responsibilities upon programme companies selling air-time and upon advertising agents and advertisers buying and using airtime. A TV advertisement can be banned at a viewing session prior to transmission, and this has even happened to a government commercial.

Three Kinds of PR Material for Broadcasting

British broadcasting—and this may well apply elsewhere—can use PR material in three ways:

1. *As news for its various bulletins.* Regional TV, local radio and ILR present both local and national news.

2. *As programme material.*, e.g. facilities for filming persons for interview; library shots (i.e. airliners, landmarks, famous buildings, ships, zoo and safari animals, ports, personalities); properties for use on sets

for plays (clocks, lamps, furniture); and give-away prizes, plus ideas for both radio and TV programmes.

3. *As whole programmes*, e.g. documentary films which may be accepted in their entirety such as those produced about industries, transportation services or tourism; facilities to make documentaries; and joint productions as when a film is made by a consortium of interests, some contributing finance or other resources and one being in charge of production.

More specifically, PR material can be provided for each medium in the following ways:

Radio

1. News can be sent direct to the appropriate Facility Unit, and if it is an item which may interest several departments or producers copies will be distributed to them. The Unit should be sent six copies.

2. Topical ideas can be sent to the producers of programmes such as *Today*, *The World at One*, *PM Reports* or *Woman's Hour*, at least a week in advance if interviews are likely to be required since these can be taped days before the actual broadcast.

3. Radio reporters can be invited to press conferences and receptions.

4. Radio personalities who give talks, present programmes or are correspondents on special subjects (e.g. science, aviation, education) can be sent new ideas for new topics and given opportunities to collect information. Programmes such as *Motoring and the Motorist*, *Gardener's Question Time* and *You and Yours* have such personalities who may welcome suggestions. The Schools programmes also require material which may well spring from PR sources.

5. Radio serials (e.g. *The Archers*, *Waggoner's Walk*) constantly require topical material. Government department PR campaigns have been able to use popular radio programmes as "platforms" for current topics such as road safety, and provided the material is legitimate information of value to audiences—like how to borrow money to buy a house or how to go about making a will which might be supplied by a building society or a bank—it may well be worked into the script. But it could be how to deal with house flies during a very hot summer, or advice on travel sickness during the holiday season. Some years ago

Guernsey and Guernsey tomatoes had the benefit of a visit by the Archer family to that Channel Island, a very nice PR tie-up with the BBC for all those concerned with Channel Island air services, hotels and glasshouse produce which demonstrated the value of PR as a marketing aid.

Radio has been reborn in some lands, thanks to the transistor, car radios and Hi-fi tuners. Introduction of the transistor quadrupled the number of radio sets in the world in a matter of twenty years, and today's total is approaching one thousand million! Rediffusion services —known as 'box radio' in Nigeria—carry programmes to thousands of listeners in cafes, bars, hotels, factories and homes. In India there are twenty two states with their own radio stations broadcasting in different languages. Radio reaches PR audiences of the following kinds and probably in this order of merit:

1. Housewives—morning mostly plus afternoons
2. Businessmen—driving to and from work
3. Travelling businessmen and salesmen—all day
4. Factory workers—throughout day where transistors permitted, or diffused music provided.
5. Teenagers—various times of day, but principally late evening.
6. Miscellaneous—various times (e.g. hotel guests, hospital patients, fishermen and ship's crews off duty).

It is a very versatile audience and very different from either the family that used to listen to the radio during the evening, or the television audience. The portability of radio compared with the immobility of television, is a factor that reconciles some of the doubts about whether there is not too much radio. And the ability of commercial radio to give instant advertising and instant news is the media revolution of the seventies. A restaurant can advertise today's menu, while the local sales —whether of livestock, second-hand cars, houses, shares or department stores—can be reviewed as programme material.

Television

1. *Personal Interviews*. This subject is introduced first because it is the personal appearance in news bulletin, current affairs or chat programme that provides most of the opportunites but more of the problems for the PRO. Any organization likely to be "in the news" needs to have a

spokesman who can go before the cameras and the glare and heat of lights, state the facts in answer to an interviewer's unexpected, penetrating and often unwelcome questions, and appear attractive, interesting, credible or authoritative as the case may be. Such a spokesman needs to be relaxed, and oblivious to lights, technicians and studio paraphernalia; frank and well-informed; and visually interesting. If television is to attract big audiences it must *entertain* and this element is present even in supposedly serious programmes. After all, the news readers wear gay shirts and ties and make quips. A good TV personality owes much to an interesting physiognomy in contrast to an interesting voice for radio. We watch one and listen to the other, and strange as it may seem television often demands the attributes of silent film rather than movie personalities. This has even spread to films which have been made with musical backgrounds but no dialogue, almost like silent films with a cinema pianist!

How does one discover a good TV spokesman? There are firms that train and select people, familiarizing them with studio conditions and interview techniques and—what is sometimes difficult but necessary—advising on who should be restrained from accepting interviews. One has only to recall how badly many of the world's leading politicians—Richard Nixon, Edward Heath and Ian Smith compared with the late John Kennedy, Willy Brandt and Lord George Brown—come across on the small screen to realize that when a choice of people is possible it pays to exploit the most suitable person. The head of the research department may not be so eminent as the chief executive, but if the latter's appearance, manner or voice creates a poor impression (a truly bad image!) this could be grossly unfair to the organization. Yet the cheerful, interesting-looking but comparatively unimportant research man could represent the image that the organization deserves.

This lesson was surely shown in that historic election-time confrontation between the smart confident, well-dressed businesslike John Kennedy and the shifty-looking, grey-suited face-in-profile Richard Nixon who evaded the camera. The making of the president, in TV terms, created a "tricky Dicky" image which may have been utterly unfounded in fact, but the viewers can form an impression only of what they see, or think they see, with their very own eyes. TV can therefore be the great disenchanter capable of provoking false impressions. For example, TV becomes the great illusion of all time when that big, fierce-looking TV interviewer is met in person and found to be a short, small-built man, a Ronnie Corbett rather than a Ronnie Barker. The compelling thing about Enoch Powell, Sir Gerald Nabarro, Adolf Hitler and Joseph Stalin is or was not their voices or their words so much as their eyes.

Strangely enough, television fails to have the magic of radio which to different audiences this century has carried the voices and propaganda of Roosevelt, Churchill and Hitler who might have been visually less successful on TV, except possibly for Hitler's magnetic eyes which have been remarked upon by most people who met him. TV is a volatile medium—McLuhan's cool medium of involvement—that needs to be treated with caution and respect. Talking into a radio microphone is like speaking on a telephone. A voice can excite thoroughly unjustified visions of the speaker (hence many people's horror at the idea of television telephones!) and the beautiful voice tends to be matched by an imagined beautiful woman or handsome man. But on TV the voice is less important and the visual impact is overwhelming or at least very pleasing. How very different from the advent of the talkies when poor voices destroyed stars of the silent screen, while archive Charlie Chaplin is just as much a winner on TV in the seventies as he was on the silent screen in 1913.

2. *News*. Although rather less featured on TV than on radio, TV news can be treated in greater depth when cameras can be used. Ability to provide picture facilities, or to have a pictorially interesting or dramatic subject, can mean TV coverage as with topics as diverse as fashions and shipbuilding. However, time and equipment factors are more critical in TV than in radio, even with the flexibility of VTR and its playback and easier editing advantages. This means that the PRO must give cameramen plenty of notice, ask what special requirements there may be, and do his best to be of service. For instance, a private room may have to be set aside for a single interview whereas a whole press party will be happy to sit together in conference. Or the TV filming may have to be done on another day, perhaps the previous day, when time can be spent on shooting and reshooting. It is very seldom that TV cameramen will be happy to operate within the confines of a press reception. Sometimes they will send along a reporter to test possibilities,

and then make a film weeks or months later for a series rather than a news bulletin. But the best advice that can be given if an event looks like good TV news is to send TV news editors an invitation four to six weeks in advance so that a camera can be reserved, making sure to ask what facilities are wanted.

3. *TV Series.* Usually, when a series appears on our TV screens, it has been researched, scripted, produced and shot long before being screened. This is particularly true when the subject is timeless, such as a weekly series on country houses or famous gardens. When there is topicality, the series is constantly in production; when there is immediacy but control, it is shot only a few days in advance; and when a surprise scoop element is essential, as in David Frost interviews, the series must be live.

Before attempting to offer ideas to TV series producers it is essential to decide not only whether the subject is suitable but whether it is physically possible for the idea to be considered. There is no point in trying to have one's subject included in a series which is already in the can, and it will have to be an absolutely up-to-the-minute idea to be accepted by a programme that relies on the unexpected. It is also wise to consider whether any benefit will result from being televised: it could be shown to the wrong audience. Moreover, television is time-consuming and quite often exasperating, and involvement in it should not be contemplated unless its demands are understood.

4. *TV Serials. Coronation Street* and *Crossroads* are the most obvious examples of British TV serials which may welcome topical material from a PR service, but sometimes topicality may be less important than broad general interest. This is because such series are exported and must not appear obviously dated. Consequently, a subject like the Open University could be introduced into *Coronation Street*, while a new system of central heating could be a talking point in many such serials. But a programme like *Peyton Place*, sold to television companies all over the world and shown years after the original American screening, would be very dated if it referred to specific events such as a presidential election. When a Coronation Street character enrolled for the Open University this was good PR in that it helped to convey the idea of the OU to the less intellectual working class which the University wished to reach, and it appeared on ITV when the instructional programmes were on BBC 2. Many months later, viewers in Australia saw the OU as part of the

British scene. If any marketer has a product or service that fits into a series or serial like this, it would be well worth discussing the idea with the producer, scriptwriter or research assistant.

5. *Library Shots.* When a TV or a cinema film is being made it is not necessary to shoot every foot, for many scenes will already exist. In Western films a lot of Red Indians have hit the dust repeatedly in succeeding films. Similarly, there is no need to film famous places, because plenty of stock or library shots exist and can be hired. The action may well be shot in a London studio and interspersed with scenes from Copenhagen, New Delhi or Hong Kong to give the illusion that that is where the story is unfolding. Thus, in films or series where the hero appears to flit from capital to capital it is only necessary to show an airliner taking off from Heathrow, flying above the clouds and landing at a clearly named international airport for the illusion of transit to be achieved. The actors need not move off the set. All that is required is some footage of aircraft from British Airways, Pan-Am, Transworld Airlines or some other enterprising airline which has seen the PR value in making sure that such shots are available. Shortly after BEA introduced the Trident there was a TV series called *The Ratcatchers* which opened every week with a BEA Trident taking off. The very successful American series *Hawai Five-O* opens with a TWA aircraft landing in Hawai. But one TV producer was a little too clever: he had the hero taking off in one airline's aircraft and landing in another's!

6. *Properties.* Property managers have to furnish sets for plays and series so that they look realistic. The PRO with such an item—clock, teapot, ornament, carpet, chair or cigarette lighter—can obtain valuable exposure on television. Of course, this is valuable only if the product is instantly recognizable by its shape. Product names are unlikely to be recognizable, but it is said that the Saint's Volvo sports car did a lot to familiarize that foreign car with British car-buyers. That the possibilities are mostly overlooked can be seen by the frequency with which sets are dressed with the same items show after show week after week. The same prints of veteran cars and old aeroplanes have been decorating interiors for a decade.

7. *Documentary Films.* It pays to make mute copies of documentary films so that frames may be cut out of them for use in TV programmes.

Good industrial films can be accepted as regular programme material, especially in the afternoons, or as "test card" material just before transmission starts. Judging by the inroads made into radio audiences by the increase in British viewing time, afternoon audiences are not to be ignored. However, as explained in the section about the COI, there are very real chances of showing films on TV overseas as part of an export PR campaign. Similarly, films from overseas are shown to peak audiences as we have seen with ones about Volvo and Daf motor production, tourism in the Seychelles, emigration to Australia, life in modern China, Indian industry, safaris in Kenya and Tanzania and insights into Japanese cities, industries and transport.

There is also the possibility of documentary films being made jointly with other organizations plus a television company, when the specialist production side is handled by the experienced TV programme company and resources and facilities are provided by trade associations, government departments and individual firms. This can also work the other way round as when the BBC made a film of the *Financial Times* which was afterwards revised and converted into a film which is frequently shown in the FT's own cinema to parties of visitors.

8. *Give-away Prizes*. One had to tread warily here because producers of these programmes have to be careful not to over-publicize prizes so that the presentation can be criticized as "free advertising". Obviously, if the marketer has a product of a value suitable for the grade of prize given he may find it very attractive to have this product presented in front of a virtually national audience of several million viewers. Sony hi-fi equipment, and Necchi sewing machines have been presented as prizes on give-away shows. They were not named or identified in any way, but their characteristic shape was sufficiently distinct for the machine to be recognized in any stockist's window. Necchi went further and, using a photograph of the winner holding the machine, very quickly produced a lithographed poster which was distributed to every stockist within a few days. But the moral of that story lies in the fact that the machines were not given to the television company free of charge: they were purchased from the makers. Thus, with give-aways, it may be necessary to convince the producer that it is worth buying the product as a prize.

In all these examples the lesson to be learned is that broadcast media are—as the name aptly implies—mass media. Any interview, film clip, idea or library shot must first of all help to please the majority of viewers, directly or indirectly. Quite apart from whether the BBC bans advertising in its home programmes or ITV programmes dare not usurp the commercial slots, it is useless for the marketer or PR practitioner to expect to gain blatant advertising outside natural breaks.

However, there has been an attempt to do this which almost contravenes the rules and has caused criticism both inside the broadcasting authorities and among the TV critics in the press. This is the buying of advertisement space round the perimeters of sports arenas, or the sponsoring of racing cars or actual events such as show jumping, tennis and golf tournaments, and horse racing so that publicity is gained when the cameras pick up these messages. In a special chapter, the PR role of sponsorships of various kinds will be discussed in detail.

There have been major examples like Omega at the Mexican Olympics, and more regular ones like the John Player Special racing car, and in fairness it may be said that these sponsors have made a substantial contribution to the sport itself and to the possibility of the event occurring at all. But the free screening of posters at football grounds tends to be seeking a strictly advertising bonus that may be thought to be offensive. It is a kind of sneak advertising, but its value may be outweighed by the fact that only glimpses of these placards are caught by the viewer and there is no monopoly of the viewer's attention.

Nevertheless, we may have to consider the subliminal or marginally conscious effect of such surreptitious advertising versus the meagre and interrupted vision obtained. Is it unfair exploitation of television or is its publicity value exaggerated? Moreover, are there PR undertones? When cigarette advertising is illegal on ITV is it cheating the law to blazon the names of cigarettes on racing cars, at football matches and tennis tournaments (so that publicity is gained on both channels)? To what extent is reputation tarnished or enhanced? The difference may be slight, until someone provokes a scandal. The marketer has to judge shrewdly for while advertising is comparatively short term, PR is definitely long term in its effects.

CHAPTER 6

Documentary Films, Video Tapes and Video Discs

THE expression "documentary" film was coined by John Grierson to describe his production *Anook of the North*. Since then the term has come to mean a non-advertising and usually a non-fiction private film. Sometimes it is called the "industrial" or the "sponsored" film, although documentaries are not always confined to industrial topics. The word "industrial" should be taken to mean "business" rather than public entertainment. On television, a documentary means a planned and edited study or report, not just a straight newsreel, but newsreel or archive material might of course be included.

As a PR medium it has few peers. It is one that helps to distinguish PR for what it is, an informative, educational and image-forming technique of communication, the antithesis of persuasive, promotional biased advertising. Advertising films, as seen on commercial TV or as cinema screen advertising, should not be confused with the documentaries and tapes or discs described in this chapter. More than that, it is foolish to abuse this excellent medium by including in a documentary blatant commercial references such as company vehicles, packages and name boards. The place for the company name is in the credits at the end of the film. Marketers have to be severely dissuaded from ruining otherwise fine films by insisting on a display of retail products at the close.

With that preamble, let us look at the essential elements of this medium. They fall into three convenient groups: *Purpose, Production* and *Distribution*, and they are so interrelated that these considerations need to be seen as a whole even though we shall analyse them here as separate entities. By whole is meant a total concept such as "To explain how our equipment works we shall show users and buyers a twenty-minute sound colour film." But that whole concept can be analysed three ways, and the sequence of study may not be chronologically the same. In the concept we have actually put the elements in the different order of *Purpose, Distribution* and *Production.*

Having made the analysis, budgeted the costs, and estimated the results we may still have to evaluate the operation against use of some other PR medium or media on a cost-benefit basis. Can we, for instance, reach the same (or a larger or a more influential) number of suitable people (a) more cheaply, (b) more quickly or (c) more effectively? Will a stand at an exhibition, a series of feature articles, an information bureau, or an external house magazine—or even paid advertisement space (like the ICI *Pathfinders* TV series or institutional press advertising)—do the job better? This campaign planning aspect belongs to Chapter 13, but is heralded here so that the reader can begin to make comparisons between the media discussed in these chapters.

Characteristics of a Documentary Film

1. It has the realism of movement, sound and usually colour.

2. Because a film has entertainment value, it is a very pleasing form of communication. Moreover, the actual showing of a film—the audience participation—also has entertainment value so that the message is conveyed in favourable circumstances

3. It is a permanent medium which can be reshown and reseen just as a piece of music can achieve growing appreciation with each successive performance. Most documentaries have a useful life of up to five years: others may live longer. This contrasts with the tendency of advertising films to bore and defy undue repetition because the action has been condensed into very brief showing time. (A notable exception is the Brooke Bond PG Tips TV commercial, with its performing chimpanzees, which retain the power to amuse even after being shown for two years).

4. It occupies a fairly large amount of viewer's conscious time, and is therefore impactive and likely to be memorable. Again, this may be compared with the transitory nature of radio, TV and much of press material. We are likely to remember one film for years but forget a press report very swiftly. This indelible effect on the mind makes the

documentary a very powerful medium, so that when confronted by what may seem an immense cost (from £3000 to £30,000) the value-for-money nature of the medium should be compared with the same expenditure on other PR activities.

5. To the viewer, the film is impressive, obviously having cost time, money and skill to make. Conversely, faults in these respects are very obvious, and extravagance as well as frugality can be a fault.

6. As we shall see under "Distribution", the documentary film can be used in so many ways that it is a versatile and flexible medium that well justifies the cost if the film is fully exploited. So, another test of a good PR practitioner is the extent to which he makes use of film in all kinds of PR activity, a good example being the showing of a relevant film at a press reception.

7. With the introduction of playback equipment it has become possible to make films or video tapes very quickly and use them for visual communication with small audiences scattered throughout a country, a continent or all over the world. Or, inexpensive short tapes can be made, supplied and stored for showing at short notice. These developments will be discussed in fuller detail at the end of the chapter.

8. Joint films are another possibility, a good example being one made by IBM and John Laing to show the application of the computer to the building industry. One of the advantages of joint films is that each partner or member of the consortium shows the film to his audiences who in turn may be interested in the products or services of more than one sponsor.

9. Films have international appeal, and language problems can be overcome by one of two methods: dubbed versions or ones without any vocal sound, vision and mime being sufficient, as with a number of Dutch films for agriculture and tourism.

But let us return to an examination of the three-point analysis:

Purpose

Why make a film? Good question! It is not always asked. Some films are little more than someone's whim or a projection of managerial vanity. Occasionally, a film may be a sort of bonus like the Brooke Bond golfing film which resulted from making a series of hilarious commercials and having a team of trained chimps available. But owning one's own film does have an ambiguous prestige value for some company directors, rather like those lush old-fashioned prestige house journals which are luckily dying out. Good PR is not just showing off. So, in this chapter we are not concerned with the idle dictates of tycoons. Production of a film costs a fair amount of money, and then prints have to be made, and after that there are distribution costs—maybe exhibition costs—to be met. We are therefore going to consider the documentary as a serious PR project, and one that can be particularly helpful to marketing.

Below is a useful check-list of possible *purposes*, some of which can be combined. The object of the exercise is to define the audience or audiences. Not every film will suit every audience, and it may be advisable to make a technical and a non-technical version of an industrial film. This was done by Smit, the Dutch tug company, which showed a full-length version of a film about international tug services to client audiences round the world, but made a shorter version for club audiences. The producer must gauge the intended audience, and this may also imply knowing their special interest in the subject and their prior knowledge if any. For example, a film about narcotics may be made differently for audiences of policemen and doctors, and differently again for audiences of young people, teachers and parents. The first two groups will need very different approaches to the subject while the same treatment may treat the second three groups whose sympathies are more similar. It can be foolish economy to try to make a film that is all things to all people. This applies to all media, as we have already seen with the press, radio and TV and shall see with different kinds of internal and external house journal. For this reason, very few documentaries are likely to suit the mass audience demands of cinema and television unless their theme is of universal appeal.

Check List of Purposes

1. Demonstrate the product or service to distributors and consumers.
2. Demonstrate a technique or a safety precaution to company personnel.
3. Tell the company story to prospective employees.

4. Produce a permanent record of achievement.
5. Show the company's contribution to social welfare, e.g. hygiene, education, safety, prevention of pollution.
6. Explain policy points at a sales conference.
7. Demonstrate the work of a voluntary organization.
8. Educate children about a product which, sooner or later, will be an important purchase for them.
9. Explain a company report and balance sheet to shareholders at an AGM.
10. Explain a government policy or service.

These are ten broad purposes covering a multitude of organizations, and the list can no doubt be extended to embrace many other purposes, In fact, this short list can trigger off other purposes more directly relevant to the reader's special interests.

How Existing Films Have Met Some of These Purposes

1. When a new car, ship or airliner is introduced a film is an excellent way of showing what it is like and what it can do. A beautiful film in this category was Sud-Aviation's documentary on their Caravel aircraft. Similarly, the services of banks (Midland), ports (Port of London), pest control firms (Rentokil, Murphy Chemicals and Cooper McDougall), countries seeking immigrants (Canada and Australia) have been and can be demonstrated on film.

2. In workplaces—like steelworks—it may be necessary to remind staff to observe safety regulations such as wearing helmets and other protective clothing. A film, shown in the works canteen, can drive home the message.

3. Recruitment may be a major issue, and a film can take would-be employees behind the scenes and show them what the company does and what the job prospects are. The recruitment film can help to increase the number of job applicants, and either select or improve the calibre of applicant. It can also help to overcome prejudice and inhibitions about certain jobs and careers. The Metropolitan Police have a very good film that tells the story of a day in the life of a London policeman. The marketer may have a special interest in such films when production is

lagging because of staff shortages. Films have been successfully used to attract immigrant labour, whether West Indians to Britain or Yugoslavs to Sweden.

4. There is nothing like a film for showing proof of what can be done, outstanding examples being Laing's *Coventry Cathedral,* and Brown's *Algerian Pipeline.* Films of this kind can enjoy a variety of purposes, ranging from general goodwill (especially if one builds humble dwellings as well as magnificent cathedrals) to demonstrating to potential clients what can and has been done. A film like *Algerian Pipeline* is infinitely more convincing than a set of progress photographs, and although this was an expensive film to make because of location shooting on many occasions it proved to be a profitable marketing exercise. And it is the sort of film that its sponsors can be proud of showing for a long time for it is genuinely prestigious. After all, if the Egyptians had been able to film the building of the pyramids it would still be worth showing!

5. Some firms suffer criticism because it is alleged that they produce dangerous products or irresponsibly contribute to pollution. The extent of the company's carefulness, or its avoidance of pollution, may make a useful subject for a film that will enhance corporate and other forms of goodwill. During conservation year, BP issued a most artistic and instructive film which showed that efforts were being made to use or transform waste products. BP's 1973 award winning *Tide of Traffic* is another film in similar vein which presents the problem of the motor car in modern cities and indicates some of the civil engineering solutions.

In conjunction with the San Francisco Police Department, and using real people, not actors, the Chemical Bank sponsored in 1971 one of the ugliest and most disturbing family shows ever seen on CBS-TV. The film was about drug addiction and death. A significant press comment was that the programme was associated with only one brief institutional message, and that it was "encouraging to find a major institution backing a program specifically geared toward shaking up the audience". Unlike drug abuse films presented from an adult viewpoint, this one was exceptional and credible because young drug abusers told of their own experiences.

6. Nowadays, original ideas are constantly sought for presenting policy decisions, sales targets and other information to assemblies of salesmen, members, delegates or others attending meetings and con-

ferences. An effective yet economical method is the production of a video tape for projection by controlled circuit television, preferably using a giant Eidophor screen. This provides big-screen audio visual presentation of a once-only performance, production costs being justified by the economy of VTR compared with cinefilm. A VTR tape is quickly produced and edited on the spot in a single operation. There is no processing of film, cutting, splicing, marrying of sound and vision, and making of prints.

7. Charity films are often sponsored by large benevolent companies, but however they are financed they form a vehicle for telling the story of the voluntary work and justifying appeals for funds. The Welfare State has tended to suggest that voluntary contributions are no longer necessary, and a big PR job has to be done by many societies. In the advertising business there is the NABS film which helps in the raising of funds for the NABS homes at Bexhill, while the Royal National Lifeboat Institute has had splendid films made for it by industry. The one sponsored by W. D. & H. O. Wills was accepted for showing in public cinemas as the supporting film to *Julius Caesar*.

8. Children have been taught the benefits of cleaning their teeth in films for schools made by toothpaste manufacturers and in such useful films there is scope for firms interested in tomorrow's market. Children can also influence the purchase of products used by adults. Gibbs pioneered the dental hygiene film in the thirties.

9. Using VTR again, and combining this with the making and shooting of animated charts, visual presentation of company results have been made for AGMs.

10. Road safety is the obvious example of film being used on behalf of a government department, but many departments (and public authorities such as the Post Office) have made sponsored films as a means of explaining policies or services.

The range of *purposes* can be very great, and it may well be that the documentary is an ideal—perhaps the only—medium for communicating a particular message. When the question is how do we reach our audience the film may be the most practical answer, subject to some of the considerations to be discussed below. These will include cost and the ability to find audiences willing to see the film. These two factors go together. The cost of the film may be negligible if enough of the right people can be found to see the film. But the cost can be prohibitive if no planned method is found to secure adequate audiences to justify production and other costs.

Some very attractive films have been given no more thought to distribution than placement in a film library and entry in its catalogue with the vague and pretty forlorn hope that unknown people will decide to borrow or hire the film for showing to equally unknown audiences. This is about as sensible as deciding to run a house magazine and then sitting back and waiting for contributions to roll in, yet both documentary films and house magazines are sometimes conceived on this haphazard basis. Film libraries are best regarded as extra outlets, unless used as distributors to whom film bookings are directed by the sponsor. All PR exercises have to be planned and executed according to defined objectives, otherwise it is impossible to evaluate results.

So now we come to the second element of *production*. While expert advice is desirable on technical matters, it is possible to define some of the variations and possibilities that are bound up in cost and treatment relative to *purpose* and *distribution*.

Production

1. Who will make the film—the company's own film unit or an outside one? There is a difference between the company-employed unit of professional film-makers and the amateur ciné-camera enthusiast who would love to make films in his spare time at the company's expense.

2. What length? Twenty minutes is a good, safe average. Anything longer runs the risk of dragging out the material. Only the simplest subjects can be covered in from ten to fifteen minutes. The twenty-minute film fits in well with other films to make up a varied programme.

3. Colour or black and white? This is a matter of cost. Black-and-white VTR is usually adequate for a sales conference or an AGM. But most documentaries are now in colour, and with colour TV there is no need any more to have black-and-white standby copies for possible usage on TV at short notice.

4. Professional or amateur actors? Acting fees can add enormously to costs: on the other hand, Denis Norden "makes" the Churchman small cigars film, *Smoke Rings*.

5. Local or distant location, one or many? The high cost of *Algerian Pipeline* lay in the film crew having to make repeated visits to North Africa as the work progressed. But if there is a choice of what can be done on the spot and what calls for air travel and hotel expenses, and cost is a deciding factor, it may be wise to choose the less sophisticated home locations.

There are two films about the RNLI which highlight the contrast in the final result gained by a "budget" versus a more generously funded film. The first, made by Petters, uses a large number of stills to tell the history of lifeboats, and is mostly a studio production. On the other hand, the Wills film is full of action and is filmed at sea. The less expensive but quite interesting film in this case is unlikely to gain the audiences won in public cinemas by the exciting Wills production. But to be fair—and one must not be ungracious about this—the Petters film is basically about engines and there is hardly any value in the cinema audience for Petters. Incidentally, Rentokil's prize-winning film about cockroaches—which do not like the light!—*had* to be made in a laboratory under controlled conditions, especially for shots of the eggs hatching out. In this case, the location was a very simple one. The major cost item was the waste footage.

6. Who will write the script—sponsor, independent writer or the film producer? Some films have been seriously spoilt by a dull, jargon and cliché-ridden script written by an inside man who knew too much about his subject and was non-creative. A professional scriptwriter, if well briefed, is nearly always best, especially for the voice-over commentary which can become more stilted than dialogue. The professional scriptwriter can add freshness and originality because he will view the subject objectively and also appreciate audience reaction and response. Home-produced scripts can read like sales literature and worse still they can resemble technical data sheets. This seems to be a particular failing of some American documentaries in which both script and commentator fail to catch the subtle nuances of an objective and creative work. Or is this just that the American tends to wear his heart on his sleeve more than the Britisher? The French, with their greater sense of culture, make beautiful documentaries.

7. Who will read the commentary? This can be a very difficult decision to make. Should it be a well-known radio or TV personality, a

voice known and liked, or will the very familiarity intrude on the veracity of the story, making it seem acted, fictitious and false? Should he or she be no more than a sincere and good speaker and preferably unrecognizable? Should a certain tone of voice be sought, a fatherly, authoritative, professional, rural, working class or regional voice, as the case may be? A Vickers-Crabtree film about their Yorkshire plant for making newspaper presses has an actor with a Yorkshire accent who becomes so lyrical and voluble that he obtrudes to the film's detriment. On the other hand, there are well-known voices that are associated with certain interests and topics and if these are sympathetic to the film such a voice can be most appropriate. However, broadcasters are picked simply because they speak well. Newsreaders past and present do frequently feature as commentators in documentaries.

9. What size stock? While it costs more to use 35 mm film it is possible to make 16 mm copies from it but the reverse is impossible. A better print results from the larger stock, 35 mm is essential for cinema use and it is preferred for telecine.

10. Will sound be recorded during filming or dubbed in afterwards? Live sound, particularly on location, is obviously more costly because of the additional production gear and personnel. Voice over commentaries are, of course, dubbed in afterwards, and this method is preferable when language versions are to be made.

11. Are foreign language versions required, calling for translations of the script, and foreign language speaking actors and commentators?

12. Will original or library music be used? If music is specially composed it must also be specially performed. Library music can be hired and dubbed in. So can sound effects.

13. Will it be filmed live or will it be animated? Or will a live film contain animated sequences? Animation can consist of simple hand manipulated charts, or stop action devices can be used (as when things appear or disappear on packages open or characters on them come alive), but cartoons require hundreds and perhaps thousands of drawings to achieve the movie effect. An alternative is the use of puppets. Some subjects could be very dull or difficult to handle without the humour, action and imagination possible with animation, a case in point being the delightful but expensive Mullard cartoon *The Electron's Tale*.

14. Can the film be made in collaboration with another sponsor with

whom costs may be shared? If this is possible, extra facilities may become available. The film may be given additional authority because of the verisimilitude gained from association with other interests. We have already touched on the "Distribution" aspects of joint sponsorship.

15. Is it intended for theatrical showing on public cinemas? If so, there are trade union strictures stating that a full professional crew must be employed.

16. Are there any export considerations such as the avoidance of any references acceptable at home but offensive or embarrassing abroad, in the script, characters or scenes?

The third basic consideration is what shall we do with the film when it is made? This is very closely linked to "Purpose": the two may be identical as when a film or tape is specially made for a sales conference. However, a film can have various uses and audiences and decision to make it at all may rest on the extent to which a great many distribution outlets can be exploited. Add to this the durability of a film, and the number and kind of audiences can be important determinants.

Distribution

1. Invited audiences are, in most cases, the primary outlet. A film should be made for showing to people we want to show it to! Audiences are invited to a private cinema, or to a gathering where the film will be projected as part of the proceedings. The showing may be accompanied by a speaker, this alone obviating the need for commercial references in the script or supplementing the film that has no commentary, and no doubt "hospitality" will be provided for the guests. As an example of this, Midland Bank branch managers are encouraged to arrange audiences to whom the Bank's many films are shown.

The Midland Bank Executive and Trustee Company made their famous film *Why Not Uncle Willy?* (slightly long at 34 minutes) "to illustrate how the officials of the . . . company carry out their duties and to dispel the belief that a corporate trustee is impersonal or unsympathetic" and it was aimed at specific audiences of married women, businessmen and Midland Bank branch managers. Distribution was by free loan from a film library service or by direct approach to the bank or the trustee company. When the film became out-dated and was withdrawn it had been booked 4000 times and seen by some 170,000 people, and in the two years following the film's release in 1965 the Trustee Company's business increased by more than 11 per cent compared with the previous two years. The film won first prize in its category in the BISFA Festival in 1966. This potted case study emphasizes the combination of "Purpose" and "Distribution" culminating in a valid assessment of results for not only did the film aim to educate the market but also to make branch managers "better able to sell the services of the Trustee Company". It was a double-headed marketing aid.

2. Can it be shown on a film loop with back projection in the company's showroom? (Other playback devices will be discussed later in this chapter.)

3. In a similar way, can it be used on the company's stands at exhibitions? Video tapes can also be shown in this way.

4. Can the film be entered for competitions? Some of these—British Industrial and Scientific Film Association Festival and the Venice International Industrial Film Festival—can create bonus interest, new audiences and help to establish demand for a firm's films. This in turn enhances the reputation of the sponsor, always provided that the mistake is not made of sacrificing basic PR purpose for award winning.

5. Does the film, or shots from it, provide library material which can be made available to film and TV producers?

6. Is the film of interest to the Central Office of Information which has a films acquisitions department. This useful department arranges foreign language versions, catalogues, and makes available British non-advertising films to overseas borrowers while at the same time assuming all rights for overseas TV presentation. If the film can help with exports, the COI can be a valuable outlet. Copies of the catalogue are held in British embassies and consulates throughout the world, through whom films may be booked.

It is then up to film sponsors to create a demand for their films in those parts of the world where they would like them to be shown. This can be done by getting local selling agents to borrow and show the film, by sending synopsis leaflets to interested organizations which could then feel encouraged to borrow and show the film, and by obtaining publicity for the film through reviews, or press reports on the winning of awards.

7. Does the film lend itself to the packaged film shows which are toured round the weekly meetings of women's clubs? A number of food manufacturers such as McDougalls and Robertsons, and package tour and cruise operators, put their films on this kind of "circuit". Guild Sound and Vision Ltd, a member of the Film Producers Guild, Upper St. Martin's Lane, London, WC2 organize these showings.

8. Can it be "road-shown", that is shown in mobile cinemas set up in market squares and other provincial centres of the sponsors' choice? This is another service provided by Guild Sound and Vision. Some firms tour their own mobile cinemas, putting on shows at outdoor gatherings such as agricultural shows, gymkhanas, flower shows and sports meetings, borrowing something from the entertainment of the old "medicine shows". They are also a very important medium of education and publicity in many parts of the Third World where mobile film shows defeat the problems of distance, scattered population groups, language, literacy and scarcity of other media, and they have great novelty appeal.

9. Can the film be taken to organizations, perhaps through members of the sale force or local branch managers who are able to accompany the film with talks and lead discussion? Women's Institutes, Townswomen's Guilds, church societies, professional societies, chambers of commerce, Rotary clubs, horticultural societies, golf clubs and so on are often looking for programme material and will gladly accept the offer of a film and speaker.

10. Can it be offered to societies that run their own film evenings and want a selection of appropriate films? A film about garden aids can be offered to local horticultural societies during the winter evenings, one about banking and credit facilities to Young Farmers Clubs, and one about career openings to youth clubs.

11. Schools warrant a separate section. Has the film a schools application? Chemical firms may have films of value to senior school students while a sewing machine manufacturer may have one of interest to domestic science classes. Should there be an announcement in the *Times Educational Supplement* when it runs a feature on films suitable for schools? Or should an invitation to borrow be sent direct to selected schools? Gas and electricity undertakings can find useful outlets among schools for their films on fuel and appliances. Again, school parties can

be invited to attend film shows. Teachers are of course great users of the catalogues of the film libraries.

12. Does it make a TV test card film like BP's famous *Giuseppina* and P & O's *Run away to Sea*?

13. Are there TV programmes that can use sequences, or can it be shown on TV in its entirety as legitimate programme material? Programmes such as *Tomorrow's World* may like such material, e.g. the European air bus. (*NB*. The Chemical Bank bought air-time to show their film on drug addiction. See page 115.)

14. Can it be used for staff training purposes, as in the example of the Midland Bank's *Why Not Uncle Willy?* An induction course exercise, perhaps? Documentaries can be very useful for induction courses if the company is setting up overseas as when Shell ran such courses for several months while its new Lagos headquarters were being constructed.

15. Has it a use in a community relations exercise, being supplied to local societies, or townspeople being invited to showings in a local cinema or hall?

16. Can it be shown to the press at press receptions or during press facility visits to the factory or other premises? It can be a good way of demonstrating the end product and the end use of the product when visitors are to see production lines in action.

17. Finally, can a bonus distribution be placement in film libraries from which it may be borrowed free of charge or at a charge by anyone who cares to apply? This should be the last consideration, not the first!

Again, the list is not conclusive, and yet with no fewer than seventeen outlets to begin with it can be appreciated how the answers to the questions posed can effect both the "Purpose" and the "Production", and also the budget. The possibility of generous showings may mean taking more trouble with production, as in the example of the Wills film about an inshore rescue boat. However, it can also mean that the budget must permit enough prints (bearing in mind that a single showing may take one print out of circulation for a week and so reduce the potential of one print to fifty or fewer than fifty screenings a year), together with their handling and maintenance. Physical distribution can be contracted out to a film library.

To these forty-three considerations must now be added the trimmings. A film is a promotable product in its own right, and it calls for its own PR campaign which may comprise the following.

PR Campaign for a Documentary Film

1. *Film premiere*. There are critics who specialize in industrial films, writing for newspapers and specialist magazines. A premiere should be arranged for them at a private cinema.

2. *Synopsis leaflets* should be printed as give-aways after performances. These help to remind people of what they heve seen, and to tell others about the content of the film. It is a way of reiterating points, and a better way of mentioning products or giving addresses than in the film itself. Supplementary information can also be given. P & O have an excellent synopsis leaflet which describes films available on free loan, illustrated with stills. So, too, have W. D. & H. O. Wills for their many films, mostly on leisure themes.

3. If the film is taken up by the COI it is a good idea to follow this up as suggested in "Distribution" (6). Translated news stories can be distributed by EIBIS (see page 79).

4. A news release about the availability of the film should be mailed to all relevant publications, accompanied by the synopsis leaflet and a still from the film.

5. Opportunities to enter the film in competitions should be taken up as, winner or not, it will be seen by important people and publicity will accrue from entry alone.

6. Locational and local interest may be exploited, captioned stills and news releases being sent to newspapers where the shooting took place, or from whence "actors" came, not forgetting the locales of the company's own units.

7. It should be offered to TV producers as background material for series, or for use in a magazine or current affairs programme.

8. In time, other press stories can be issued about the number of people who have seen the film, the countries in which it has been seen, the length of time of the waiting list (if it becomes very popular like Laing's film of Coventry Cathedral), and details of any awards it may have won. Meanwhile, whenever company staff organize a showing at

which they are present they should send a brief report to the local press, mentioning the sponsors of the film show, the title of the film, the sponsor of the film, and a resumé of its content.

Thus, a documentary film is a versatile PR medium if it is made to work hard. As with all planned PR, nothing must be left to chance, no opportunity must be missed, and as Lord Geddes once said the orange should be squeezed until the pips squeak.

The initial cost can be spread over a number of years, as can production work and it will be cautionary to close this section by emphasizing that the idea for a film may well be conceived at a contract or order stage, long before there is anything to film. A long-term project may require shooting at intervals over several months or maybe years. Laing's *Coventry Cathedral* took nine years to make. There would have been very little worth filming, from Laing's point of view, when the work was completed. The initial and vital decision may therefore be one of great courage, foresight and conviction. In the case of the Laing film, the decision was made ten years before the Queen eventually performed the opening ceremony, and more than ten years later the film is still doing a big PR job. That's a span of more than twenty years.

International Use of Documentaries

Where language or illiteracy is a handicap to easy communication, the documentary can be a primary PR medium. Filmed action, whether live or animated, can communicate information speedily and convincingly, and this can be important to the marketer who needs to demonstrate a product, prove its value or achieve its correct usage. A shirt may look very smart in its plastic wrapping—a great improvement on old ways of packing shirts in brown paper parcels done up with string—but in a film a man can be seen enjoying leisure pursuits while wearing the new shirt. The film can project usage. No-one has to say a word. Mime can replace words, and in some films ballet has been used.

However, if speech is necessary it is neither difficult nor costly to produce foreign-language versions of films, the same film being dubbed with different sound. Dubbing is always superior to sub-titling. But it is seldom wise to have commentators speaking in languages other than their own: better to have foreign-languages spoken by natives, and foreign film-makers are usually careful to prepare both English and American versions!

The speechless film has interesting possibilities, making use of sounds relative to the action, or music which may have been specially composed to create the right mood. Such films are international in appeal, can be shown in any country or to audiences of mixed nationalities. They are ideal for international delegate conferences, overseas trade fairs and assemblies of multi-national company staff or sales agents. The lack of commentary usually requires brilliant editing and a kaleidoscopic effect to maintain continuity and attention. In the Common Market situation where different language versions cannot be screened simultaneously, the technique of doing without words has obvious advantages. But it does call for a highly disciplined shooting script because the pictures must often speak for themselves, avoiding confusion, ambiguity and misunderstanding and this may require symbols which help to tell the story.

In very different parts of the world, such as the villages of Africa, Asia and South America, the touring film show is an attraction that can serve the marketer for either advertising or PR purposes, probably a mixture of both. Government PR units have promoted birth control by this educational medium in Malaysia and India, and the change-over from left- to right-hand driving was similarly explained in Nigeria. The mobile show with song and dance team, product demonstrations and documentary film is ideal when communities are scattered in clusters of villages or compounds. In West Africa, travelling banks have been promoted in this way. Road shows have all the elements of novelty, surprise, entertainment and contrast which appeal to simple-living people. Yet, despite the simplicity of, say, Nigerian villages, the sophistication of their purchases and possessions is the result of the manufacturer or trader seeking out the market. Even in remote desert dwelling places, the Arab herdsman has his transistor radio.

On a larger scale, when a contract service or a public works service is being promoted abroad a mute film supported by an on-the-spot commentary in the appropriate language—perhaps read from a translated script—can whittle down communication barriers. For instance, it may be that the head man speaks English, but his counsellors, fellow directors or executives, do not, and their understanding, appreciation and approval can be gained by demonstrative moving pictures that explain swiftly what may be laborious in translation. In this way, many nationalities and tongues can be made to understand the message.

Films and International Companies

When a company sells to the world—often because its home market is too small to justify mass production—the film is an excellent way of creating a corporate, product or service image on an international scale. A company famous in its own country is frequently little known, if known at all, overseas, and the film can demonstrate the size, importance, efficiency and so on of the company on its home ground. Here are a few examples:

1. *India* does not have a industrial image in the West, yet castings, machine tools and other engineering goods are being exported to Europe and elsewhere. A film about Indian state-owned engineering works has been showing at engineering exhibitions in London, and other Indian industrial firms have been seen on TV, endeavouring to replace the "elephants and Taj Mahal" image with something more modern, and showing how the traditional crafts and skills of the Indian are being adapted to modern technologies.

2. *Italian* Necchi sewing machines are made at Padua in Italy and sold the world over. The company's 100-year history, and the modern plant at Padua, feature in a film which has been shown round the world to show the authentic background. This is very important when a product sold in, say, London, Los Angeles and Lagos is made in a far-off city perhaps better known historically than industrially.

3. The *Dutch* tug company Smit Internationale serves ship-owners throughout the world, and films have been screened in international ports to demonstrate the nature and facilities of Smit's fleet of large, fast ocean-going tugs. Originally, films were used to explain the costs of ocean-going tug services, clients not realizing the class of vessel and size of crew involved.

4. The *British* company Rentokil sent directors on foreign tours, prior to the setting up of their present subsidiaries, and they went armed with films to show to audiences often organized by British Government trade officials. This was some of the spade-work that eventually

resulted in today's international network of Rentokil companies and sales agents.

5. Bovis, another *British* company, produced a 16 mm film in 1973 which it showed simultaneously at thirteen different centres in the UK, South East Asia and Canada so that 3000 employees could be told about the change-over to fee work. The medium was picked for its ability to present the facts clearly and to communicate management thinking, Bovis chairman M. F. Sanderson and chief executive Bernard Heaphy making personal appearances in the film. Production and screening of the film was achieved in a matter of fourteen days, something usually done nowadays only with videotape.

6. Co-inciding with Britain's entry into Europe, six films on finance in Europe were jointly sponsored by the *British* National Westminster Bank and the distributors, EMI, who are making available films for management. These 16 mm colour films cover the financial institutions of Europe; the City of London; the Euro-Currency Market; International Money Management; the Eurobond Market; and Expanding in Europe. Copies may be bought or hired from EMI Special Films Unit, 7 Soho Square, London W1V 5FA. Experts from ICI, Philips, BP, Warburgs, Rothschilds and NatWest appear in the films.

Closed Circuit TV

Mention has been made of the use of films and tapes at business conferences and sales meetings, but the showing of tapes through conventional TV receivers (instead of projecting films onto screens) lends itself to many situations which are more like a drawing room than a cinema. Hotel lounges, hospital wards, business offices, works canteens, schools and colleges, exhibition stands and showrooms, board and committee rooms all offer themselves as temporary and quickly adapted venues for small audience presentations. A number of possibilities will now be discussed, and proceeding from the well-known technique of showing on a TV set what is being simultaneously shot on the premises by a TV camera—or conveyed from an outside location to the receiver by means of a Post Office landline—we shall also consider the more modern playback and recording devices using film, tape or disc.

Modern Playback Techniques

A variety of electronic techniques are now on the market, and others are being developed—mostly in Europe, USA and Japan—for the playback of prerecorded film or videotape programmes, and for the recording of TV programmes. With these units it is possible to organize showings to fairly small audiences, to do so simultaneously if required, or to provide a library of material which can be played whenever desired. The medium is therefore extraordinarily flexible, less costly in production than film, more compact for either despatch or storage, when tape is used, but with one kind of playback device it is also possible to use film in a more compact fashion. However, VTR does mean that programmes can be made in the camera, projected on a conventional TV screen, and the tape wiped and re-used (if wished), thus eliminating costs of stock while cine-apparatus is not required. With backward, forward and stop frame controls, both film and tape playback devices provide full control over presentation.

There are two basic videocassette devices. First, there is the *electronic video recorder* (EVR) which uses an 8.75 mm film enclosed in an automatic loading cartridge. The film has two tracks, one for the monochrome image and the other for colour encoding. Alternatively, the second track can carry a different monochrome programme and therefore the cartridge will show half-an-hour in colour or one hour in black-and white. Magnetic sound stripes along the edges of the film can provide stereo sound for colour reproduction. This device lends itself to, say, packaged tour operators whose agents can give realistic shop counter demonstrations of resorts and hotels or modes of transport.

The second system, *video cassette recorder* (VCR), has wider applications. Many different formats of cassette/cartridge/tape speed are already announced but the most important are Philips $\frac{1}{2}$ inch VCR, Sony $\frac{3}{4}$ inch U-matic, RCA $\frac{3}{4}$ inch Magtape, Cartrivision $\frac{1}{2}$ inch and Matsushita $\frac{1}{2}$ inch. Prerecorded material is consequently cheaper to produce, having the benefit of instant editing instead of requiring the processing of film, rushes, reshooting and so on to achieve the final result. This is a medium that has been advanced in recent years by devices such as the Sony and Philips VCRs.

For example, Ford in America have supplied 6000 US dealers with Sony VCRs, and every month one or two new programmes are supplied.

Some cassettes can be used to demonstrate cars to customers, others provide a library of tapes on servicing so that engineers can run a tape on a TV receiver to check how to carry out a particular job. Printed service manuals promise to become a thing of the past when such a visual demonstration is possible, and communication is so wonderfully improved. American drug companies are also providing video cassettes to hospitals to demonstrate treatments, and the obvious advantage of such a means of up-dating the knowledge of general practitioners is an obvious encouragement to the British National Health Service to sponsor this method of medical re-education.

Another development adopted by tanker and cruiseship owners is the Telmar Programme Service whereby current British TV programmes, including football matches, can be shown to off-duty ships crews within ten days of being seen on home screens in the UK. This is a major move in industrial relations, especially since tanker crews are away from home for very long periods. There is surely scope for sponsored documentaries too.

VCR devices cost from £400–£750 but prices may well be halved as their versatility increases demand. Advertised internationally is the Philips VCR N1500 which has a built-in TV tuner, and a time switch, so that it can be used to record and replay TV programmes. A programme can be recorded in one's absence or while watching another channel so that programmes need not be missed and the recording may be seen whenever the viewer wishes. Programmes can also be retained for further showings in the future. This lends itself very much to schools and Open University programmes. It uses a cassette about the size of a paperback book, and, just like an ordinary cassette tape recorder, it can be stopped to exchange cassettes, and has the familiar reverse and forward controls. Prerecorded cassettes can thus be played on a conventional TV receiver as well as recordings of TV programmes. A library of cassettes can be created, or they may be borrowed or hired. The only limitation is the size of the screen—the system is one for small audiences capable of watching a TV screen in comfort, although one player can feed five receivers. For large theatre audiences, the giant Eidophor screen can be used for simultaneous screening of a conference speaker as at the annual conference of the Institute of Directors at the Albert Hall, London.

Yet another development from both Telefunkun-Decca (TED) and Philips is the *video disc*, rather like a gramophone record capable of playing both vision and sound. This will provide an alternative to the video cassette just as the LP stereo record is the alternative to the stereo musicassette.

In Denmark, a subsidiary of Philips, Telscan Television Inv, 33 Grønnegade, DK 1107 Copenhagen K, is operating a production, leasing and renting videotape service for exhibitions, in-house or external information, PR presentations, export promotion and conventions. Telscan has mobile production units able to move to any location inside or outside Europe. A fully-equipped studio exists in Copenhagen which can produce films and tapes and has capacity to copy per hour fifty cassette copies with 30 minutes playing time. Playback equipment can be rented on a short- or long-term basis. This suggests an interesting service for any marketer who wishes to have, say, regular up-dating visual contact with a dealer network in common market countries, or short-term VCR facilities at exhibitions, press conferences or technical seminars.

Information About Industrial Films

In 1973 the British Industrial and Scientific Film Association and the Association of Specialized Film Producers published a guide "Exploitation of the Industrial/Sponsored Film" price £1.75 from ASFP, Nascreno House, 27 Soho Square, London WC1 5FL.

Advice on film production and roadshow distribution in the UK may be obtained from the Film Producers Guild, Guild House, Upper St. Martin's Lane, London WC2.

Useful commentaries on industrial film-making, and reviews of new films, are given by John Chittock in the *Financial Times*, and by Kenneth Myer in *Public Relations* and *Marketing and Advertising News*.

Film Libraries

The Central Film Library has a main catalogue containing some 1000 films and a *Films for Industry* catalogue listing some 900 films available on hire or in many cases on free loan, from Government Building,

Bromyard Avenue, London W3 7JB. Makers of industrial films may be able to obtain inclusion in the Central Film Library by arrangement with the Films Division of the Central Office of Information, Hercules Road, London SW1. The majority of films in this Library are government-sponsored ones.

Guild Sound and Vision Ltd, 85-129 Oundle Road, Peterborough PE2 9PY (telephone Peterborough 63122 (STD Code 0733) operate the library service most widely used by owners of industrial films, and apart from the actual showing of films (as described on page 122), Guild will take over the entire distribution of films, handling requests, despatch and maintenance, and acting upon the instructions of the owner who is thus relieved of the task of running a film library, booking, despatch and servicing department. The owner still retains control of the showings.

CHAPTER 7

Sponsorships

THE marketing value of sponsorship is twofold. An immeasurable amount of publicity results from a popular sponsorship, mainly of a name-plugging kind. The Schweppes, Mackeson's and Whitbread's gold cups and trophies in horse racing, the *Daily Mail* Air Race, the *Daily Telegraph*, Dunlop, Players, and Benson & Hedges golf tournaments and the dozens of sponsored awards at show-jumping events are of unspecific advertising value. Yardley exploit them to the full by announcing in their outdoor advertising the motor races for which their car has been entered, while Midland Bank display posters on their own premises to announce their participation in sponsorships.

But on the whole, these supports are investments in goodwill, for without such philanthropic gestures many of the events would not exist, and the standards of the various interests might be less in the absence of competitive attractions. Many sponsorships are not unlike one-time patronages of the arts. They are services to sport and other interests, and so earn their own prestigious award. It works both ways: no award would be worth winning if it were made by a disreputable company. To be able to sponsor at all is to have arrived. The marketer will therefore be jealous of his ability to sponsor, and not surprisingly there is often a clamour to be accepted in this way.

In some cases, then, there is public recognition of respectability, responsibility and status. One's product is associated with youth, beauty, health, leisure, pleasure, or one's company is seen to patronize the arts, encourage research or promote learning. Sometimes there is great philanthropy like the Nuffield Trust, financial support for new universities, purchase of art treasures for the nation, or the endowment of medical research. Successful companies acknowledge a debt to society when they contribute to social developments or causes, whether it be the library of the London School of Economics, a cathedral restoration fund, or a hospital unit. At Ibadan University, the impressive hall was the gift of the United Africa Company while Rootes Hall at Warwick University marks another gift from industry.

Sydney Opera House attracted commercial sponsorships when it was opened in 1973. Benson & Hedges of Australia financed the opera *War and Peace*, and ran a nation-wide TV advertising campaign using a 60-second commercial costing A$7,500 to make apart from time-buying costs. Pioneer Concrete (whose chairman and managing director is Italian) also sponsored the opera *Il Tricittico*. The Ampol Group of Companies sponsored the Sydney Opera House's first ballet, *Australia-Australia*, and this wholly owned Australian company invested A$30,000 on the project. It was Ampol who financed Donald Campbell's land and water speed record attempts in Australia in 1964.

In the USA, Gillette engage in major sponsorships of which the annual Miss America Contest is the most spectacular and is heavily backed by the Toni Personal Care Division. It is fascinating, therefore, that while it might be expected that a British company like John Player should sponsor its cricket league to the tune of £65,000 a year it was the American firm of Gillette that helped to rescue British county cricket from bankruptcy and obscurity. There is a parallel between the changes for the better in British county cricket and the success of Gillette's product diversification and marketing programme since 1962.

In 1962 Gillette made razor blades and little else, while county cricket was in the doldrums, a three-day game with vanishing public interest and attracting financial support only from philanthropic enthusiasts. In 1973 all but two county cricket clubs were making significant profits. And Gillette are now manufacturing and marketing male and female toiletries, and ball-point pens as well as newly styled razors and their blades or cartridges. Less than 50 per cent of their turnover is now in razor blades.

Gillette adopted a generous attitude from the start. Their philosophy on sponsorship was to provide the necessary financial backing and let the sportsmen get on with the game to the benefit of the sport and the enjoyment of the spectator. For £15,000 a year Gillette enjoyed a well-deserved halo effect, preferring not to become involved in high pitched marketing and promotional campaigns which placed more significance on its image and its products than the sport itself. Cricket, thought Gillette's management, was an old and dignified sport that should stay that way.

So they launched the Gillette Cup which has three rounds, semi-finals and the final match in September. In the first eleven years it brought in seventeen of the nineteen minor counties, and while most of the matches were completed in a day—and two ended before 2.30 pm!—only 44 out of 205 matches took longer. The competition stimulated exciting cricket, with spectators fairly confident of knowing the result at the end of day. In three matches the winning side didn't even lose a wicket, and there were level scores in two others.

The Cup "invested Gillette blades with all the healthy, open-air clean-shaven charisma that cricket conveys", according to a study of sponsorship published by the PR consultants, Daniel J. Edelman Ltd, who handle Gillette's PR and are the London end of Daniel J. Edelman of Chicago.

The first eleven years of the Gillette Cup was celebrated with the anniversary of three centuries of cricket by means of a merchandising offer of three reproduction prints of eighteenth-, nineteenth- and twentieth-century cricket plus a 32-page booklet about the Cup. This offer was promoted on Gillette razor blade, cartridge, Foamy, Right Guard, Foot Guard and The Dr. Look packs, three tokens being required. Retail displays showed miniatures of the prints.

There is therefore good reason why the marketer should look at the PR value of sponsorship, the halo effect of being a distinguished organization meaning that products and services, including staff behaviour, need to reflect the status of a well-known sponsor. Sponsorship, in this light, is a privilege, something to live up to. In fact, while branding means that a manufacturer stakes his reputation on the product, sponsorship goes much further and implies that the reputation is established. Sponsorship, to be worthwhile, is not therefore for the raw, brash newcomer, the unknown or the unproven.

It is therefore of some significance when a comparatively new but successful newspaper like the *Sun* is able to present TV Awards, when the annual awards by Pye might be expected, or when a successful new business like Alpine Double Glazing makes a premier horse jumping award alongside well-known prizes from the *Sunday Times* and Ronson.

From this general look at the broad field of sponsorship, and its marketing-PR implications, let us consider definite areas of support, some of which may be more suitable to some organizations than to others. Without suggesting any order of merit, the following may be discussed: (a) books; (b) exhibitions; (c) education and research; (d) expeditions and adventures; (e) sport; (f) culture; (g) causes and charities; (h) local events; (i) films; (j) professional skills.

Books

The sponsored book is an excellent PR medium which in recent years has pulled itself up from that position of abuse when firms used to perpetrate dull company histories and commemorative tomes. Even so, over the years, there have been some noteworthy sponsored books to mention only *Pears Encyclopaedia* and the *Leica Manual*, while more recent successes have been the remarkable *Guinness Book of Records* and the mass-selling Spectator books on cookery and handicrafts. However, the intention may not be to produce a best-seller but simply an authoritative account which adds prestige for its sponsor because it adds to the recognized literature on a subject. The Rentokil Library of books on timber preservation and pest control fall into this category, and are described in the case study section.

If books are taken to include publications generally we can include diaries, guides, maps and similar printed items short of house journals which have their own chapter.

One pocket or desk *diary* is very useful, but more than one becomes an embarrassment. The danger with diaries is that the sender is never sure that his is the first received and therefore the most likely to be put into use. The best way to overcome this problem is to issue a first diary in a substantial loose cover (bearing the sponsor's *and* the recipient's name!), and then to supply refills in subsequent years. This method makes the diary act as a piece of permanent goodwill, rather than as one of those tiresome Christmas gifts, and money will not be wasted. While the diary does serve as a Christmas gift it is also a form of sponsorship which can foster goodwill over a long time if it earns the appreciation of the recipient.

The splendid pocket *guides* to London and elsewhere produced by Francis Chichester Ltd are useful for presentation to overseas visitors, or strangers to the city. Similar pocket guides are available in cities round the world, banks being among the principal sponsors. Useful and long-lasting, they exude goodwill.

Maps and guides like the Shell and Michelin editions, and inexpensive paper road maps sponsored by petrol companies and sold at garages, are a mixture of money-spinners, self-liquidating offers and service-to-motorist customer relations exercises.

The most comprehensive guides used by tourists in the USA, giving unbiased ratings to hotels and resorts, are the Mobil Travel Guides. Published annually in six volumes, they sell about a million copies. The project is of major proportions, and its only equivalent is the Guide Michelin in Europe. Self-liquidating, the sponsorship is a service to the traveller and so enhances goodwill towards Mobil Oil.

Sponsorship of *popular books*, that is books selling to the consumer mass market, can involve four kinds of distribution: (a) bookshop; (b) mail order; (c) direct selling through own outlets; and (d) free distribution to customers and other interested readers.

Probably one of the best examples of those sold through the book trade is the annual *Guinness Book of Records* which had a print order of 690,000 copies for the 1973 edition. It is published by Guinness Superlatives Ltd, a wholly owned subsidiary of Arthur Guinness Son & Co (Park Royal) Ltd. The editors, McWhirter twins Norris and Ross, were given the job in 1955 when Sir Hugh Beaver, then managing director of Guinness, could find no means of verifying the speed of the fastest game bird. The book is printed in English, French, Spanish, Italian, Czech, Dutch, German, Danish, Swedish, Norwegian, Finnish and Japanese, and has sold close on seven million copies.

A firm which has become closely associated with sport sponsorship is Rothmans, and their football annual is to be seen displayed in popular bookshops at Christmas while their tennis annual is promoted in the Spring and Summer. The *Rothman's Football Annual* had a print order of 80,000 for the 1973/4 edition, ran to over a thousand pages, sold in twenty countries and had a subsidized price of £1.30. At £2.50, the *Piccadilly World of Golf*, is a slightly more up-the-market hardback. These books are promoted with press advertising which is also subtle, oblique advertising for the cigarette itself. Clearly, there is an excellent seasonal market for inexpensive books of this kind, of which other examples are the *Daily Mail Year Book* and the beautifully produced *ITV Yearbook* which contrasts strikingly with the sedate *BBC Yearbook*.

Mail order selling of sponsored books can be achieved in two ways. First, the book can be offered in a press advertisement inserted by the sponsor (for cash like the *Spectator* and Rothman books or free of charge like the Midland Bank's *Riding For The Gold*), and, as with the Spectator books, further sales can be obtained by inserting tear-out order cards at the back of the book. This has been and can be done with books on wide-interest topics such as cookery, dress-making, gardening, home handicrafts, decorating and car maintenance.

Direct selling is possible when the sponsor has his own shops or door-to-door sales network, provided the book is directly related to the firm's normal trade. For example, a manufacturer with his own outlets, e.g. paints, wallpaper, knitting wool, kitchen furniture, can sponsor books on home decorating, knitting or room-planning.

The Dutch supermarket chain, Albert Heijn, produced a meat cookery book *Het volkomen vleesboek* on a self-liquidating retail sales basis. In Britain, the Fatstock Marketing Corporation sponsored Helen Tullberg's *Economical Meat Cookery* which sold more than 50,000 copies at 30p. The book showed housewives how to enjoy cheaper cuts, thus doing a PR job for meat and butchers while helping the sale of the whole carcase.

Free distribution is comparatively easy, but may be prohibitively expensive unless it is perhaps linked with a merchandising offer which at least promotes selling out. On the whole—because production costs are considerable—sponsorship of books needs to be at least partially covered by sales.

A variation on this is the *textbook* which brings together industrial authors (with technical resources) and publishers (with renowned imprints and distribution facilities). A typical arrangement is for the sponsor to pay for production costs and to receive royalties on retail sales, or to agree to purchase a certain number of copies, the balance being retailed in the usual way. There can be variations on these agreements to suit both sides. In this way a specialized book with a limited print order of a few thousand copies can be produced to a high standard permitting, say, good paper and generous illustration. The sponsor distributes his copies to clients and staff.

Advance Electronics, for instance, published an educational book privately with some success, but generally it pays to combine the resources of author and publisher if the book is to gain the widest possible distribution and find acceptance as a legitimate contribution to the literature on the subject. The danger of private publication is that the book may suffer from promotional bias (which the publisher's editor would erase) or have the misfortune of appearing to be a book that had to be issued privately because no publishing house would accept it for his lists. The publisher's imprint is therefore an important recommendation.

Exhibitions

Sponsorship of exhibitions by trade associations, professional institutes, government departments, newspapers and magazines has become a means of proclaiming their authority and repute. This endorsement may come about by exhibitors co-operating through their own trade association to put on an event for their own benefit, such as the *Business Equipment Exhibition*. Without this joint sponsorship there might be no event at all, and it also guards exhibitors against inefficient and dishonest organizers. Meanwhile, from the visitor's point of view the show promises to be of a high standard with representation from leading people in the business. Good examples are the *Motor Show* and the *Commercial Motor Show* which are sponsored by the Society of Motor Manufacturers and Traders and supported by an IPC journal in each case, while the *Do-It-Yourself Exhibition* is sponsored by the journal of that name, *Hotelympia* by *Caterer and Hotelkeeper*, and *Ideal Home Exhibition* by the *Daily Mail*.

Education

The endowment of bursaries, exhibitions, travelling scholarships and other higher education awards is usually a mixture of social responsibility, inspiration for original research and sometimes a means of attracting graduate personnel. In the USA, a large number of technical books have resulted from industrial sponsorship which has enabled high level research to be undertaken, often in vocational subjects, at American universities. Study bursaries are awarded by United Tobacco in South Africa. Unfortunately, British universities tend to be too academically and too little vocationally biased—a matter of different histories and cultures—to attract anything like the sponsorship that American universities woo from American industry. There are a few notable exceptions in Britain, such as BOC and Guinness. But there is a wide-open field for more sponsored industrial research fellowships at British universities, even if it is less spectacular than a motor race, and even if the need is for pure rather than operational research. One would have thought that the Common Market alone warranted marketing/PR orientated bursaries at business schools, polytechnics and universities to encourage valuable research and publications.

A long standing educational sponsorship is that of the Japanese Mitsui Group and the Faculty of Commerce and Social Science at Birmingham University. A number of Japanese students attended the British University, and in 1923—in appreciation of the education received—the Mitsui family endowed the Mitsui Chair of Finance with the sum of £5000, a generous sum at that time. In 1947 the chair was changed to Economics. Anglo-Japanese links have extended to professorial lecture visits to Mitsui and Kejo Universities.

When Japanese prime minister Tanaka visited the USA in 1973 he presented ten million dollars to American universities on behalf of the Japan Foundation. During his subsequent tour of Europe Tanaka gave cultural exchange funds of one million dollars to universities and research institutes in each of three countries, Britain, France and Germany, to promote understanding of Japan among Europeans and also to promote study of Japan and the Japanese language. This cultural sponsorship has obvious marketing implications in respect of both import and export trade.

The Australian Ampol Group is the major sponsor for the annual Summer Science School at the University of Sydney, and Ampol also present an annual geology scholarship at the Australian National University for post-graduate work.

An inexpensive sponsorship by a large organization has been BP's scheme of road safety talks to schools.

Expeditions and Adventures

This form of sponsorship is open to abuse when firms are expected to provide almost everything down to the bootlaces free of charge and with little hope of the slightest reciprocity. In contrast, the yacht *British Steel* was a major sponsorship. In some cases, the sponsor has to accept that he is being generous in a worthy cause, and leave it at that. But it may be that the undertaking will help to prove the qualities of a product, and this was the case when Hillary used a Smiths watch when climbing Everest, and a Smiths watch proved to be an unexpected steering aid for John Ridgway and Chay Blythe when they rowed the Atlantic. So, while explorers and other adventurers may seek no more than free supplies, there can be suppliers who seek opportunities to demonstrate, say, that their processed food withstood extremes of temperatures, or that a material proved its strength and durability. This, of course, is very true of motor rallying and safari rallies, and the success of Datsun and SAAB must have done much to enhance their export sales, especially Datsun in Africa.

Sport

With rare exceptions such as Rugby Union, almost every sport welcomes the patronage of firms willing to contribute prize money. Sport sponsorship the world over is big business and amounts to £5 million a year in Britain alone. In addition to prize money and trophies it includes provision of training facilities, equipment and clothing, funds to cover the expense of attending events, and contributions to club funds.

There is a close link between sport sponsorship and television which has vastly increased the audiences for sporting events. Horse and motor racing, show jumping, golf, tennis, cricket, football, athletics and aerobatics have their sponsors. Motor racing is one of the more costly areas because it is not only prize money that is funded but actual racing teams such as those of Players, Rothman and Yardley whose teams cost around £200,000 a year to maintain.

But when it comes to prize money, Rothmans in association with the London *Evening News* inspired the richest motor race in Europe with a total of £50,000 in prize money—first prize £10,000—at Brands Hatch on August Bank Holiday Monday 1972.

The Japanese are also involved in motor sport, and in 1973 the Hitachi electronics firm helped to add a new venue to the world championships by introducing the Hitachi Grand Prix of Sweden as the seventh round of the fourteen-round contest.

Labatt's, the Canadian brewers, signed a contract in 1972 to sponsor the Formula One race at Mosport Park, and prize money in the 1973 event amounted to $220,000.

There are other types of motor racing sponsorship: Ford have filmed world championship motor races, and Martini set up special marquees for spectators.

Motor racing attracts a great variety of sponsors. The crowds are big and the TV viewing audience is large and there is plenty of news coverage in the press and on radio. While horse racing has more meetings and individual races, and relatively inexpensive sponsorship is possible, motor racing attracts backers as diverse as newspapers, airlines, banks, cigarettes, toiletries, petrol, and car accessories. The psychological impact of the sports is particularly interesting, for while horse racing is a popular form of gambling, motor racing associates a product with manliness, endurance and adventure. The psychology of sponsorship is important and certain sports, activities and interests are chosen for their connotations.

According to Sally White in *The Times* on 30 June 1971, "The company name reproduced in newspaper headlines and stories, and staring out of television screens" is what it's all about! Moreover, as the Racing Information Bureau says in its booklet, "sponsorship represents a novel opportunity of bringing the company's name to the attention of the public, with the assistance of the communications media. It is done in a relaxed atmosphere amid pleasant surroundings and gives them an opportunity of entertaining their clients and their employees."

Many sporting events are sponsored in South Africa, and there is the Rothmans Derby, the Castle football cup named after Castle beer, the big walks supported by the *Rand Daily Mail*, and tennis sponsorships by S. A. Breweries and Clows Garages.

Canada has national sports which attract special sponsorships. For instance, the Bank of Montreal in 1971 and 1972 supported the national ski team and sponsored the 1971 World Cup Race in Canada. It invited bank customers to make donations to the team, set up booths at major ski shows in Toronto, Montreal and Vancouver, and sent Canadian world ski champion Nancy Greene on a personal appearance tour.

Curling is a major Canadian ice sport which Joseph E. Seagram & Sons have sponsored since 1965 with the Seagram's Mixed Curling Championships of Canada. More than 30,000 curlers participate in local, regional and provincial play-downs. Nationwide TV coverage is given to the event. The annual cost is $75,000.

In Britain, the USA, Canada and South Africa golf is a leading sport that owes much to commercial patronage, and there is massive coverage by all the media. Presumably American influence is responsible for Japan's ten million golfers. However, golf is still a novelty in France, and when the perfume firm of Lancome ran its fourth annual golf tournament on a private course 15 miles outside Paris it was still the only one in the French calendar. Lancome's sponsorship has aroused French interest in golf to the point that in the mid-seventies the first public course in France was laid out in the Paris suburbs between Melun and Senart Forest. Meanwhile, Lacome's 1973 tournament produced the headline "U.S. Golf Pros Present Rare Sight for French" in the European edition of the *New York Herald Tribune*.

With so popular a sport capable of gaining literally hours of coverage on TV and columns of reporting in the press, golf sponsorship lends itself to makers of popular retail products. Not surprisingly, British sponsors include John Player, Piccadilly, Dunlop, Senior Service, Sunbeam Electric, Daks and Martini. Alcan were once very big sponsors and their stake was as high as £65,000, which became prohibitive for a company with few retail products with which the public could associate their name.

For many years Seagram in Canada sponsored the Canadian Open Golf Classic and were spending $160,000 a year when they relinquished the privilege to Imperial Tobacco who went on to invest more than $200,000 annually in the Peter Jackson Canadian Open Golf Tournament. In 1973—their third year—80,000 spectators came to see Lee Trevino, Arnold Palmer, Gary Player and other stars playing for prize money of $175,000. Imperial Tobacco also support regional tournaments in all of Canada's ten provinces, and according to a national survey conducted in September 1973 30% of the Canadian population associated the product name of Peter Jackson with golf.

In North America an interesting development in the world of sponsorship has been the series of annual awards made by the Life Insurance Advertisers' Association for PR activities. At the Association's annual meeting in Washington, DC in October 1973, Prudential Insurance of America won an award of excellence for public relations in recognition of its role in promoting table tennis.

Snooker is the sport sponsored by Norwich Union Insurance with its world open championship attracting 24 of the world's leading champions to the Piccadilly Hotel, London, during November 1973.

The 1972 20th Olympic Games in Munich had more publicity tie-ups and sponsorships than any previous Games, mainly because of the Bavarians' frantic need to recoup some of the fantastic costs of the specially built stadium. How much of the symbol buying and supply of free goods and services merited the title of PR sponsorship is somewhat difficult to assess. Much of it was of the give-away publicity kind, nearer to advertising products than maintaining corporate images and building goodwill.

The marketer does need to define the *purpose* of his financial support. Quite legitimately, it can be to plug a brand name and maximize sales, as when Coco-Cola augments all kinds of publicity in connection with a sporting event, but the PR *purpose* of seeking acceptance of a particular public, namely youth, is also adopted by the same firm. Both are part of the marketing strategy, and sponsorship can operate on both levels sumultaneously. Coca-Cola have consequently adopted athletics and swimming for their sponsorship, and this provides much local interest and press coverage.

W. D. & H. O. Wills support so many sporting events that they publish a sports world calendar covering angling, cycling, flying, golf, horse racing, powerboat racing, rally cross, Rugby League seven-a-side, show jumping, speedway and tennis. As we shall see later, these events also provided subject matter for films much enjoyed by sports clubs. John Player & Sons, who are associated with a great variety of leisure-time sponsorships, run the John Player Information Bureau at 240

Oxford Street, London W1N 9DE (Telephone 01-629 9266) which will provide details of all manner of seasonal events, supporting this with a seasonal calendar (interspersed with events sponsored by Players) in the weekend colour supplements.

However, Wills dropped their £30,000 of tennis sponsorship in September 1973. Other sponsors such as Rothmans, John Dewar and Commercial Union continued to contribute to the £400,000 invested in UK tennis sponsorship. The Wills decision was not so much disenchantment with tennis or with sponsorship but disagreement with the various tournament organizers and representative bodies. In some cases the PR of promotors can be imperfect! Rothmans have supported international tennis since 1963, and do so to the tune of £100,000 spread over thirteen tournaments. As a result, tennis tournaments are now held in Holland, Italy and Germany. Dewar specialize in the indoor Dewar Cup tournament with televised finals at the Albert Hall, and feature it in their consumer advertising. Rothmans in Canada have sponsored tennis in that country since 1970. They gave $100,000 in prize money to the Canadian Open in Toronto in 1973, and $80,000 to the World Doubles Tournament, while also sponsoring the Canadian Closed tournament for amateurs.

Some companies are stuck with a limiting image. Gillette had a problem with its Feel Free feminine deodorant, despite the Toni association. And Yardley had the double problem—how to make men accept a name famed for feminine products and at the same time leave behind the lavender water image. Sponsorship is Yardley's way of educating the market, but having done that they believe in spending three times as much to capitalize on their PR achievement. The Yardley toiletries market is the 25-year-old, and sponsorship of the Maclaren racing car (which is also blazoned with Goodyear, Champion and Gulf like a mini-cab covered with advertisements!) aims to create a "racier, more exciting, dynamic image". Yardley's have certainly accelerated from their pretty picture link with old-time London street sellers and their cries.

It may take a long time to set up a new sporting event, and the *Financial Times* Clipper Race in the Autumn of 1975 was launched by Alan Hare, managing director of the *FT* at a press conference in London on 2 March 1973. With this magnificent international event at least three types of sponsorship are envisaged, that of the race itself by the newspaper, that of prizes, and that of the yachts themselves. Sponsored entries are permitted subject to the approval of the International Yacht Racing Union. Any yacht with a full crew and with a maximum rating of 70 foot under the International Offshore Rule may compete, this upper limit being set so that an owner, building a yacht for the *FT* race, will also be able to compete in the other ocean races. The minimum size permitted is 45 foot IOR rating. Sailing from London (where the public will be able to see them start), the yachts will sail to Sydney via the Cape of Good Hope and after a stay in Sydney, return via Cape Horn, taking about five months to complete the course. The PR reasons for this international event are two-fold: to gain world-wide publicity for the newspaper, and to interest *FT* readers, many of whom are sailing enthusiasts.

In 1973, firms were looking for new sports to sponsor. Clarks men's shoes division took up basketball, a sport with more than eighty million players all over the world. Bata Shoes in Nigeria also took up sponsorship of basketball in 1973, this coinciding with the opening of the new sports stadium in Lagos, and providing one of the many topics in a PR film made by the Nigerian company. In this sponsorship there is clearly a very direct link between product and sport, and in major contests teams can be fitted out with sports shoes.

Culture

In this realm big business represents the aristocratic arts patron of bygone days, and it is one of the oldest forms of commercial sponsorship. In the USA, Ford have bought air time for broadcasts by symphony orchestras, a very laudable patronage since American radio has no BBC to ensure regular music programmes like our Radio 3. TWA also sponsored the European tour of an American orchestra.

Symphony orchestras seem to attract the most cultural sponsorship, with Peter Stuyvesant paying the London Symphony Orchestra £12,000 a year, and W. D. & H. O. Wills giving the London Philharmonic Orchestra £10,000. In addition, Wills pay £18,000 a year for six recordings by the LPO on budget price EMI Music For Pleasure discs, specially labelled *Wills Embassy Series*. Here—on the record sleeve and on posters advertising LPO concerts—Wills receive reciprocal advertising. Wills also run Brass Bands Championships in which a hundred bands compete.

The Midland Bank also went musical by sponsoring promenade performances of *Aida*, *Arabella* and *Cosi Fan Tutte* in April 1973 at the Royal Opera House, London, This meant stripping the stalls of seats to allow the traditional promenade arena. Attractive posters displayed in the Bank's branches announced seats from 50p to £3.80 and 650 stall promenade tickets were available one hour before curtain up at 50p. Thus inexpensive opera was offered to a wide public and given the additional publicity among bank customers. Players have also sponsored "proms".

A different cultural sponsorship was Players' support for an open painting competition and exhibition in 1968 which drew nearly one thousand entries from the UK and Europe, the sponsor creating a special gallery in Nottingham for the purpose. Two thousand people attended the show, and in 1969 the paintings went on tour. Players have also sponsored film celebrity discussion evenings at the National Film Theatre, which have been televised. The same company has sponsored annual summer seasons of plays at the Bankside Globe Theatre, off Southwark Bridge, London, where Sam Wanamaker the American producer and director is seeking to "recapture the vitality and spirit which was so characteristic of the stage in Elizabethan times". The 1973 John Player Season, running from mid-June until September, offered fare as original as Ionesco's *Macbeth* translated and directed by Charles Marowitz.

The House of Seagram in Canada sponsored the creation and display of the huge Seagram collection of paintings of Canada. This collection toured North and South America and also Europe. It had dual PR and marketing pay-offs for it helped to make Canada better known and also created awareness of Canadian whiskey.

Also in Canada there is the Du Maurier Council for the Performing Arts which Imperial Tobacco established in 1971. A minimum of $1 million over five years was pledged to cover grants. But that was not all: each beneficiary was offered the services of the company's PR consultants. In 1972, thirty-four groups benefited from these PR services in addition to the grant, and so received designs for programme covers, showcards, posters and other promotional aid for their performances.

The Craven Foundation was founded in 1972 by Rothmans of Pall Mall Canada Ltd to help preserve historical and cultural objects and collections. The Foundation has acquired a collection of sixty-four antique and classic motor cars worth $¾ million, restored them and shown them in exhibitions across Canada.

In South Africa the Rembrandt Group has established an important art collection.

In 1971, Whitbread, in association with the Booksellers' Association, introduced £1000 literary awards for fiction, biography or autobiography, adding a children's book category—largest of its kind in the world—in 1972. The standard of judging is shown by the 1973 panel which consisted of Elizabeth Jane Howard, Laurie Lee and James Pope Hennessy who won the biography award in 1972.

Causes and Charities

This must be the least directly sales-promoting of all sponsorships, but some firms have made valuable contributions. It is of course dangerous to be seen to be getting publicity out of helping a charity! Yet association with a reputable business name may inspire confidence in the charity itself, rather like seeking a royal patron. In the chapter on films mention was made of the Petters Engine and the W. D. & H. O. Wills films for the Royal National Lifeboat Institution. The Wills film, *Bequest to a Village*, is an exciting one that bestows due credit on the lifeboatmen of Sennen in Cornwall, and it was awarded a certificate of merit at the 1970 British Industrial Film Festival.

The Midland Bank gave its support to the Wild Life Trust by sponsoring a book which was displayed and publicized in the bank's local branches throughout the UK.

Surf life saving associations in South Africa are supplied with equipment by United Tobacco.

Local Events

Good community and employee relations may be bound up with support for local events. Public relations is rightly said to begin "on the doorstep", and sponsorship of activities of local interest can help to make a company "belong". This is all the more important when the company is an outsider, as in development areas and on trading estates to which expanding or multi-national firms have set up an outpost. Philips have been established in Croydon for a great many years but it is not exactly a "local" firm, so that when it saved the Royal Russell Schools from being closed down its loan of funds was a much appreciated gesture of community relations.

When Volkswagen set up their offices in a new building that was a landmark in Purley on the outskirts of Croydon, the name in blue lights high up on the face of the circular office block, deliberate efforts were made to become involved as responsible residents so that hint of the company's possible to move to Milton Keynes produced sincere local regret.

Building societies (e.g. Burnley) award prizes at flower shows in areas where they have branch offices. Sewing machine companies (e.g. Elna) provide judges and prizes for dressmaking contests organized by regional newspapers; swimsuit manufacturers run beauty contests in conjunction with holiday camps, local department stores and swimming pools; agricultural feed and implement firms offer prizes at county agricultural shows; and in resort towns local traders (including branches of chains) subscribe to town publicity funds. Similarly, pharmaceutical companies often sponsor local hospital needs, while industrial firms supply equipment to technical colleges, polytechnics and Universities, and food manufacturers link baking contests with gas and electricity showrooms.

An internationally famous sponsored event is the planting out of hundreds of flower beds with every kind of Spring bulb in the glorious Keukenhof Gardens in Holland, something which in a smaller way has been imitated by local rose growers and nurserymen in other countries who have beautiful local parks, traffic islands and road verges with free displays of their produce.

Participation should be willing, interested and generous if it is to be made at all. A somewhat worthless advertisement in the "rag" magazine or gala programme is a poor effort compared with heading the subscription list, having a float in the Chamber of Trade carnival procession, or acting as a judge in the beauty contest.

Films

Just to show once again the versatility of the documentary film, there is the special interest film which is not directly related to the sponsor's business interests, nor is it a charitable production.

One of the finest examples is the series of 16 mm sports films and the "To Win" series available on free loan from the W. D. & H. O. Wills Film Library. The topics are all sporting, outdoor, healthful pursuits, typical of the tobacco companies' PR practice to promote health-giving activities to compensate for the unhealthy image created by the cancer connection.

Obviously, this enterprise has a direct marketing implication. Does it contradict the Government's anti-smoking campaign? Is it cynical? Or is it fair to say that when there are many other possible causes of cancer, from motor car engine fumes to saccharin, a deterrent may well be to indulge in sport, and that the healthy person is less likely to be a victim and may still enjoy the pleasure of smoking? However, all the PR in the world will not deny the most practical of all reasons for not smoking, and that is the voluntary gift of so much tax to a spendthrift government! One really has to be ultrapatriotic to indulge such a penalized pleasure!

However, some of the sponsored schemes associated with these Wills films are unusual, *Fourpence to Fly* telling how nearly one hundred men without any previous flying experience were trained as private pilots, the winner of the Wills Flying Scheme being presented with a Cherokee four-seater aeroplane.

Professional Awards

Finally, a prestigious field for sponsorship is the granting of awards for professional excellence, this enhancing the reputation of the sponsor who is seen to be encouraging high standards. Two such awards are made annually by the *Financial Times*. The *FT* Architecture Award is presented every November and in its first seven years since 1967 more than 500 buildings were examined by the assessors. The 1973 award went to the Horizon factory project, Nottingham, for John Player & Sons. The designers were Arup Designers, builders Bovis Fee Construction.

The *FT* Industrial Photography Awards, covering several categories, have been able to demonstrate with colour reproductions in the newspaper the high standards that can be (but rarely are!) achieved in this important field of communication. This is a contest which, one hopes, will help to raise the at present lowly standards of PR photography, most of which is abysmal. Awards are not the monopoly of the press, but another interesting one is the *Guardian* Young Businessman of the Year Award, which in 1973 was won by 36-year-old Sir Hugh Fraser, chairman of the House of Fraser.

In a different way, business houses also offer cash prizes, trophies and medals to those attaining distinction professional examinations.

Sponsorship has therefore become very much part of our way of life, and many large-scale activities would be impossible without the patronage of those who command wealth in the twentieth century, whether it be governments of all political hues sponsoring space travel or local stores putting up the trophies for music and drama festivals. By the number of sponsorships, many of them regular or continuous rather than *ad hoc* efforts, their value is clear to marketers, even if Alcan did find the cost excessive and withdrew from golf. But the marketer does have to make up his mind whether he is patronising for PR or advertising purposes or both. Some of the cigarette firms' sponsorships are doubtless aimed at recovering their inability, by law, to advertise on television, while others are aimed at exploiting the huge television audience on all channels. If sponsorship is a form of below-the-line advertising, a substantial budget (in a proportion of 3:1?) may be necessary to obtain the greatest possible mileage. There are clearly sponsorships and sponsorships, and in this chapter many examples have been quoted to show the extent of application.

CHAPTER 8

Exhibitions

THE public or trade exhibition, and the international trade fair and Joint Venture, comprise advertising media in which space is rented and filled with an exhibit which has to be designed, constructed, stocked and staffed. It can be a very important part of the marketing mix, given special attention by the sales manager. Some exhibitors even go so far as to conduct a direct selling operation. The costs so far involved belong to the advertising budget.

But, as with all advertising, and as with most aspects of marketing, there is a PR element. The face-to-face confrontation with visitors is in itself a PR experience. And as shown in Chapter 4, exhibitions have their press relations responsibilities, neglected though these so often are, or handled badly when press rooms are supplied with uncaptioned photographs and unwanted bumper press kits.

In this chapter, exhibitions will be discussed in three ways: (1) use of public or trade exhibitions for PR purposes; (2) PR support for exhibitions and exhibitors; and (3) special PR exhibitions.

Use of Large Exhibitions for PR Purposes

Trade associations, professional bodies, special interest societies, government departments (e.g. Department of Industry and Trade, Export Credits Guarantee Department, Customs and Excise) and other organizations may use exhibitions as a means of telling their story, offering their services and creating understanding and goodwill. Similarly, foreign governments and industrial development agencies may use the medium for PR purposes.

PR Support for Exhibitions and Exhibitors

It is the task of the exhibition press officer to make the show known to potential visitors and to win news coverage during its run. Unless exhibitors co-operate, his is an impossible task; yet exhibitors generally either overlook or abuse the available services. This is foolish. Often, the press officer is operating from one event to the next and can achieve advance publicity on an international scale if supplied with really useful information by those participating. The moment the marketer decides to book stand space he should also inform his PRO or PR consultant.

The first move may be to seek the advice of the exhibition press officer, and this should be done at least six months before the show opens. A programme of PR support needs to be planned to cover feature articles, news releases, pictures, trade and press invitations to the stand, tie-ups with government information and radio services, press room material, press day arrangements, and press receptions plus the possibility of the stand being visited by the official opener and VIPs.

The usual bad practice is to ignore PR support until it is too late, and then provide something more or less useless for the press room as if it is a minor matter. Worse still, the advertising agency may be asked to produce an elaborate press kit which neither exhibition press officer nor visiting journalists want. The essential material for the press room consists of two things: a good newsy story on one piece of paper and a very good captioned photograph. Both are extremely rare in exhibition press rooms, and a first-class opportunity to enhance the value of the stand with additional publicity is so often thrown away. Exhibition press officers are usually only too pleased to explain what will be most beneficial to the exhibitor.

Special PR Exhibitions

The real purpose of this chapter is to discuss the use of exhibition techniques for PR purposes and we shall look at (1) mobile shows; (2) portable shows; (3) in-store shows; and (4) exhibition centres and permanent exhibitions.

Mobile Shows

Mobility implies some means of conveying the exhibit by road, rail, sea or air to audiences in many places at home or abroad. It also means something that is especially applicable to PR: the audience (or publics) can be of various kinds and in small numbers. The mountain goes to Mahomet instead of the exhibition being a great focal point to which thousands of strangers throng. While strangers may still be attracted, special audiences, locations and times can be selected for the mobile show. Audiences can also be sought at places at home or abroad where exhibitions are not normally held or where the firm would find it uneconomic to take part in a general event.

The *motorized* vehicle may be a caravan, trailer, specially constructed vehicle or a converted double-decker bus which can park in market squares, car parks, school grounds, hotel yards, or at agricultural shows, sports meetings and other outdoor events. It can also travel abroad, thanks to roll-on-roll-off ferries and hovercraft, which means that firms can penetrate areas and countries more directly and intensely than they can with, say, press relations tactics, linguists being preferable to translated press stories. The press can also be invited to the travelling exhibit. With films, video tapes, slides, models, products, literature and demonstrations and lecturers, the story can be told, questions answered, doubts and criticisms handled. This is not a selling operation, but enquiries can be passed to local agents, and agents can be appointed.

The converted bus lends itself admirably to this activity, and has been used by tourist organizations. With double-decker buses, trailers and custom-built vehicles, one floor can be used for the exhibition, and the other as an office, reception room or cinema. Kitchen furniture, double glazing, central heating, television receivers, garden and floral equipment, and banking services have been successfully toured in this way. The decision has to be made whether to hire a vehicle for a touring season, or to buy one for regular use. There is also the question of finding and training staff who are willing to work away from home for long periods of time.

The *train* is to some extent a less flexible vehicle, yet if placed in a station bay and publicized it can be a good way of bringing visitors to an exhibition that needs perhaps two or three coaches to do it justice.

EXHIBITIONS 155

A snag is that it is seldom visible to the man in the street, and depends largely on an invited public or on the expense of advertising. It has been used by manufacturers of laminates and of course by the railways themselves.

The *ship* is even less flexible since its venues are restricted to those ports able to berth it. There have been successes and failures with this medium, chosen mainly where promoters have sought many visitors or a consortium of participants. Successful ship exhibitions have been those which have concentrated on a theme or a particular promoter. For instance, the ship itself was the show when the first Thoresen car ferry was toured round Britain and visited by organized parties of travel agents.

Probably one of the best-ever examples of this kind of mobile exhibition is the Japan Floating Fair, organized by the Japan Industry Floating Fair Association of Tokyo whose first ship visited Europe in 1964 and whose new, larger 13,900 tons *Sakura Maru* brought another Japanese trade show to ten ports in ten European countries in 1972.

When it came to Europe in October 1972, the Floating Fair's exhibits represented every kind of exportable product and while a primary objective was to find European buyers (and also importers to Japan) this custom depended on achievement of a second primary objective, goodwill. As the president said in his message published in the exhibition catalogue: "We hope this Floating Fair will serve for the promotion of friendship and goodwill which will lead to the progress of co-prosperity common to European countries and Japan in the future."

The total of 148,685 visitors to the Japanese ship in October 1972 was made up as follows: Amsterdam, 19,170; Copenhagen, 17,522; Helsinki, 13,940; Stockholm, 10,870; Gdynia, 12,427; Oslo, 11,417; Hamburg, 15,887; Antwerp, 14,765; London, 13,343; Le Havre, 19,344.

These figures may see rather odd. Why did more Finns than Britons visit the ship? The answer lies in the location of the ship: Tilbury is not the most convenient place to visit, but apparently the organizers rejected advice to moor the ship at a more accessible berth further up-river.

Portable Shows

These are extremely flexible and can be adapted to a variety of PR exercises. They can be complete entities or used to augment other activities, as we shall see. Compact panels and frames can be made or bought which are detachable so that they can be packed into the boot of a car or at most into a small van or shooting brake. Ideally, the displays should be given independent lighting. The panels can be made up with captioned pictures and messages in clear large type. Such displays are particularly suitable for goods or services that can be demonstrated with either actual examples or pictorially. To take two extreme examples, business forms can themselves be displayed on panels, while impressive civil engineering works can be demonstrated with photographs, plans and maps. The display panels can also act as background to bulky objects which are nevertheless transportable. With fairly compact objects, three-dimensional displays are possible by fitting transparent plastic containers to the panels, or by standing exhibits on shelves obtruding from the panels. The ingenious designer can conduct all manner of ways of presenting samples or models for showing in confined spaces, and for easy transportation.

The main thing is that the exhibition can be created in one place, dismantled, packed, transported and re-assembled at different venues whenever wanted, all with the minimum amount of trouble. It can be kept up-to-date, and replicas can be produced for additional uses.

The portable exhibition can be mounted at press receptions, and press visits; in public halls, public libraries, schools and hotels; and at mini-exhibitions associated with annual conferences. It can be a back-up for dealer and customer seminars, film shows and product launches, or toured from one branch, depot, or factory to another. Some railway stations have concourses specially designed to contain small exhibits. So do some of the larger airport lounges. It may be a model of a building under construction, a plan of a proposed new motorway scheme, an exploded or open-sided model of an aircraft or ship, or a collection of books, pottery or tableware. Moreover, it can be one of the simplest and most convincing ways of proving, explaining or demonstrating something which is otherwise difficult to communicate.

An example of the latter, which is very attractively presented, is the Rentokil mini-exhibition of timber decay which may be seen from time to time in the windows of building societies, most appropriate high-street venues for such displays. This kind of mutual display leads us to the placing of portable exhibits inside shops.

In-store Exhibitions
These have become very popular when they can be linked with stores that supply the goods, and department stores are often the venues for displays of foreign produce linked with air lines and tourism. British weeks, French fortnights and so on are to be seen in many parts of the world, and shoppers and passersby are attracted by in-store presentations of German wines, Danish pottery and furniture, Dutch cheeses, Italian glass and Irish holidays. These shows are usually run by government trade promotion departments, Chambers of Commerce and trade associations, and are therefore co-operative efforts supported by individual firms.

Exhibition Centres
These centres exist, like the Japan Trade Centre, United States Trade Centre, Danish Bacon and Cheese Boards, Dutch Dairy Bureau, Ceylon Tea Centre, the Swiss Centre, while numerous national tourist offices give space to trade shows. Throughout the world most countries maintain premises where imports from the home country can be displayed, special exhibitions can be mounted, film shows and lectures given. Some of these centres can have multi-purposes as when the Indian Engineering Export Promotion Council has mounted a press reception at the Indian Tea Centre.

The exhibition centre can be used for either permanent exhibitions or for short-term events, but while the official centres mentioned above are a mixture of sales promotion and PR the following examples are principally PR exercises.

Such was public ignorance in the fifties and sixties about the nature and incidence of timber decay, and the hazards of infestation by rodents and insects, that British Ratin Company Ltd, and Woodworm and Dry Rot Control Ltd (eventually being re-named Rentokil Laboratories Ltd, a PR feat in itself) set up a network of joint Pest Control and Woodworm and Dry Rot Control centres in the chief cities of the UK, with a major centre, first in Bedford Square and later in Dover Street, W1. To these centres the public were invited to bring their infestation problems, even to the extent of harassed housewives posting their beetles in tin boxes to the nearest centre, often being reassured that the seemingly dreaded common furniture beetle was but a mere carpet beetle. The object of the centres was educational for how could products and services be sold if the public, industry, government departments and local authorities did not understand their need? PR was seen as an integral part of marketing.

These advice centres became the venues for customer receptions with talks by experts who showed the company's documentary films and handed out reprints of feature articles published in the technical press, thus combining a range of PR techniques. For visitors to the head office at Felcourt, near East Grinstead, there is also a permanent exhibition of the company's services and products which include insulation and hygiene as well as timber preservation, and insect, rodent, bird and weed control.

A number of organizations maintain display and enquiry centres at focal points where they can be easily visited, and even though they may be largely sales-orientated they do have a considerable PR content which should not be overlooked. They permit the means of "meeting the company", understanding its diversity of associated interests, and so adopting a correct image.

In countries where national industries are also profitable tourist attractions, exhibitions and conducted tours are arranged, instances being Disneyland in the USA; the Guinness brewery in Dublin; the diamond works, Delft potteries, clog workshops and bulb growers in Holland; perfume factories in France; and wine cellars and festivals in France and Germany.

Some organizations build permanent exhibitions at their premises, typical examples being that of Smiths Industries at Cricklewood which tells the story of the company and its achievements in a surprising number of fields. At the Shell Centre, Waterloo, and at BP's City headquarters, technical exhibitions may be seen and there are first-class cinemas. For visitors to Lloyds in Lime Street, London, there is the unusual Nelson Room which houses relics of Nelson and Lloyd's Patriotic Fund, with displays of original documents, silver plate and swords. The Port of London possesses a magnificent scale model of the London Docks which is a semi-permanent semi-mobile set piece that sometimes emerges from its permanent home to appear on exhibition stands.

Two of the most original and hard-working permanent exhibitions which, apart from their subject matter, are worth visiting solely to study the application of so many audio and visual aid techniques, are the Independent Broadcasting Authority Television Gallery in Knightsbridge, London, and the Evoluon exhibition which N. V. Philips' Gloeilampenfabrieken created at Eindhoven, Holland, in 1966 to mark the 75th anniversary of the founding of the company. Both exhibitions have a fair claim to that overworked word "unique".

The IBA Television Gallery cleverly makes use of an awkward floor area with many pillars, and has been so constructed that the visitor finds himself continually changing direction to be surprised by yet another outstanding presentation. There is an historical section explaining the invention of television, and a reconstruction of the early BBC studios at Alexandra Palace, a beautifully sculptured and modelled set piece on the conception, creation and shooting of an ITV series, a fascinating twelve-screen presentation of *News at Ten*, and a special display sequence on colour television. A tour of the Gallery takes about ninety minutes, and each weekday two parties are guided round in the morning and two more in the afternoon, the maximum number per party being thirty and the minimum age sixteen. Advance bookings for parties can be arranged by telephone or letter by application to the IBA Television Gallery, 70 Brompton Road, London SW3 1EV (opposite Knightsbridge Underground Station and Harrods), telephone: 01-584 7011.

Two things strike the visitor when approaching the Evoluon in Eindhoven. The large building resembles a flying saucer, while the flag on the mast is not Philips' but one bearing the special badge of the Evoluon itself. The visitor will also note the large number of motor coaches in the car park. Inside, the exhibition is distributed over three ring-shaped floors and two balconies, there is a cinema and restaurant, and a hydraulic forty-passenger lift in a glass shaft. The whole scene is one of colour, light, movement and wonderment. The aim is to give the visitor an impression of the possibilities which modern science is creating today and of what the future is likely to bring. All this is made utterly fascinating by the scores of opportunities to participate in operating the equipment so that to see and do everything would occupy fifteen hours. The emphasis is on young visitors, and the coaches in the car park have brought parties of "young scientists" from schools all over Holland and from even further afield. In a year, 500,000 people attend, and on one day there were 6700 visitors between 10 am and 5 am, all paying the admission fee of 2.50 guilders.

Springing directly from the Evoluon concept is the international Young Scientists and Inventors Contest. There are national heats, and a final which in 1973 took place at the Science Museum, London. In addition, there is a young scientists laboratory, and weekend courses are held on energy problems, computers and other electrical and electronic topics. Philips' Evoluon is therefore a PR exhibition of constructive educational value, very discreetly presented so that it is hard to find any exploitation of the company name or its products. But Eindhoven is rather like other industrial towns where one company predominates, and it is hardly likely that anyone would fail to be appreciative of Philips' gesture in making such a splendid exhibition possible. Well-travelled visitors have remarked that there is nothing like it anywhere else in the world.

In contrast, yet another type of useful PR exhibit is the scale model of a proposed civil engineering or building project, or of one actually under construction. The model can be used to demonstrate what is intended—it could be controversial!—or to help raise funds for its construction (or cleaning or restoration in the case of an historic building)—or, like the inspection platform, to explain what is going on on a building site, and so divert curious onlookers from causing obstruction or risking danger.

BP have a scale model of an oil rig which cost many thousands of pounds to make and it has been used in the company's London offices to demonstrate an oil rig to the press, government members, and visitors and for staff training purposes.

And even with the use of nothing more than existing equipment, vehicles and uniformed or professionally dressed people, excellent exhibits can be mounted in tents or in the open air at agricultural shows and other outdoor events, or in public parks. The police, nursing services, various farm produce boards, Forces recruitment, government departments, garden furniture makers, rose growers and many enterprising voluntary and charity institutions regularly make good use of this easily devised medium, ready-made audiences being exploited at outdoor events, in public places or at holiday resorts.

Attendance at Private Exhibitions

Attendance at the events described in this chapter will depend on three things; knowledge of their existence, appeal and accessibility.

How are visitors to be invited? Will they be sent written or printed individual invitations? Or will there be party visits? Is it to coincide with a convention, invitations being inserted in delegates' documentation, addressed to them via the pigeon holes at the porter's desk at their hotel, or placed in their hotel rooms? If it is more than an *ad hoc* event, whether permanently sited or travelling, advertising may be employed.

However the guests are attracted, two factors are of paramount importance, these being that the event should be attended by enough people and of the right kind. For instance, a concrete formwork system could be successfully shown to small groups of men from different contractors, whereas a holiday exhibition depends on being broadly attractive. Where the interest is specialized it may be best to be selective, not just mail a list of architects some of whom may be irrelevant to the event. This precaution may be necessary when a touring exhibition is aimed at people invited by the firm's local managers. The PRO usually needs to vet local invitation lists taken from, say, directories or membership lists as local staff may not appreciate the meticulous care which should be part of the PRO's professional make-up. Invitations should not, except where the object is to invite local customers and known prospects, be left to the initiative of local people. Supervision is wise to avoid, for instance, attracting the wrong people from the right organizations.

But having been invited, will they attend? This will depend on at least five things, namely the explicitness of the invitation, the attractiveness of the programme, the date, time of day and the venue. The programme should show evidence of good planning, yet not be overdone so that it appears to be either over-socialized or too much of a publicity stunt. It should be of value to the visitor. It pays to plan a timetable of happenings such as reception, introduction, talk, demonstration, buffet, coffee, and this can be set out on the back of the ticket or in the letter of invitation. In other words, the event has to be marketed and guests can seldom be bribed to come along.

The mistake can be made, and too often is, of employing smart gimmicks and lavish entertainment as a bait. The chances are that guests will come—for the entertainment! This is where salesmen and PROs operate on different levels, as when the salesmen entertains clients and calls this public relations, or so-called PROs are engaged solely to socialize those with the power to grant contracts. This is only another form of salesmanship, and has nothing to do with PR. There is a world of difference between bribery and goodwill. Reverting to exhibitions, the event itself should be sufficiently interesting in itself to attract acceptances.

However, let us look more closely at the five factors for success.

1. *Explicitness of the Invitation*

The letter or card should make two things clear; (i) the sponsor's identity and (ii) the nature, content or range of the exhibition. There should be no pretence that the show is "official" or non-commercial, no attempt to hide behind a "front" such as an "advisory bureau", unless the firm's name is clearly stated. (It would be an offence to do so if the organizer was a member of the IPR.) What people will see should be well explained, both in respect of its comprehensiveness and its limitations. It should be neither undersold nor oversold, and teasers are inadvisable.

2. *Attractiveness of the Programme*

The presence of technical advisers and speakers, the showing of a film, the use of interesting demonstration techniques and other attractions should be fully exploited so that invitees are made aware of the benefits of attendance. Equally, the organizers should make certain that the best possible attractions are included, and that they are well presented. It should be a good copy of the film shown with a reliable projector: so often the film arrives too late for a trial run-through.

3. *The Date*

While it is not always easy to avoid clashing with other events, the date should be convenient to the guests rather than the host. It will pay to research dates very carefully, checking with authorities such as civic information services, published diaries of events, newspaper information bureaux, Chambers of Commerce, public libraries and so on to avoid undesirable dates.

4. *Time of Day*

The most suitable time of day may depend on the commitments of guests, how far they have to travel, and whether their homes are far from their offices. Those working in the metropolises are usually commuters who live between five and fifty miles from their offices, so they do not like evening engagements in town, but conversely suburban shopkeepers cannot leave their shops to attend an event in the centre of the city in the daytime. In provincial cities evening events may be practicable since travelling distances are shorter. Guests may go home and come back to the centre of town in the early evening. Receptions can often be duplicated in the provinces, with one at lunchtime and another in the evening. Local habits vary and careful consideration of custom will help to maximize acceptances. Again, the chosen city may be a focal point for a whole area, making an evening meeting preferable to one in the daytime. If uncertain, the advice of the hotelier or the opinions of a small sample of clients may be invited. It is not the prerogative of the host to fix times to suit himself.

5. *Choice of Venue*

Most cities have venues which are good or bad for special reasons such as: public room facilities; catering standards; car-parking; privacy; audio-visual and other equipment; co-operative management; ease of entry for equipment; accessibility by all forms of transport. Few places combine all these virtues, but it is a useful check-list. Choice may result from a combination of the most important items as they affect the event and the location. That is, unless a specific advantage must be secured, and that might well be car-parking in the middle of the day!

CHAPTER 9

External House Journals

THE majority of privately published "house" magazines are issued for the benefit of employees, members or supporters, and may be termed *internal house journals*. Some may also have outside distribution to specially interested people, including relevant sections of the press. But this chapter concerns wholly external private magazines that can be marketing aids, and serve as one of the best links between PR and marketing. Staff magazines and newspapers are by no means the only kinds of house journals, although that false impression is often given in articles and on courses about the subject.

The *external company magazine* is much less common than the staff journal, and there are the lavish prestige journals for outside consumption which tend to ruin the whole idea of a hard working marketing-orientated "external". It is useful, then, to analyse the precise publics to which externals can be profitably directed. Their value as marketing aids should then be more readily understood. This breakdown may also suggest other possible readerships which the marketer and PRO can reach through this flexible, versatile and often astonishingly economic medium. Some of these journals may, of course, be suitable for a combination of outside readerships, *The Forge* (Brockhouse Organization) being a good example of this as we shall see.

Analysis of Readerships of External House Journals

According to the BAIE House Journals 73 survey compiled in the UK for the British Association of Industrial Editors by England, Gross & Associates Ltd, sponsored by John Player & Sons, Lyon Group Ltd and RHM, 21 per cent of the sample had dual internal/external circulation, 59 per cent had mainly internal and 18 per cent primarily external circulation. The report is quite candid in stating "there was some confusion on this question". Presumably this means that even within the professional body people do not really understand the significance of the external, most industrial editors being familiar only with the staff journal. As an aside on this, it is true that in some companies the internal house journal is edited by an editor attached to "personnel" or "PR" while the external may be produced by the "marketing" or "advertising" staff, even by the advertising department. This is a mistake and both editorships should be PR responsibilities.

The BAIE report is also vague about the type of external circulation, since nearly a quarter of this part of the sample offered no information. However, the principal reader groups were as follows and in this order of priority: people within trade/business; customers; prospective/potential customers; shareholders; agents/overseas agents; door to door/ local newsagents/bookstalls; educational sales/higher education/schools.

As the author has made a special study of external house journals let us therefore go into this subject in greater depth than was found possible by those conducting research for the BAIE survey published in March 1973, excellent though that is in its presentation of statistical information about the editing, production and distribution of member journals. Five major groups are studied, with references to actual journals addressed to them.

1. *Consumers, Customers, Clients and Patrons*

Under this broad umbrella can be gathered all those readers who finally buy the product or service, and this is the area of customer relations which no efficient marketer dare ignore. (Incidentally, for the purpose of this chapter, "readership" and "circulation" are taken to be synonymous, although the terms are used differently for advertising purposes, readership meaning the total number of readers per copy as distinct from the audited net sale of copies.) Typical examples of company magazines addressed to this public or readership are:

(i) Hotel magazines, usually placed in hotel bedrooms as a service to guests, or sent to conference organizers and other users of hotel services.

British Railway Hotels publish a very good one. The Sheraton Heathrow Hotel mails a newspaper to potential clients.

(ii) Retail store magazines, sometimes sold to customers. Foyles the booksellers have published a journal for some forty years, while symbol grocers and supermarkets issue customer magazines.

(iii) In-flight magazines, issued to airline passengers but also posted to airline users at their home addresses, to mention only those published by British Airways, Pan-Am, Sabena and Swissair, all varying tremendously in their format and content. Some aim to provide passengers with enjoyable reading matter, others to promote tourism, and some to give businessmen useful information.

(iv) Client magazines produced by consultants, such as advertising agents, and sent to their actual or potential clients. Usually, the content of these journals and newsletters is about political, economic and marketing matters, interspersed with discreet references to the sponsor's facilities, services and successes.

(v) Investor magazines for members of building societies, unit trusts and clients of banks, insurance companies and other financial institutions. *Sign* (now bound into *Europa Magazine*) is distributed to American Express credit card holders, while *Standard Bank Review* gives excellent economic reports on countries where it has branches.

(vi) End-user magazines aimed at helping customers to enjoy the product or service, e.g. old-established ones like *Kodak Magazine* and *Gibbons Stamp Monthly*. This is an area where the motor industry excels with journals such as *Quest* (Duckhams Oils), and *Pronto* which Fiat (England) Ltd brought out in the Autumn of 1972. Throughout the world, *The Wheel Extended*, is distributed by Toyota Motor Sales Company Ltd, Tokyo. *Haylin News* was produced by Winkler Marketing Communications in the Summer of 1972 as part of the campaign to launch garment rentals from James Hayes & Sons Ltd (part of the J. Lyons Group), the garments being manufactured from Dacron supplied by the Italian firm of Klopman.

United Glass communicates with users of its containers and closures with *Packaging Forum* which is issued every eight to twelve weeks, either as a magazine or as a special report on a topical subject (e.g. fruit juices). The 3000 copies cost between £1100 and £1200 according to the number of colour pictures. A questionnaire card was inserted in one issue, producing a 12 per cent response and indicating to the editor (a) the number of readers per copy (which proved to average four) and (b) the popularity of certain types of content.

To the question, "which kind of articles do you find most useful", the replies were:

Specific packaging products	30
New developments	65
Own market and competition	44
Market research	32
All or most	51
No comment	94

(vii) Entertainment magazines issued by entertainment promoters which describe forthcoming events and the artistes taking part, such as those sold in cinemas by the owners of circuits, fan magazines for pop stars, and *Cassette News* issued by Phonogram Ltd (Philips).

(viii) Children's magazines such as those issued by toothpaste manufacturers and distributed via dentist's waiting rooms, schools and junior libraries.

(ix) Cookery magazines issued by either makers of kitchen aids or foodstuffs, which can be sent to domestic science teachers or distributed through gas and electricity showrooms.

(x) Gardening magazines sent to customers by rose growers and other horticultural suppliers including some of the catalogues which are full of practical advice.

(xi) Pet owners magazines issued by pet foods manufacturers.

(xii) Do-it-yourself magazines published by paint, wallpaper, laminate, tool and other home decorating and handyman suppliers.

The list could be even longer. An advantage of the medium is that there is unlikely to be much or any competition, and so it is well worth exploiting if a monopoly situation can be enjoyed. But if the same readers are known to receive several such journals from rival firms the impact is bound to pall. Another drawback may be that the potential readership is so great that the print order would be prohibitively costly, but ways of controlling this may be to charge a cover price or to supply request copies only. But this is a field so little exploited that it is wide open to most marketers who can make practical use of the technique.

2. *Dealers, Franchisers, Agents*

Once again we have an umbrella heading which comprises "the trade", that is all those who distribute, represent or sell our goods or services. "The Trade" consists of a huge number of different classes of people such as wholesalers, bottlers, franchise holders, retailers, agents and brokers, the middlemen and retailers, those who invest in franchises, and professional consultants. The opportunity of publishing an external dealer-type house magazine is a very real one for those who need to improve their relations with the trade. Rather than detail the possible readerships any further it will be more helpful to consider the purposes of this kind of external.

(i) To link together isolated distributors. Some organizations rely on the loyalty and enthusiasm of a great many people who seldom meet one another and have very little direct contact with the supplier's head office. They may not be sole agents and their loyalties may therefore be divided. The regular external magazine can provide the essential link, and America's oldest company magazine *Protection* is a splendid example. It is claimed to be America's oldest house journal (although Dickens refers to *The Lowell Offering*, launched in 1842 by the Lowell Cotton Mills). *Protection* was first published in 1865, a year after the formation of the Travelers Insurance Companies of Hartford, Connecticut. Every independent agent and broker receives a copy, and 30,000 copies are mailed monthly. Editor Glenn W. Caywood says "the very best means of communicating with every Travelers representative on a regular basis has proved to be *Protection*". Of special marketing value is the offer of reprints of articles printed in the magazine, readers ordering reprints for distribution to their clients. Thus the magazine acts as a vehicle for further and wider dissemination of information of interest to the market. This is an idea marketers may well copy, and it shows how excellently a really practical PR technique can serve as a marketing aid. In a slighty different way, Ingersoll-Rand have sold reproduction rights of their house journal articles to the international trade and technical press.

Another type of distributor to whom a journal can mean a valuable link is the franchiser, whether he is running a drain or carpet cleaning service, a cooked food shop or a bottling plant and distribution centre.

Heineken of Amsterdam despatch their *Bulletin* to 5000 importers in overseas markets and its trade relations success is measured by the lively reader response that results, including voluntary notifications of change of address! *Western Auto Dealer*, from Kansas City, seeks to stimulate trade through the company's franchised retail hardware stores. But for sheer brash sales promotion, Dr. Pepper's *Clock Dial* is perhaps the epitome of the American-style franchiser magazine. Published since 1938, *Clock Dial's* marketing objective is "to provide franchised bottlers and members of their organizations with information about Dr. Pepper, about Dr. Pepper Company and its programs, and to disseminate information among 512 franchised bottlers about the programs, events and successes of these various operations. News of and about these activities helps recognize people for good accomplishments and motivate others to strive to achieve more." A survey of readership (not unlike the United Glass questionnaire already described) showed three readers a copy. Every two months 16,000 copies are mailed in bulk lots to the 512 bottlers.

Similarly, in yet another field, the Norwegian quarterly *News From Tandberg* is mailed in an English language version to Tandberg radio and TV dealers in the English-speaking world, while Scandinavian dealers receive the Norwegian version. Its aim is to keep the Tandberg dealers and representatives well informed about what is happening at the factory, what is new, why products are being launched, the philosophy behind a new product and its selling points.

(ii) To educate stockists. Some products are simply handed across the counter on demand, or taken from the supermarket rack, but others require the knowledge, advice and demonstration skill of the shop assistant. This applies to products as different as cosmetics, paints, toys, sewing machines, lawnmowers, Hi-fi equipment and cameras. There is, consequently, a multitude of opportunities for educating main dealers and appointed agents so that they are better able to present products to customers. In the USA, *Kodak Dealer News* is a colourful, lively journal which sets out not only to discuss products but also ways of promoting products with examples of in-store schemes. This is one of the oldest dealer magazines, first being issued in 1915 as *Kodak Salesman*, and is yet another example of the supremacy of American use of the external company magazine. Forty thousand copies are mailed every two months to dealers, retail staff, Kodak marketing personnel and overseas Kodak companies.

Obviously, some stockists may carry so many lines that the arrival of too many company magazines would be unwelcome and wasteful. Before launching one the sponsor would be wise to research the competition, if any. However, if the product is a principal line, there are strong reasons for expecting dealer loyalty or, conversely, if the lines of communication are weak (as happens when there is wholesale distribution) a dealer magazine may be a splendid marketing aid.

When, as suggested above, there is a distant relationship between producer and distributor—because of wholesaling, agencies, foreign manufacture, long journey cycles or other reasons—the company magazine can be one of the most impressive ways of fostering goodwill, especially if participation is invited through window display contests, publication of dealer news and announcements of bonus prizes to dealers in consumer contests. It does not have to be an elaborate publication. Obviously, colour is important in the cases of the United Glass and the Kodak dealer magazines, but some are inexpensive black-and-white litho productions, and others are newsletters or broadsheets rather than bound journals.

3. *Opinion Leaders*

The house journal may well carry a convincing message to politicians, teachers, clergy, broadcasters, journalists and many other "opinion leaders". These influential "experts" may form a fringe or secondary readership for some staff journals and user/consumer externals. But it could be a marketing objective to educate those whose authoritative (or opinionated!) statements, or power behind the scenes, may be detrimental to an organization because they are poorly informed. Ignorance and prejudice bias the attitudes of anyone who lacks knowledge and understanding. It is easy to be wrong, and in the absence of correction to perpetuate false ideas. The "external" may be the best way to create a true image in the minds of people whose attitudes matter.

But anything resembling the "hidden persuader" must be resisted. If there is a fault with some externals, it is that they are seen to be a promotional exercise, sales literature dressed up in journalistic style rather like a reader advertisement. This publicity-seeking emphasis springs from their being edited by publicity managers rather than industrial editors. These non-PR-minded editors have yet to make the mental somersault necessary to construe the difference between copywriting and journalism, between advocating purchase and reporting facts. Contents, treatment, style, format all matter, and it is no use putting a fancy masthead on a sales catalogue and calling it a magazine. The contents of these advertising journals are therefore suspect to the opinion leader who feels that this sort of journal is no more than disguised direct mail advertising. It is hard to comprehend why the marketer ruins his external in this way, except to take it as yet another example of the world of difference between advertising and PR and in particular the unfortunate antipathy between marketing and PR. If an external is to be accepted by the opinion leader it must seek to tell, not sell.

Lots of the banking magazines do, of course, provide valuable information for certain opinion leaders as well as businessmen, while food technology journals can be enlightening to dieticians, home economists, doctors and other specialists.

A typical objective here may be to educate readers about the range of interests of an organization which was once famous for a certain product. Diversification creates many problems calling for a communication solution, the external magazine being an admirable one.

4. *Suppliers and Sub-contractors*

It may be important to communicate with suppliers of services, raw materials or components, or to present a progress report to subcontractors, suppliers, financial institutions and government agencies, especially in the course of a long-term project or contract. Civil engineering, ship building and aircraft projects lend themselves to use of the external. On a major construction job, a weekly, even a daily, news sheet has often proved an excellent way of keeping everyone informed and so helping all concerned to make their contributions more efficiently. Roberts Construction Group of Companies of Johannesburg have produced individual journals such as *Copper Chronicle*, *Reactor Review* and *Platinum Post* for separate construction jobs.

5. *Buyers, Specifiers, Formulators, Technicians, Users*

Purchasing officers, architects, quantity surveyors, engineers, designers, scientists and others concerned with choosing and recommending items need to be constantly informed of the availability, modification and introduction of hundreds of products. Trade magazines, data sheets, catalogues and directories all help but sometimes basic details are inadequate, and a magazine can carry articles, pictures and drawings that will demonstrate actual uses and prove the value of the product in practice.

Magazines in this category include the beautifully produced *ICI Plastics Today* which is published in English, French and German editions and is aimed at "all users and potential users of plastics materials and articles made from them". The English edition also carries summaries in Spanish, Portuguese, Russian and Italian. About 70 per cent of the 22,000 copies go overseas, and it was originally published in 1959 as an export marketing aid.

The Swiss *Brown-Boveri Review* is a highly technical austere-looking journal printed in English, German and French editions, and part of the circulation is free and part by retail or subscription sales. The contents include technical papers on hydro-electric equipment and similar topics

Inco-Nickel is an engineering review featuring the uses of nickel containing materials and is published in various language versions throughout the world where International Nickel have offices. Its marketing objective is to help maintain the market and the company's share of it. The company also publishes the more elaborate *International Nickel Magazine*, produced basically in New York with several overseas editorial offices of which London is the principal one for the printing of English and foreign language texts. This is a full-colour offset-litho journal with a circulation in excess of 80,000 copies quarterly. It represents an immense international PR/marketing concept.

The British magazine *GEC Journal of Science and Technology*, which began in 1930 as the *GEC Journal* and has since seen a variety of content and title changes following acquisitions and mergers, is a very substantial technical journal aimed at supporting the company's technical prestige on a world scale without being overtly sales orientated

Every quarter, 21,000 copies are mailed to senior scientists, technologists and University libraries in 140 countries, a three-language synopsis of articles being tipped into certain overseas copies. Typical contents are features on electron microscopes and microprobe: a new analytical instrument, and thyristor-converter drives for dc hoists. The text is of post-graduate standard, with plenty of pictures and charts, a second colour being used judiciously.

An interesting division of circulation occurs with another British quarterly, *The Forge*, from the Brockhouse Organization which has thirty-one operating companies in the UK, Europe, Canada, South Africa and the USA. Of its 7500 copies 5000 are sent to customers and contacts, 500 to the trade and technical press, and the balance to members of the staff and also to visitors to their stands at exhibitions. The emphasis is on *external* distribution. The press copies contain a memo size news release summarizing the contents and stating "Use may be made of any of the material in this issue and photographs are available from the Brockhouse Press and Public Relations Office."

A policy decision has to be made about the freedom with which other editors may use house journal material, and it is worth noting here how the policy varies from one journal to another, presumably for well-deliberated reasons. Ingersoll-Rand syndicated their articles in typical publishing house fashion, thereby earning an income from them. Brockhouse invite free reproduction and are obviously anxious to get the widest possible use of their material. But *ICI Plastics Today* states: "Application for permission to reproduce in any form any matter contained herein should be made to the Editor" and seeks to control usage of material, but the implication is that permission is unlikely to be refused. The word "application" could be taken to mean that requests for permission are invited! Toyota are even more cautious and print the following: "*Editorial Statement.* Articles in *The Wheel Extended* are restricted to translations from Japanese arranged for by the Editors."

Ideally, with all PR material, there should be complete freedom of publication, otherwise why send anything to the press? However, if it is imperative to know how, when and where material will be produced the "permission" restriction may be stated in each issue. Even then there is no legal restriction on small extracts being quoted with acknowledgement as has been done in this paragraph. The general rule in PR is that anything submitted to an editor—news releases, articles, illustrations, speeches, reports, house journals and so on—are submitted free of copyright so that he may use the material if he wishes. This rule is understood and applied by the Brockhouse Press and Public Relations Office. But to send an editor interesting material and then tell him he cannot use it without first seeking permission or paying a reproduction fee is guaranteed to raise his hackles and mutter about these "bloody stupid PR people".

The Dutch magazine *Tug* was first introduced in 1967 as part of the PR campaign recommended by the Rotterdam PR consultants, Bureau Hartogh, which has more recently been converted into the international consultancy, Hartogh Relations Publiques (HARP). Its aim was to show clients of ocean-going tug services just what these services meant in terms of vessels, crews and operations. This helped to change the average clients' image of a tug service, justify its costs, and broaden the marketing base. Subsequently, the sponsors—L. Smit & Co's International Sleepdienst—became involved in much more than towage and salvage, especially with the servicing of North Sea oil rigs, and the co-ordinating company is now known as Smit Internationale. The magazine *Tug*, and other PR activities since 1967, have contributed to the marketing strategy which has resulted in a modernized and enlarged international organization. This was the company concerned in the *Pacific Glory* salvage operation. A feature of this Dutch magazine is that all its 4000 copies are printed in English, an interesting commentary on British and American firms which go to a lot of trouble to produce foreign language versions, although GEC go no further than to offer very brief foreign language digests in French, German and Spanish which occupy only three pages.

Another skilful use of the external is the quarterly *Vigilance* published by the Manchester firm of National and Vulcan Engineering Insurance Group. First published fifty years ago as *Vulcan*, the name was changed with the merger of the National and Vulcan companies. Most of the 30,000 copies go to insurance brokers, consulting engineers, architects and plant operators throughout the world, and engineering construction and machinery case studies are used in a PR/marketing job which associates NV insurance policies with the projects described.

From these examples the use and value of the external company magazine as a marketing aid can be judged. Some are monthlies, quite a few are quarterlies. Of these described only *ICI Plastics Today* and *International Nickel Magazine* can be described as "lavish", but all are professionally produced and offer worthwhile reading. They are private magazines, not sales literature. This is a medium worthy of development provided the editing is treated as a serious publishing venture rather than an extension of advertisement copywriting. It is one of the most rewarding of PR techniques if a proper policy is laid down for intended readership, content, format, distribution and budget.

Two points are of special interest in the examples given above: (i) the external is not a new idea—neglected though it tends to be—and some of the journals described have existed for anything up to a hundred years; (ii) the external is well used by companies long experienced in overseas trading.

Future Trends and Prospects

For many years, famous firms anxious to communicate with customers, prospects, users, agents, investors and others scattered throughout the country, a continent or all over the world have used this medium. Today, two special opportunities encourage the use of the external, these being the Common Market and the Third World. Let us discuss each in turn.

Externals and the Common Market

We have already shown in Chapter 4 that there is a dearth of trade and technical journals, despite the enterprise of IPC. The simple reason is that it is not a business proposition to publish a highly specialized journal in a small country with its own language. Revenue can come from either advertising or cover price, but when there is little advertising and the cover price has to be prohibitively high—a French professional journal is usually four times the price of its British counterpart and France is a large country—such journals are not viable. So, while British publishers like IPC have been venturing into Europe, there is likely to be very inadequate press coverage for the majority of British, American and other firms interested in educating the European market about their organizations, policies, products, services and people. The answer, as firms like ICI and others mentioned in this chapter have long ago discovered, is to publish a private external magazine with its own controlled circulation. It is even possible to make the external financially inexpensive or even profitable by carrying advertising from non-competing firms interested in the same market.

But is it necessary to print in all the languages of the EEC? Can we get away with English alone, or no more than French and German as well? No answer is absolutely right: so much depends on whether a firm can sell equally well in all markets or only in some, and also on the linguistic standards of the readers. For while a highly technical magazine will reach a large proportion of English-speaking readers, a consumer magazine may not. There are questions of cost, courtesy and correctness, and the latter may be fundamental to successful and sympathetic communication. The ideal is therefore to print in the reader's own language, but a rough compromise is that an English language version may serve North Europe but native language versions are advisable in South Europe with the possible exception of Greece.

English is the commonly-used business language in Scandinavia, and the common second language in Holland, Belgium, Germany and increasingly in France, Italy, Spain and Switzerland. No doubt this is due to the spread of American multi-national companies, the entry of Britain into Europe, and because of Europe's increasing contact with countries like Japan, India and Nigeria which use English as their international trading language. Is it not significant that the Dutch magazine *Tug* is printed in English, and that the Brussels-based British-owned *Electronic Product News*, circulated throughout Europe, is printed only in English? It is perhaps no exaggeration to say that the rapid increase in car ferries since 1965, the greater exchange of visitors between Britain and Europe, and the thousands of school-children who exchange language-study visits, are all helping to break down language barriers so that more and more English is predominating as the international language. While it still pays to translate news releases, there is practical scope for the English language external house journal with a European circulation.

Externals and the Third World

In the developing countries of the world there is usually a very meagre press coupled with a considerable clamour among the better educated for technical reading matter. Visitors to China invariably comment on the avidity with which technical literature is devoured. Prospective buyers are literate and mostly English speaking. There is great scope for promotion of export markets, setting up of subsidiaries, or coming to royalty agreements in many African, Asiatic and Latin-American countries, especially if this will encourage the development of local talents and boost the national economy. British firms have been curiously lax about such developments, with the notable exception of firms like UAC and Guinness, but the British motor industry has made a gift of exports to the more enterprising Japanese. Such is the strength of Japanese motor-car PR that it is believed that the Japanese will make a bid for British Leyland unless Labour is returned with power to nationalize them! The African motor-car scene is becoming predominantly Japanese, and in twelve months the Nigerian market was swamped by Datsun, Mazda and Toyota who swiftly exploited the favourable situation created by the change-over from left-hand to right-hand driving in 1972 which British manufacturers refused to believe would actually happen.

It is in this intensely competitive international marketing environment where, almost unnoticed by British industry unless it reads the economic reports in the *Standard Bank Review*, African states like Nigeria are developing fast while Zambian copper will find its outlet to the sea and to China because only China would invest in the Tan-Zam Railway. Indian films, Japanese cars and Chinese railways, that is the story of black Africa today!

Here is surely scope for the combined PR/marketing operation of the educational technical journal, perhaps in editions specially addressed to each of the three continents, printed in English, mailed direct to prospects or supplied in bulk to local agents for local mailing. Such journals would be appreciated as supplementing the education of technicians and executives, and the contents could be partly about the sponsor's interests and partly about management and marketing topics which readers in these countries would relish. Not only are technical magazines scarce but so are text books (because of exchange control restrictions), and sponsors of externals could enhance their reputations by supplying part-work supplements on, say, business management, equipment maintenance, safety and protective clothing, hygiene and so on according to the nature of the sponsor's business.

CHAPTER 10

Seminars and Conferences

CONFRONTATION with clients or prospects, including distributors, is a PR technique much used by those with either a technical product that needs demonstration and thorough explanation with discussion, or a new proposition that requires quick, effective presentation. Seminars and conferences of various kinds make use of combinations of media such as documentary films, slides, videotape, exhibits, visual aids, printed literature and organizational techniques similar to those of a press reception.

The three essentials of a good PRO—ability to communicate, get on with people, and organize—come to the fore in the use of this method.

Unfortunately, it is a technique which has sometimes become hackneyed, abused by advertising agencies which have converted PR occasions into sales promotion junkets; while there are those who imagine quite wrongly that the cost of running a seminar or conference is prohibitive.

The chief merit of the exercise is the psychological effect of face-to-face confrontation, of taking the organization to the public, as with a VIP walkabout. The seemingly distant, monolithic corporation is seen to consist of interesting, knowledgeable, sympathetic human beings, while the clients are revealed as rather better than irritating ignorant boneheads. The curious wall of antipathy between companies and customers (whether distributors or consumers) can be demolished. In other words, PR is seen to be what it really is, human relations. The author saw this actually happen with an organization whose sales manager was convinced that local authorities were opposed to the company and would never buy from it. Yet a PR programme consisting very largely of "one-day schools" with films and technical speakers produced a situation where today it is unlikely that any local authorities (and other buyers such as hospitals) in the UK, and also in many parts of the world, are not customers of this growth company.

The idea, then, is to invite a selected party of guests to attend a meeting at a convenient venue on a suitable date and time, attracting them with a programme that has been set out in the invitation letter or card. Careful choice of guests, venue, date and programme is essential to the success of the event, and the remarks on this theme in the chapter on exhibitions may be reiterated here. The following are the five essentials when organizing such an event:

(i) *Guest List*

Haphazard preparation of the invitation list may result in either a disappointing response or a curious mixture of acceptances. This dual warning is made because it is all too simple to mail the wrong people and have an attendance of people delighted to drink your cocktails but unable to influence the purchase of your goods. There are also (although this applies only to British class-ridden society) certain people who do not socialize, e.g. builders and architects, and it is wise to invite them to separate events. Moreover, a list of professionals will consist of numerous specialists, many of whom are irrelevant to the occasion although their specialities may not be defined in the list. This could apply to doctors, architects and teachers while as we noted before there are all sorts of "engineers".

A central organization may be organizing a series of local seminars through the auspices of local staff whose responsibility it may be to obtain the audience. Where the list consists of known customers and prospects there will be little risk, but when the unfamiliar task of creating an original invitation list is thrust upon a field sales manager or branch manager, the disasters outlined above may occur. These remarks tend to repeat what has already been said when inviting people to attend an exhibition, but inviting people to a seminar can be more critical as there will be more intimate participation in general questioning and discussion and in socializing. An exhibition can be a more open affair with a more mixed attendance.

The best audience is therefore a hand-picked one, conscious of the privilege, and treated as special guests. Postal invitations can be followed up by personal approaches by the company's local senior staff or representatives. Or personal invitations can be made in the first place. An example of this is the way in which computer firms invite prospects to attend courses in computer techniques which, in the case of IBM, require a week's attendance at a residential course.

(ii) *Venue*

Either the guests come to the host, as when a company has its own training centre, showroom or attractive headquarters, or the host goes to the client by holding the event at a local hotel. In special circumstances, there may be an especially acceptable venue such as a building centre, conference hall, livery company hall or club. If the company's own premises are used, care should be taken over transportation and timings to avoid inconveniencing guests. Sunday travel may be bad, and it may be better for a course to start on a Friday, Saturday, Monday afternoon or Tuesday. When local venues are used they should have their own or adjacent car-parking facilities, a rarity sometimes if the hotel is in a city centre. There are cities where only one hotel meets this requirement, although others are seemingly more attractive and eligible, and it pays to visit the venue and check out every need. Proximity to a railway station may also be important.

A good PRO will make it his business to know which provincial or international hotels have the right combination of facilities for PR events, location, size of rooms, audiovisual facilities, catering, car-parking, and so on. There are certain cities in the UK where these factors are critical. This is equally true in venues as different as Dublin, New York, Hamburg, Rotterdam and Lagos. It is also dangerous to take for granted that just because a hotel in a certain group proved to be excellent this will be so of other hotels in the same group. If on-the-spot advice is difficult to obtain there are usually state information agencies (e.g. the very helpful Convention Bureau of Ireland which brings conventions to Ireland from the USA, Britain and Europe) which will be willing to assist.

The venue may not be of one's own choosing, and it may be possible to take advantage of the fact that prospective guests will be attending some other function such as a large exhibition or conference, and so are available to attend a private seminar held on the same premises or at a nearby hotel, while an "after hours" event may be held during the run of the larger function.

(iii) *Date*

The date should always suit the convenience of the guests, not the company VIPs who may be taking part. Once again, care is required to make sure that it is easy for people to attend, and that the date does not clash with important local events which may be sports meetings, festivals and shows which can usually be discovered from the civic PRO. Overseas, it may be necessary to avoid the frequent religious holidays in Catholic countries, "independence" and other celebrations in former colonies, and special holidays and celebrations like New Year's Day, Labor Day and so on which are peculiar to particular countries. Anyone trying to organize an international itinerary for an export programme will need to take a lot of advice, and this can be had from sources such as the Department of Trade and Industry, or information officers and commercial attachés at embassies and consulates.

(iv) *Time*

Some guests may prefer a daytime or lunchtime engagement, others like to attend during the evening. Much depends on local habits and how distant people's homes are from the venue. This, again has been dealt with in some detail in the chapter on exhibitions. But if an all-day event is being run, special consideration should be given to such details as provision of hospitality on arrival, and the amount of time that can be spared for lunch, a sit-down affair usually taking longer than a cold fork buffet.

(v) *Programme*

Some of the best seminars offer only sherry and biscuits by way of hospitality, but if held during the morning or at lunchtime, a buffet is necessary. It is foolish to woo an audience with the promise of champagne or exotic foods, although original catering (such as national or local specialities) can be thoughtful and pleasant. The hospitality should be just right for the occasion without dominating as the prime attraction. It should be a courtesy, not a bribe.

There should be a timed programme of precise activities so that guests know exactly what they are being invited to. A good programme should secure acceptances more than anything else. Speakers should be rehearsed, timed and controlled either by a reliable chairman or by the PRO acting as discreet "master of ceremonies" from the back of the room. There should be some measure of entertainment, whether it be a film, a celebrity, a competition, an exhibition or photographic display or something which captures the attention and interest of guests. And there should be plenty of opportunities for questions and discussion so that problems may be aired. Such an event can be a once-in-a-lifetime chance for company and customers to get together, and the resultant value can be like a ripple on a pond, going far beyond the original moment of contact.

Assuming that the titles of talks and films, and the names of the chairman and speakers would be stated, the following are outline plans for a one-day conference and an evening seminar:

One-day conference

Delegates assemble	9.30
Introduction by chairman	9.45
Talk by Mr —— on ——	10.00
Discussion	10.45
Coffee	11.00
Film, "——"	11.15
Talk by Mr —— on ——	11.45
Discussion	12.00
Cocktails	12.45
Buffet lunch	1.00
Re-assemble	2.15
Talk by Mr —— on ——	2.20
Discussion	2.45
Tea	3.00
Film, "——"	3.15
Talk by Mr —— on ——	3.45
Discussion	4.15
Chairman's summing up	4.30
Close of seminar	4.45

Evening seminar

Reception, cocktails	6.30
Introduction by host	7.00
Film or demonstration	7.10
Talk by Mr —— on ——	7.30
Discussion	8.00
Bar and buffet	8.30
Coffee	9.30

Some Uses of Seminars and Conferences

How to win the confidence of customers may be the PR problem with some products or services. If only the customers could see for themselves, or have personal contact with the promoters! This is as true of tourism as it is of farm implements or data processing. Generally, then, the PR foursome of apathy, hostility, ignorance and prejudice can be challenged through the medium and technique of the seminar or conference.

It has been used with renowned success by the marketers of kitchen furniture, pesticides, computers, educational aids, wines, electronic components, business print, forklift trucks, office equipment, banking and insurance, building materials and concrete formwork.

But if one is marketing a product with a limited number of outlets, as with a secondary product which is part of a primary product made by only a small number of manufacturers such as domestic appliances, motor cars, carpets, paper or television receivers, a gathering of rival buyers may fail because they will not speak up and so disclose their interests to their competitors. In these circumstances, individual client seminars may be worth setting up, a team being invited from each company.

We have tended to speak primarily of the reception-type seminar occupying only two or three hours, but half-day or whole-day "schools" or conferences can be mounted (as suggested in the programme layout on page 183) when the sponsor can put on an educational event which is beneficial to the guests. This is possible when the company has the resources of good speakers or demonstrators who are technicians, not salesmen, and whose authority gives credence to the day's proceedings. In other words, if the speaker is a designer, research chemist, engineer or someone else who can give an authentic "backroom boy" account, this can be a fascinating experience for the members of the audience.

For example, when Dennis & Robinson ran seminars in building centres and hotels to discuss kitchen units with speculative builders, the main talk was about meeting the recommendations of a government report on achieving maximum storage space in a flat or three-bedroom house.

For many years Rentokil have mounted conferences for hospital staff, property managers, medical officers of health, housing managers and others concerned in their daily work with pest control and timber decay problems. The programmes have included eminent scientists as speakers, supported by award-winning films, and technical exhibits. The only time a product is named is in response to questions from the floor. With commercialism kept to the minimum, important information—such as the cause of a fungal attack or the characteristics of a destructive or unhygienic insect or rodent—form the topics discussed by the speakers who also explain the results of laboratory experiments and the range of techiques and formulations that are available for cures and treatments. Quite large audiences of around a hundred people have been attracted to Rentokil "schools" held at strategic points throughout the country.

Those responsible for advising on or actually buying school equipment can be brought to similar conferences—usually in the late afternoon or "twilight hour"—to hear good speakers and see demonstrations over tea and cakes. Products such as sewing machines, cooking utensils and teaching aids are suitable for this kind of event.

The PR aspects of these events is stressed because they can be ruined if regarded as a form of "soft selling". Marketers sometimes mount selling operations in the guise of seminars, gilding the premises with banners and advertisement material, and using glib salesmen as speakers so that suspicion rather than confidence is alerted. The audience feels it is being "got at". The purpose of the PR seminar or conference is to inform and invite impartial opinion so that understanding is obtained. This understanding may require knowledge of the organization, who runs it and how it behaves. A lot of misconceptions may have to be removed. All this is much more subtle than selling. For example it may be necessary to explain the causes of a problem, and the research that has gone into providing an answer before it is possible to show that a given product offers a solution. This background work can then become the forerunner to eventual sales. But the temptation is ever so great for the marketer to plunge straight into selling before the guest is receptive. By that it is not meant that PR is a brainwashing exercise but that it is much harder to sell something that is misunderstood or not understood at all. This was the sort of difficulty facing the Midland Bank Executor and Trustee Company, and they found their answer in the film *Why Not Uncle Willy*? and the technique of the film-show-talk-and-reception kind of seminar.

With a PR operation, the risk has to be taken that the guest may remain unconvinced, just like the person who never will go up in an aeroplane, stay at a holiday camp or take a package tour. All the seminar (or any other PR activity) can do is present the facts. It exploits the marketing theory commonly adopted by computer firms that you cannot sell to someone who does not know and understand what you are selling, and this prior education of the customer is a PR technique which the marketer can adopt as an ice-breaker.

CHAPTER 11

Printed Literature and Printing

HOUSE styling enters into the question of print, and a uniform typography, colour scheme and symbol, name style or logotype is one of the first PR considerations of printed literature. However, in this chapter it is the use of printed literature as a PR medium that we have to discuss.

It is a correct if hackneyed saying that print is a company's ambassador, and while this is so its PR purpose goes beyond serving as a goodwill messenger. Printed material usually has a reasonable life span: it is not ephemeral like radio or TV material, and it is certainly more enduring than stories in the press. By means of reprints, the life and readership of magazine articles can be extended for perhaps five years or more.

Sponsored books, diaries and guides are PR literature, and so, too, are house magazines. In this chapter we shall deal with other types of print which have not been covered in earlier chapters. Some of the examples may not be produced by the PRO, but they are forms of communication that clearly have a PR content, whether it be an instruction manual or a glamorous Christmas calendar. A brief look will also be taken at the principal printing processes, bearing in mind that the print world is one of constant change and innovation.

The following is a breakdown of the remaining types of PR print.

(i) *Calendars*

The Christmas calendar was once the goodwill gift of the small shopkeeper, but today it has become the coveted collector's piece from Pirelli or Pan Am. The merit of the calendar is its prominent display throughout the year, a regular reminder of product or service, and a handy reference to address and telephone number. Those rather obvious merits have to be stated because it is very easy for the expensive calendar to decorate a wall without performing any PR service whatsoever. The calendar, costing thousands of pounds to produce, is one of the easiest ways to waste money, and it is no excuse to write it off as part of the below-the-line advertising budget. Some calendars become a habit best forgotten. Others are distributed indiscriminately so that recipients receive more calendars than they can use, and spare ones end up in Lil's bed-sit or mum's parlour. Wise distributors are very selective, and some go so far as to offer calendars rather than mail large numbers that may not be wanted.

In recent times a number of art studios and photographers have sent out calendars which may have been examples of modern art but which failed to make it easy to check the date. Such perverse publicity is scarcely good PR and hardly recommends the studio for its understanding of the principles of communication.

An interesting calendar in 1973 was that of ICI Holland BV which was printed in red and black on Melinex polyesterfilm, demonstrating the versatility of the material. There was a limited run of only 200 copies.

The most famous of the PR calendars was undoubtedly the Pirelli which celebrated its tenth birthday with the 1974 edition. The calendar revealed camera-struck nudes cavorting in the Seychelles without a spare tyre between them. The 40,000 copies cost £1.50 apiece or a total of £60,000. Two thousand went to privileged outsiders, the bulk to motor traders. Mr. Antonio Rosetti, managing director of Pirelli, considers it good PR that the black market price is up to £55 a copy, even though all 40,000 copies were given away free. No doubt a vintage copy will one day fetch a remarkable price at Christies. Is such a calendar worth a cost of £60,000? Was there a danger that Pirelli could have become better known for calendars than for tyres? Yes and No answers lie in the arithmatic that the tenth and last calendar projected the Pirelli name 365 days of the year at a cost of 3p per calendar per week.

Girlie calendars are not uncommon, but a modest competitor for Pirelli is now Godfrey Davis with their truck rental calendar that pictures roadside sexual fantasies. Eight thousand copies were printed of the 1974 calendar at a cost of £10,000. Romantic gipsy pictures, shot for a photo fee of £10,000 near Grasse in the South of France, made Avon's 1974 calendar attractively original. Total production costs were £16,500 for 30,000 copies. Another calendar with sophisticated models is that for General Analine Films (GAF), while Ciba-Geigy go quite the other way with more demure and lavishly dressed ladies in settings of Impressionist delicacy.

The calendar can be either a splendid way of cementing goodwill or a splendid waste of money. It probably works best when its receipt is anticipated and appreciated, maintaining a friendly relationship over the years. That is rather different from being just a costly publicity gimmick.

(ii) *Posters, Wall Charts*

Having some of the display merits of the calendar but also having wider application and being capable of reaching very different audiences is the visual aid in the form of a large poster, chart, map or other large area of print. Supplied flat, rolled or folded, it can be fixed to a wall or screen, or even framed, as an informative and fairly permanent or at least long lasting display. The information bureaux for many food promotion councils issue them for schools, and generally they are of an educational nature, whether for schools, factories, public libraries or other places where they may be seen by appropriate audiences. Excluded from this category is, of course, the purely advertising poster, although some of the tourist posters have a PR value in their decorative use in canteens and rest rooms. Such is the collector demand for advertising posters that some firms actually sell copies.

(iii) *Educational Folders, Booklets*

Because of an awareness of scholastic interest in industrial enterprises, print may be produced solely for younger readers and many firms produce special booklets or complete kits of thesis material. Domestic science teachers also welcome PR material from manufacturers of foodstuffs. But adults may need educating too about organizations, products or services, whether it be garden pests, do-it-yourself products or financial services. In these three fields alone, excellent examples of informative booklets may be found on the counters of horticultural and do-it-yourself supply stores, banks and building societies.

(iv) *Recipe Books, Leaflets*

How to use the product and how to vary its uses is very much the prerogative of the food industry. Most housewives appreciate recipes, and this kind of print is bound to enjoy a long life. It has also been adopted by the makers of aluminium cooking foil. It may be given away in the food store or offered in a press advertisement or on the pack, and cookery books can be sponsored and sold in bookshops or by mail order.

(v) *Handy Aids*

There is a temptation here to produce the give-away gimmick, but some may have lasting PR value such as calculators for working out quantities of wallpaper. Valuable aids can also be sold.

(vi) *Instruction Leaflets, Manuals*

Few things can cause illwill more quickly than incomprehensible instructions, including ones that are printed too small or explained too technically. The ability to win instant understanding is very much a PR responsibility. Since successful use of the product is bound up in repeat or recommended sales, it is an after-sales service which the marketer should give thoughtful attention to. Regrettably, this is an area of communication that is too frequently neglected (if not totally overlooked) by firms so anxious to market their products and bring in revenue that they do not stop to consider the anti-sales effect of customer frustration. Some of the manuals for continental cars are very poor, but there are electronic instruments for which no manuals exist at all.

(vii) *Annual Reports and Balance Sheets*

The lavish annual report and balance sheet, with full-colour plates and perhaps foreign language summaries, is a costly undertaking, almost a fetish, once recommended by PR consultants. However, reason (if not budget!) has prevailed and the best PR-inspired annual reports are those which are well-designed typographically so that the information is easily understood. There is a difference between a wasteful piece of prestige print and a document that invites shareholders and others to take an interest because the facts are clearly presented.

(viii) *Postage Stamps and First Day Covers*

A number of small countries, such as oil sheikdoms, are prepared to issue sets of commemorative postage stamps sponsored by commercial concerns. Specially designed covers can be printed for use with new stamps or special postmarks, such as the inauguration of a new transportation service or the opening of a new building, and these can be sent to clients, prospects and other interested people. The first day cover idea has been used regularly by a famous charity, and has also been used by hotel proprietors and airline operators. They can usually be organized in conjunction with a specialist stamp dealer (e.g. Philart Productions Ltd) and the Post Office, which is also able to offer special cancellation facilities.

Special stamp issues have also been made to introduce metrication in Australia and right-hand driving in Nigeria.

(ix) *Press Kits*

The press kit or wallet should not really come in this chapter because the best ones are plastic wallets bearing no print at all. A press kit should not be turned into an advertisement. Expensive cardboard press kits, with cunning cut-outs, embossings, multi-colour printing and nasty sharp corners may be the advertising agency's idea of PR, but that is all. They are a waste of money, serve no useful purpose, and bring PR into disrepute. It is not necessary to advertise to journalists.

Translated Print

When print is required in more than one language version (and remembering the differing lengths of copy when translated) it is a good idea to print the pictorial material by offset-litho and to overprint the text areas by letterpress, one process being economic for large quantities, the other for short runs. However, even this strategy is being superseded by the versatility of offset-litho and the capacity of litho printers to accept shorter runs. With the Common Market, and the world trade of most countries, foreign language printing has become the speciality of certain printers. It is important to use a reliable specialist printer who can offer: (a) foreign language type from stock, rather than buying it in from a trade typesetting house; (b) compositors who are at least familiar with foreign-language type and are capable or using these types; (c) printers' readers who are able to correct proofs in these types. In the UK, for example, there is a minority of perhaps three or four excellent printers with high reputations for this sort of work. Moreover, they work the other way round with overseas customers sending them work to translate and print in English.

Printers of all kinds are listed in *Advertiser's Annual*.

Printing Processes

The chief processes are letterpress, photogravure, lithography and silk screen (sometimes called screen printing), and the print buyer—and the marketer may well have to be his own print buyer!—needs to understand the elementary reasons why and when each process may be used. Most of the reasons are quite logical, and it is not a case of "liking" one method more than another. As with the purchase of photography, it is rarely wise to use the same firm for every job. In fact, most printers tend to specialize in well-defined classes of work such as stationery, sales literature, posters, labels, books, cartons or newspapers. Even the more general or "jobbing" printers tend to do better at certain jobs than others. It is difficult to generalize about this because the printing industry is continually changing, and it pays to talk to printers and ask to see specimens of their work before accepting estimates. The choice may depend on quantity, but it may depend on quality or the kind of surface that is to be printed, for the printer that will print on a drip mat is unlikely to print on a drinking straw!

For example, photogravure would not be used unless the quantity (say a quarter of a million upwards) justified the cost of plate making, while silk screen would be ideal for printing on materials other than paper or with non-flat surfaces such as bottles or balloons. It is not, therefore, a question of "calling in a printer" but of using the right process and the right printer for each different print job. That is why large users of print employ a print buyer, and there are trade journals devoted to this speciality. The journal in the UK is called *Print Buyer*.

However, it is essential that marketers and PR practitioners should have a working knowledge of printing so that they can work *with* printers. A lot of money is wasted because corrections are made at the proof stage when they could have been made quite easily on the typescript, for such corrections not only incur re-setting or hand-composition corrections but also overtime costs to meet the delivery time. The person who has a basic understanding of the subject will find it easy to get the best out of printers: he will also cut his print bills and get good quality work delivered on time.

Letterpress is an extremely versatile process. There are all sizes of machine from a small platen for jobbing print to giant presses that produce newspapers and magazines. The process will accept any kind of paper so that a great range of printing qualities is possible, according to machine. This is achieved pictorially by the system of half-tone screens whereby a combination of tiny dots and art paper will give a superb reproduction while a combination of large dots and poor paper will produce the typical newspaper picture. In between, the process lends itself to a variety of jobs ranging from labels and packages to catalogues and books.

The basis of letterpress is a raised or relief printing surface which when inked and pressed on to paper produces a print and this is not unlike the operation of a typewriter character or a rubber stamp. Because of the constant contact with the paper the printing surface is subject to wear and deterioration of impression, hence there are certain limitations regarding quantity. To some extent this can be overcome by the making of duplicate plates known as stereos or electros. Also, fullcolour work requires expensive plates for each colour (usually four), and unless it is a very modern heat-set machine which dries one colour after the other, the second, third and fourth colours cannot be printed until the previous ones have dried. It is a process that is at once versatile, yet limited, capable of printing a business card or a really glossy magazine while there is the remarkable machine that prints *Reader's Digest* with a veritable rainbow of coloured inks. For many years letterpress dominated British printing, but in recent years both sheet-

194 MARKETING AND PR MEDIA PLANNING

fed and web offset-photolitho (introduced from the USA) have become great rivals.

Generally speaking, photogravure will be used for vast quantities and offset-litho for medium to large quantities, compared with letterpress which may be uneconomic beyond runs controlled by the wear and tear of printing plates. However, these questions must be discussed with printers because so much depends on the machines they have, and this may mean the size of sheet that can be printed and the number of copies cut out of a sheet, unless they are reel or web fed.

With each process there are ways of identifying its results. Because of the pressure of the letterpress printing metal on the paper there is usually some indentation which can be felt on the reverse side of the paper, while a halo is likely to be noticed round the edges of printed characters. When judging whether a piece of print has been produced by letterpress or lithography the simple test is that no halo will be found round characters or letters printed lithographically.

Photogravure is used at its very best in the printing of postage stamps (with a magnificently fine 400 screen!) and art reproductions, but commercially rather poor quality gravure is used in the production of the popular women's full-colour magazines on cheap, slightly polished, supercalendered paper. It will be appreciated how wrong it is to refer to such journals as *Woman, Paris Match, Oggi* or *McCall's* as "glossies", a term so rightly belonging to a minority of high-class journals printed by letterpress. With mass-produced photogravure printing, which includes the colour magazines of the *Daily Telegraph, The Observer* and *Sunday Times*, and many of the world's womens and general interest magazines, backgrounds are usually velvety and ill-defined, and the 150-line square grid or resist gives ragged edges to the type, making the text wearisome to the eye if too much is read at a time or under bad conditions as when travelling. The image is etched into the surface of the curved plate or sleeve, the resist of tiny squares forming the grid-like plate surface. Each minute cell is etched to a depth required to take the quantity of ink necessary to print each tonal value. Thus a pale grey area will have shallow cells holding little ink, and darker areas will have deeper cells holding much ink. A spirit ink is used.

The great advantage of this process is that very large runs of full-colour work can be produced economically, and it came into prominence with the printing of general interest picture magazines, the now forgotton filmgoer magazines, and the majority of the popular women's magazines. It is an interesting example of the choice of processes that *TV Times* should be printed by photogravure but *Radio Times* has gravure colour pages and letterpress black and white pages.

Photogravure work is very easily distinguished by the ill-defined rather flat pictures, type with irregular edges, the smell of the spirit ink, and the polished paper quality already mentioned. Colour imperfections are common—a problem for advertisers requiring specific shades —and the same picture may reproduce quite differently in magazines produced by different printers. The classic case of this was when both *Woman* and *Woman's Own* printed Annigoni's painting of HM the Queen. They were two different pictures so far as the colours were concerned. Nevertheless millions of weekend readers appreciate the colour supplements, and they are certainly a boon to advertisers whose products call for the realism of colour.

Lithography carries the printing image on the surface of the "stone" or plate, and nowadays most lithography is photo-offset litho, the metal plates being prepared photographically. A rotary press is used, with a blanket cylinder which receives the print from the plate and offsets the impression on to the paper. In this way the metal plate is preserved and long runs are possible. With web-offset, reels of paper are used instead of flat sheets so that the process is practical for the rapid printing of newspapers and magazines, the machines being more compact than web-fed letterpress presses. It is a feature of litho that the machines are compact, and this has made possible the setting up of litho print shops in urban areas where space is scarce and costly.

Big improvements have been made in litho machines, inks, papers and plates while the dot screen for tonal pictures is usually 120–150 lines to the inch compared with the much coarser 65 screen for letterpress-printed newspapers. Good examples of comparatively inexpensive but good-looking offset-litho work may be found among holiday brochures, horticultural catalogues, mens tailoring and ladies wear sales literature and car brochures. Many weekly newspapers, using poorer paper, some evening papers and many magazines, including house journals, are printed by web-offset-litho. The latter innovation was introduced into the UK from the USA by Woodrow Wyatt, and on the whole British newspapers printed in this way are superior to their American counterparts printed on similar machines.

Like letterpress, lithography is a versatile process and small office machines may be used for in-house jobbing work. It is used for printing stationery, posters, cartons, sales literature, paperback books, full-colour books and brochures as well as newspapers and magazines.

Litho work may be readily recognized by the lack of halo or indentation round the characters which are perfectly shaped and free from the battered faces and "picking" (uninked white flecks) that occur with letterpress. Litho inks are noticeably glossy, and small pictures—or details in large pictures—enjoy good definition. The paper used for printing newspapers by web-offset is usually of a slightly harder texture than the newsprint used for those printed by letterpress.

Silk Screen is an ancient process originating in the Far East where the original screen was made of human hair. The modern press may use an organdie or metal mesh. It is a stencil process, paint or thick ink being pressed through a hand-cut or photographically produced stencil onto the paper. Very usefully, the process can be adapted to print on non-flat surfaces such as soft drink bottles, and it is used for the printing of drip mats, book jackets, showcards, posters and window bills. It is very suitable for over-printing on plastic surfaces such as wallets for press kits. Unless varnished, the printed surface is rough to the touch when coarse-texture paint is used.

This of course is but the barest sketch of a complex subject, but the attempt has been made to indicate that it can be of practical help in marketing and PR to know as much as one possibly can about printing.

Information about printing may be obtained from the British Printing Industries Federation (formerly the British Federation of Master Printers), 11 Bedford Row, London WC1R 4DX who have been particularly helpful about metrication problems and the Common Market. An excellent short, simple illustrated guide to printing is *Printing Reproduction Pocket Pal*, published by the Advertising Agency Production Association, c/o 51-53 Brick Street, London W1, at 50p. Anyone dealing with printers should possess and use a set of proof correction marks, and these are clearly explained in *Pocket Pal*. The UK edition is based on that of the International Paper Company of America.

CHAPTER 12

Metamarketing — A Marketing Myth?

WHAT is metamarketing? The offered definitions seem to depend upon the professional bias of the definer. Metamarketing tends to be one of those curious mongrel terms for a bundle of things otherwise understood under more simple and self-evident terms. The word metamarketing is therefore in danger of falling midway between a semantic hoax and a marketing myth. Together with metamarketing we shall therefore consider corporate PR, corporate advertising, corporate identification, and social marketing.

The topic was thought to be sufficiently important for Philip Kotler, Professor of Marketing at Northwestern University, USA, to add a special 18-page chapter to the second edition (1972) of his monumental *Marketing Management*. He defined metamarketing as the "marketing of non-business products" and as "the furthering of organizations, persons, places and causes". He included such things as travel, celebrity and nation promotion as if they had only recently adopted marketing techniques.

How do these things differ from a business product? Isn't tourism a product? Surely Hollywood was marketing film stars before the First World War? True, it was often done supremely well by the techniques of press agent and fan clubs. Why should the marketing of a pop group differ in principle from the marketing of their discs? Like the Hollywood film stars, pop groups are promoted by press agentry, which is not to be confused with either advertising or PR, and is a legitimate marketing technique in its own right. If metamarketing is to have any logical meaning it does not apply to "non-business products" at all and Kotler is off on a false tack of his own choosing.

A more practical approach to metamarketing is desirable or marketers will find themselves backing into a cul-de-sac of academic pretensions.

Presumably, what Kotler means is this: scientific marketing techniques are now being spread to other than consumer or industrial products or services, a classic example being "the making of the president" when an advertising agency is called in to treat a candidate (in any country, not just the UK or the USA) as a "product" with its unique selling proposition. Well, the whole theory of maximizing press coverage by marketing stories more efficiently could also come under the heading of metamarketing but why bother with coining yet another bit of jargon? As we shall see, Kotler actually admits to doing just this! It is commonsense—if rarely adopted—to give the press what it wants how and when it wants it and so achieve publication. That is applying marketing concepts to PR, which is what Chapter 4 of this book is all about. There is no need to call this metamarketing. Not unless one is trying to create a scientology of marketing.

For the past forty years the presentation of an organization by PR practitioners has been called corporate public relations. For an even longer period advertising practitioners have produced institutional, prestige or corporate advertising (and the Institute of Practitioners in Advertising publishes a booklet on the subject), while specialists like Lippincott and Margulies in New York, Toronto and London, the British firm of Martin Warnes and others concentrate on corporate identification. The promotion of causes (and nations) has been called propaganda ever since a committee of Cardinals in Rome introduced the word in 1662. Is metamarketing the integration of salesmanship, advertising, PR and propaganda to serve the marketing process of selling what people will buy? This is an unsatisfactory explanation, yet seems to be what Kotler implies.

Philip Kotler's rather Rip Van Winkle approach to corporate PR really has to be re-read to appreciate its naivety. Thomas Cook's celebrated a century of marketing travel *ten years ago*! The British Government started marketing Britain to the Americans during the First World War with a special staff set up in Washington itself. Mr. Winston Churchill promoted himself with whole-page advertisements in the *Evening Standard* when, in the late thirties, he found himself in the political wilderness.

More broadly, the author's more realistic definition of metamarketing appeared in his *Dictionary of Marketing and Communication* (1973). For instance, including what Kotler says but extending beyond it is the definition that metamarketing is the application of marketing concepts and tools to the marketing of products, services, organizations, individuals and places in order to achieve an exchange relation. That is beginning to mean something, taking marketing into the promotion of a port like Baltimore, London or Rotterdam—or into "the making of the President"—but also into the marketing of anything business or non-business. After all, there have been development committees to promote tourist centres ever since the advent of steamships and railroads. Mississippi showboats were promoted just as much as Barnum and Bailey's circus. But perhaps without the "concepts and tools" of modern marketing. Thus metamarketing can mean the application of sophisticated selling and promotion techniques resulting possibly in the revelation that it is better to play a pipe (like the Pied Piper) than to beat a drum in order to attract patrons. It is likely that modern methods such as programmed decision models can be applied to non-commercial marketing. One of the marketing tools that can now be applied is public relations, even though there was never such a good PR technique as the circus parade through the streets so that the circus image was instantly established. There are times when marketing, for all its models and mathematics, lags behind the direct communication of PR!

So is the above definition any more satisfactory? Is there any need to invent a term like metamarketing when marketing itself will do? There is nothing new about marketing "non-business products".

Perhaps a better definition from the *Dictionary of Marketing and Communication* is the systems view that metamarketing implies taking a company as a total integrated business system, not a number of separate functions or units, and so seeing the whole business (or other organization) as a marketing entity.

Well, this is where marketers and PR practitioners may disagree, both feeling that theirs is a management function. To avoid hair-splitting, it may be better to accept metamarketing as no more than what this book is all about, namely, marketing-PR, a fusion of marketing communication.

Now it is possible to see that top management needs to have this marketing-PR philosophy if it is to face up to the special pressures of modern society upon any kind of organization, commercial or otherwise. In other words, the civil servant, doctor, lawyer, architect, institute official, celebrity, philanthropist, politician and so on also has to be marketing conscious. He has to understand what the market needs and try to meet the need. An effective benefactor has to market his will-making.

In these circumstances, metamarketing becomes slightly more meaningful as the application of marketing techniques in fields which may well have shied away from such tactics. Even so, a hospital does not need to advertise for patients, but may well use PR techniques to disseminate information about remarkable surgical achievements such as heart transplants, plastic surgery and kidney treatments. But marketing techniques could be used to make the best use of the hospital's equipment or skills, or to attract to it the most complementary personnel, and also to gain financial aid for the development of its pioneer work.

The earlier chapters of this book may well have suggested that PR has been in the vanguard of metamarketing: it is certainly an important part of the areas that Kotler specifies for metamarketing.

But the most disputable part of metamarketing is surely the idea that an organization, person or place can be "sold" to various markets which are unsympathetic to it, such as to the consumer movements, state departments, TV commentators, and other critics and opinion leaders.

This is where the marketers fail to understand the outstanding role of PR. When it is in trouble an organization does not have to be "sold" like a product. Publics should "buy" the organization along with the product or service. A new flour is bought because the consumer has faith in the miller. The two go together. But it is impossible to sell a president, road safety, cancer research, or anything else which has no exchange relation in the conventional sense of value for money. A vote does not provide a mercenary benefit. A vote expresses a personal choice, and it is totally wrong to sell a politician like a consumerable commodity. The politician has to remain unbought.

The mistake has been made in a number of countries of handing politicians over to advertising agents. What these candidates needed was the advice of a PR practitioner on how to present a clear image of themselves and what they stood for: instead, the adman sought out

USP's and plugged them to death. Nowadays, politicians are oversold and found wanting. The most sensible thing Edward Heath did during his premiership was to avoid appearing on TV too often!

The tragedy of politics in all parts of the world—in the Third World no less than in Europe and North America—is that politicians, some of them better men than the marketing prophets have permitted them to be, have lost their credibility through what Kotler would apparently call metamarketing. Men cannot be used and abused like products, programmed to maximize votes. The philosophy of maximizing profits is anathema to men who must act more pragmatically.

Sales resistance is still the bogey of the most scientific marketing. It is a phenomenon of the human mind, not of instincts and emotions, and the overcoming of prejudice, apathy and hostility is something that requires the human relations techniques of PR. Such resistance requires a state of cognitive dissonance when the disliked becomes the liked, not through persuasion but through the removal of false ideas and misinformation. PR seeks a justified change of mind. This is totally different from the persuasion tactics of marketing and advertising in particular. And it is different again from the brain-washing methods of propaganda which have now been discredited in too many wars, revolutions and elections the world over. Metamarketing seems to be mischievous in its splendid disregard of follies long since denounced, especially by the incredibly wise younger generation who have seen through it all in the fifties, sixties and seventies.

Metamarketing has the right intentions but falls into the trap of overselling. It is bad PR. It is shockingly bad marketing. The president has been oversold too often. This is not the fault of the mass media but it is the fault of those who will abuse communication media by creating over-exposure, distrust and even boredom.

In metamarketing, marketing has sold itself short. Organizations cannot be sold to hostile publics. Why? Because the way to overcome the Naderism, Women's Lib, Friends of the Earth or whatever may be the hostile public is to remove the cause of the hatred. That philosophy comes naturally to PR practitioners because PR is a two-way process of communication. Metamarketing has value when it enriches promotional activities with scientific methods, but it is valueless when it imposes biased one-way selling tactics for the two-way skills of PR.

Metamarketing is inferior to corporate PR when it seeks to exceed its tolerance and modesty. The need is for marketers to understand the place of corporate PR in communicating organizational policy to hostile publics and so achieving credit for genuine achievement. Or credit for finding solutions to pollution problems, putting their houses in order, correcting follies of industrial relations, improving or modifying products that have been condemned and so removing the causes of misunderstanding, criticism and opposition.

It is right to realize that a misunderstood or maligned firm, person, place or cause needs to be understood and respected. But marketing concepts and tools are not enough. No business is so socially insignificant that it is nothing more than a mercenary marketing entity. Marketing is not the only purpose of business activity. Instead of metamarketing being a development there is a danger of it making foolish claims. These excesses could ruin the efforts of corporate PR and institutional advertising to create understanding and goodwill and establish reputation, which is very different from the compulsion, persuasion and influencing of selling. Instead of the possessive claims of metamarketing there is need for marketers to understand how much PR can do to serve the many strands of marketing endeavour. Marketing and PR need to work together. Metamarketing tends to be salesman with a six-gun trying to sell spectacles to a blind man.

When Philip Kotler says that "pharmaceutical firms... find they have to sell the idea of medicine, not just particular drugs; and textbook companies have to sell the idea of textbooks, not just particular textbooks" he is describing what PR has been contributing to marketing for decades. The only difference is one of language: the PRO does not "sell" ideas for he is an educator and informer. The teacher in the classroom does not "sell" geography, any more than the newsreader on radio or TV "sells" the news. And this is a very different matter from "selling the sizzle, not the sausage". It is one of the supreme arguments of marketing-PR that advertising will not work unless people understand what is being advertised. By means of PR techniques and media, the market can be educated. Now we are told that this is metamarketing. This is not so. It is very elementary communication.

If metamarketing means "the application of marketing concepts and tools to the marketing of organizations, persons, places and causes as well as business products and services" there is no point in creating a new word, metamarketing for something which, as Kotler admits, has been going on for a long time. For example, he himself says that celebrity marketing has a long history going back to the Caesars, so why bother to call it metamarketing? For many years this author has been saying that the exclusive PR feature article should not be written speculatively, but should be negotiated with an editor. That is to say, it should be marketed, but there is no sense in renaming this metamarketing.

Kotler confounds himself by admitting in his section on Organization Marketing that this is a new term, a more traditional one being "public relations". So now we have the low down on metamarketing! There is perhaps a simple answer to Kotler's confusion, and it lies in the differences in the USA and the UK concerning many of the things he puts into his strange category of "non-business organization". In the British Welfare State we have long become accustomed to these organizations—the British public health service compared with private medicine in the States—and so public relations have served them in ways that Kotler sees his so-called metamarketing serving American institutions.

Yet another glimpse of the difference between American and British techniques lies in his comment that an art gallery "received a lurid public relations blast". Apart from his contradictory language, he appears to be talking about some form of press agentry or publicity stunt which would not be regarded in Britain as PR. Yet, he quotes an acceptable American definition of PR, and observes that it shows "the similarities between marketing management and public relations".

We can therefore discount Philip Kotler's ideas on metamarketing as being no more than the discovery of the long discovered and the attempt to wrap it in the many-coloured cloak of salesmanship. He writes like a marketing man who has found PR but prefers to rename it metamarketing. This is a sort of scientology of marketing. His approach is understandable because a reversal of attitudes towards marketing and PR does exist in the USA and in Britain. It is one of the problems experienced by American companies when they seek to operate in the UK. Britain adopted PR sooner than America and professionalized it more rapidly. Two examples of this are the facts that the British IPR and the American PRSA were both founded in the same year, 1948, and even in 1973 (as shown at the IPR annual conference at Eastbourne) the PRSA was obliged to make its own film on a shoe-string budget and—from the land of Hollywood—it was a pretty pathetic little film. The IPR might not have the funds for such a film but British industrial film-making is of such a high standard that one would expect a better quality film about British PR. In contrast, marketing was adopted in the USA well before World War Two and with the birth of mass production it dates even earlier. Marketing was, in the main, a post-Second World War concept in Britain, despite the various pre-war marketing boards. No doubt the war retarded the development of marketing in Britain while accelerating that of PR. In this curious history Philip Kotler's attitude is better understood, odd as it may seem to the British reader.

Social Marketing and Social Awareness Marketing

With this in mind, it is significant that a British marketer, Norman Marcus, who frequently lectures in the USA and knows Kotler, has rechristened metamarketing as *social marketing*. Kotler apparently acepts the new name. Out of all this, a social marketing foundation has been set up as a focal point for research and the interchange of information.

Marcus is more realistic, and has something to say, even if it seems to be resurrecting traditional PR in the guise of new marketing. Perhaps the PR profession should be grateful for this oblique recognition! And maybe the truth lies in the scares set up by consumerism and conservationism so that marketers are finding the need for a corporate conscience when PR people have been urging companies to adopt PR in depth and corporate PR in particular. Reputation can stem only from good behaviour. When a company behaves well, when it is seen as a contributor to and not the robber of society, its reputation will be ever so great. Brought back into modern marketing parlance, it means that just as a company needs to market at a profit what people want so must it be seen to behave as people expect a responsible company to behave. They do not like learning that a company has bribed politicians, underpaid coloured workers, negligently disposed of waste products, or uses production methods that are dangerous to the health of their workers.

Norman Marcus contributed a chapter on Social Marketing to *Marketing Concepts and Strategies In The Next Decade* (1973), edited by Leslie W. Rodger, Professor of Business Organization at Heriot-Watt University, Edinburgh.

With Marcus' vision of social marketing it is possible to say that while PR adds a new dimension to marketing (and in the Kotler sense brings non-business products within the scope of marketing), the promotion of propositions adds a new marketing dimension to management. That dimension could be termed a business conscience. And once again we see the affinity between marketing and PR, for PR is very much to do with the way a business behaves, or is seen or thought to behave. It is the job of PR to be jealous of reputation, to provide management with feedback on the attitudes held by different publics. PR is concerned with more than trade. It is therefore very difficult to distinguish between corporate PR and social marketing. We are playing with words. In fact, a better term for both social marketing and corporate PR is not public affairs (as some American firms call it) nor external affairs but simply management communication. But Marcus has a nice label in social marketing which in itself is probably easier to market than any other. Social marketing does imply associating a social conscience with the old adage of maximizing profits which does smell of pollution, over-charging and asset stripping and invites the onslaughts of consumerists and conservationists alike. In these days of Simon's counterplea that a good many businessmen are willing to settle for satisficing, social marketing suggests the respectability and professionalism of the efficient marketer.

It can be concluded from Norman Marcus's contribution to Rogers' compendium, and especially when he writes of "corporate marketing strategies", that marketing and PR are converging into what he calls social marketing. Yet this is the message of this entire book, and if marketers were to adopt PR more comprehensively they would automatically embrace social marketing as a natural extension of their activities. That this calls for bold boardroom acceptance of such a philosophy only places PR where it should belong as a management function. PR should serve every facet of a business, not just marketing, but when marketing itself becomes involved in corporate behaviour this is emphasising the communication role.

This also leads to the question of social cost which immediately returns social marketing to the realm of marketing proper. It is all very well saying that the NCB should have prevented Aberfan, but most pollution, conservation and public safety issues are in the end ones of cost. Who pays—society through taxation or consumers through prices? Does the public pay indirectly and indiscriminately as they pay for public golf courses, toilets and maternity benefits (whether they use them or not) or do customers pay directly in relation to their usage? Social marketing may well have to explain to soft drinks customers that there is a convenience cost to the once non-returnable plastic bottle which can now be collected and either converted or destroyed. The PR element is here concerned with the dual conscience of manufacturer and consumer.

Marcus is also concerned about advertising. Codes and statutes, including those for the control of broadcast advertising, have abolished most of the abuses. It is, after all, the advertiser and not advertising who is guilty of misleading the public. There is therefore very much a social responsibility here. But whereas the reader can discriminate between one press advertisement and another, he does take the full impact of broadcast advertising so that he is more advertising conscious and more willing to be resentful. One of the peculiar differences between advertising and press relations is that while a press advertisement can contain vague or emotional generalities, a news release must confine itself to cold facts. Unfortunately critics of advertising tend to regard the generalities—the "legitimate puffs"—as facts.

Fundamentally, social marketing is about improving the quality of life, of business responsibility, of negating the old idea of "that's business, that is" in condoning the sharp practices of profit-taking. It is no more than a full-time PR job. The best case for a good reputation is not only the performance of the product but the behaviour of its maker. But someone has to pay for social marketing/corporate PR. It can come out of profits, reducing the company's financial performance. Or the buck can be passed to the Treasury, the nation being responsible for cleaning up the messes of private industry and commerce. The more practical answer is that the manufacturer should take the initiative in being socially responsible, and the cost should be built into his pricing policy.

There is one other possibility: that the abuse can be abolished profitably as when the gravel pit owners Hoveringham set up their leisure organization for the conversion of eyesores into places of pleasure. Social marketing could mean investment into laboratory research and feasability studies to see what can be done with waste products, effluent, and other industrial excrescences. It could mean more thorough research into the possible side-effects and residual dangers of drugs and chemicals. With safety changing from being a negative to a positive selling point, there is encouragement to foster the social element in marketing.

Already, there are many examples. The high hygiene standards of many stores in which smoking is banned; the dating of packaged foods; packaged fireworks and posters setting out the firework code; inbuilt safety factors in modern cars; warnings on gramophone sleeves that plastic covers should be kept away from children, and so on combine the demands of legislation with the voluntary efforts of marketers to be socially responsible.

But Marcus has now gone further: he distinguishes very rightly between *social awareness marketing* which makes buriness more socially responsible (which we have discussed so far in accordance with Rodgers' book), and pure *social marketing* in which business and marketing strategies are applied to social programmes. This distinction is perhaps what Philip Kotler really meant when he applied metamarketing to the "marketing of non-business products". Many non-profit making undertakings—and even some like local government trading—borrow marketing techniques but lack a coherent marketing communication programme.

Two British Government examples come to mind. The Conservatives utterly failed to market rent rebates for pensioners, and then Labour adopted the sledgehammer tactic of TV advertising. Jimmie Saville, familiar in quite another role, was used on TV for the fairly useless "clunk-click" safety belt campaign (at great cost to the tax paying viewer!) when, as Marcus says,*had the target audience been researched it might have been discovered that it was "one that could not be best reached with TV . . . the question could be 'can they be reached through advertising at all' . . . marketing communication is no longer merely advertising." Common ground seems to exist here between Norman

* *1st International Driver Behaviour Congress*, Zurich, October 1973.

Marcus and the author, even if we differ ever so slightly in our terminology. There would seem to be a vast future for social marketing using the PR tools of communication and the marketing aids of research. That is no myth but a prophesy. It applies to central and local government, charities and causes, trade associations, trade unions and professional institutes, Universities, hospitals and social services—to the great non-commercial world which is already the greatest user of PR, however modestly it may be employed!

PART THREE
Planning PR Programmes

CHAPTER 13

Planning PR Programmes

IN Part One we discussed the role of PR in marketing and related it to specific aspects of the marketing mix, while in Part Two we analysed the principal PR media and showed some application of marketing needs. Now, in this third and final Part we shall first of all suggest some practical ways of planning, costing and testing PR programmes, and then give some short case studies which demonstrate marketing-orientated PR in action and specific use of media.

To those who regard PR as something intangible, the value of it being difficult to assess, the logical answer is that tangible results can only be measured against clearly defined objectives. Seen in this way, most objectives seek qualitative rather than quantitative results, attitudes, knowledge and understanding rather than pounds or dollars, *but not always*. With image building it may be necessary to mount an opinion survey to measure the shift of opinion as a result of PR activity, but with a product publicity story for a new building component, children's toy or cosmetic the result may be measured by reader and stockist enquiries.

But let's be fair: how many marketing activities can be isolated? Are they not parts of a whole which have an accumulative effect on final trading figures, if not on monthly targets? What we have to do is minimize costs and maximize cost-effectiveness, and this is a matter of skill like deploying military forces in a battle. The more the marketer knows about the forces at his command, the more skilfully can he direct them. Of these forces, PR has been one of the least understood by marketers, and even in a topical, new and otherwise excellent book *Communicating With EEC Markets* (Kegan Page, 1973) Gordon Bolt can spare only two-and-a-half pages to a description of PR as an EEC marketing tool without actually describing the characteristics of PR in

Europe at all! On the one hand, PR is often neglected in marketing and marketing education, while on the other it is an inexpensive marketing aid compared with others that the marketer accepts without question.

The argument about intangibility probably has more to do with physical purchases than precise or sterling results (even where these can be shown) as when the marketer can see his TV commercial but cannot see the man-hours spent on running a press reception. But just as he can only quantify TV audience figures (and not until after the event!) and not exact sales figures, so he will know the attendance figures at the press party but not the actual volume of influence resulting from the press coverage, even when this has been measured in column inches. In both cases the final trading figures represent a host of influences. What is important is to make the best possible use of PR, bearing in mind the various faces of PR such as the process of behaving in a responsible fashion, creating a corporate image, and educating different publics so that the more commercial acts of marketing can succeed. Neglect of PR results in the marketer bashing his head on the brick wall of sales resistance. A lot of so-called marketers do this all the time.

The strategy for a PR programme spanning a period of six or twelve months, but up to three years if there is a major construction project for an aircraft, ship or public works contract, should follow a pattern such as this:

1. Appreciation of the situation
2. Definition of objectives
3. Definition of publics
4. Choice of media and techniques
5. Budget
6. Evaluation of results.

(In the scheme of work for lecturers taking the subject of Public Relations for the CAM Certificate in PR, a slightly different formula is given for operational PR, namely:

1. Investigation
2. Appraisal
3. Objectives

4. Targets
5. Methods
6. Recommendations
7. Budget
8. Progress reports.

This is similar in effect, and perhaps more applicable to the PR consultancy, but the author's more compact model combines Investigation and Appraisal as Appreciation of the Situation, and also combines Methods and Recommendations as Choice of Media and Techniques.)

However, the valid point is that this sort of sequential pattern is desirable, and it is a management discipline that should be sensible and familiar to the marketer. It also supplies the perspective that PR, to be effective (and also to be comprehensible to anyone asked to authorize expenditure on PR), cannot be haphazard and must be planned. Obviously, the unexpected will happen and plans will have to be modified, and this is easily done if there are regular progress reports and meetings to monitor the programme and make changes in the light of experience. When a consultancy is employed, regular monthly progress meetings are essential, and it is up to the client to demand them if the consultant is vague about such reporting.

Moreover, when a system of job numbers is introduced it is possible to give each new action (e.g. photography, news release, feature article, exhibition) an identity such as A101, A102 and so on which can be used on all purchase orders, incoming and outgoing invoices, for the items on the agendas for progress meetings, and also on the all-important follow-up contact reports resulting from meetings, telephone conversations and other contacts between consultancy and client. In the consultancy, job numbers will also be linked to time sheets that relate to the time bank produced by the manhour-based fee.

Consultancy-client progress meetings occupy time and expenses which have to be paid for out of the PR budget and fee, unlike the usual experience with advertising agencies when their meetings and many other services are covered by the income produced by the "commission system", unless fees on a manhour basis are being charged. Not being "ten percenters", PR consultants charge professional fees, generally computed on an hourly rate basis. When budgeting for PR, man-hours, overheads, materials and expenses are the chief costs, and in that order, whether there is an internal PR department or an outside PR service. We shall look again at these costs under Objectives and Budget. Let us now develop the simpler six-point model:

1. *Appreciation of the Situation*

Before anything is proposed it is imperative to know the present score. How is the organization regarded? What opinions are held by people whose goodwill matters? What is the state of misunderstanding, hostility, tolerance, esteem and understanding? This is likely to call for some kind of survey using desk research, interviews, postal or telephone questionnaires or a discussion group. We may be lucky enough to already have survey findings gleaned for another marketing purpose. Dealer audit and consumer panel reports may be useful. Perhaps it will be worth "piggy-backing" on to a regular consumer panel survey to discover the facts we need for our appraisal of the situation.

On one occasion the author conducted a survey which revealed that, far from there being any antagonism towards the client, he was utterly unknown. This produced the opinion of typical conservative-minded respondents that being unknown he was probably no good! On a second occasion, the author doubted the feasibility of a new product and advised that a survey be conducted prior to the holding of a press reception launch, and this resulted in the product being abandoned! On yet a third occasion, the author was associated with a joint PR-advertising presentation when an initial image-study showed that far from being the efficient modern company that its management believed it to be the company, in contrast with rivals, had a fuddy-duddy image with buyers. These examples illustrated the problem often faced by PR practitioners that the people who know least about a company are often those running it.

Because PR consultancy fees tend to be low, and accounts are quite wrongly obtained on a competitive basis—would we ask three doctors to quote for a treatment?—this initial investigation and appraisal is seldom undertaken. The result is that much of the first twelve months' work has to be taken up with some degree of research, and the original recommendations may turn out to be useless, or a campaign may be carried out almost like constructing a building without any knowledge of the site. Consequently, there is a lot of haphazard *buying* of PR services with consultants having to operate in the dark—often with inadequate finance—so that sooner or later this leads to a disgruntled client, a lost account, and unfair criticism of PR as a waste of money. To get the best out of PR, something like £2000–£3000 at least should be devoted to initial research to gain a realistic appreciation of the situation. Anything less than this minimal research expenditure at the onset is like buying a car but not the engine. This comment may be accompanied by the observation that it is not really surprising that the bulk of PR work is not conducted by PR consultancies (unlike advertising and the use of agencies), but is an in-house operation with staff PR personnel. When this is the case, initial investigations become much more the normal practice.

2. *Definition of Objectives*

Objectives have to be defined for four reasons: (1) To set targets for PR operations; (2) To measure the manhours and other costs involved; (3) To determine priorities which will control the timing of operations; and (4) To decide the feasibility of carrying out all these declared objectives in the light of available resources such as existing staff and equipment, and the budget (including the time-bank represented by a consultancy fee where outside services are used).

Two things are apparent here: the declaration of total objectives and the elimination of those that resources will not permit. This process is essential, but astonishingly rare, with the disastrous result that PROs are constantly expected to dissipate their efforts so that a little of everything is attempted and nothing very worthwhile is achieved. Such nebulous PR is certainly intangible.

3. *Definition of Publics*

To whom are we to direct the PR effort? Basic publics are the community, personnel, suppliers, the money market, distributors, consumers/users, overseas buyers, and opinion leaders, but each of these will break down into many sub-categories for different types of organization, while for some organizations there will be special publics to mention only educationalists, trade unions and local/central politicians and government officers.* "Community" to a department store has a different connotation from that of a toffee factory, while motor car manufacturers have fewer and better defined distributors than match manufacturers. Again, resources may call for concentration on a limited number of publics as defined by the objectives, or the PR may be deliberately aimed at publics not directly reached by advertising.

4. *Choice of Media and Technique*

Unless the objectives and publics are known, the media and tactics cannot be plotted. For example, unless the marketing objective is to sell sewing machines to domestic science teachers there is no point in addressing press relations to the educational press or organizing a seminar of needlework advisers to education authorities.

Evaluating media and techniques on a benefit factor basis will help here, and also with budgeting. We can take all the plus and minus factors in each case and so arrive at a numerical appreciation of qualitative values, which can then be costed and compared with other items in the budget.

Let us assume each factor is given a value of 5 or −5, but a semantic differential scale could be given to the positive factors in column one below, with gradings such as Very Good +3, Good +2, Fairly Good +1, Fair −1, Poor −2, Very Poor −3. To some extent it depends on the nature of the factors which mark system is used.

Plus Factors (5 points)	Minus Factors (−5 points)
1. Reaches required public(s)	1. Reaches unidentified public(s)
2. Low manpower required	2. High manpower required
3. Lasting effect	3. Transient effect
4. Great impact	4. Weak impact
5. Regular impact	5. Irregular impact
6. Easily controlled	6. Not easily controlled
7. No or little competition	7. Much competition
8. Colour	8. No colour
9. Sound	9. No sound

* Examples of such breakdowns are given in the author's *Planned Public Relations*.

Plus Factors (5 points)	Minus Factors (−5 points)
10. Movement	10. No movement
11. Sampling/demonstration facilities	11. No sampling, demonstration facilities
12. Personal confrontation	12. No personal confrontation
13. Economical	13. Uneconomical
14. Short term planning possible	14. Long term planning required
15. Can be done internally	15. Needs outside help

Without a definite situation any demonstration must be arbitrary and distorted but nevertheless here is a fictitious calculation for a documentary film compared with an external company magazine, assuming costs to be the same over twelve months.

Factor	External Company Magazine Score	Documentary Film Score
1	5	5
2	−5	5
3	5	5
4	5	5
5	−5	5
6	5	5
7	−5	5
8	5	5
9	5	−5
10	5	−5
11	5	−5
12	5	−5
13	5	5
14	−5	5
15	−5	5
Total	25	35

This reckoning (which could vary from company to company and circumstance to circumstance) indicates that when a choice has to be made a calculation of advantages and disadvantages can be made to compute a valid solution more satisfactorily than the mental weighing up of pros and cons. In this instance, the magazine, is shown to be preferable to the film. High location and acting costs might strengthen objections to the film, while airmail postages and translation costs could operate against the magazine. It is at the point where costs are equal that factor analysis and evaluation are useful. But if the factors are subject to more intensive analytical evaluation, a semantic differential scale will be more exacting.

5. The Budget

There should be an overall budget, and "shopping list" budgets for each separate allocation of funds, The target sum budget is often appropriate in PR, that is the calculation of what it will cost to achieve a certain task. But a suck-it-and-see type budget may be a good beginning when there is some initial uncertainty about what can be achieved.

A typical annual budget for an internal PR department in a large organization might be as follows, the salaries being relative to the man-hours required to carry out the work load indicated by the activities set out, other man-hours being covered by fees to freelancers, consultants, studios, film producers and others who may be employed:

SPECIMEN ANNUAL PR BUDGET
Large Organization With Own PR Department

	£, $, etc.
Salaries: PRO, assistants, house journal editor, secretaries	00,000
Overheads: Rent, rates, lighting, heating, cleaning, switchboard and other shared services	00,000
Depreciation: Furniture and equipment	0,000
Press Receptions: All materials, catering, hiring, expenses	00,000
Staff Journal(s): Editing, designing, illustrating, printing, despatching	00,000
External House Journal: Ditto	00,000
Documentary Film: Treatment, script, actors, music, shooting, editing, prints, distribution, maintenance	00,000
News Releases and Information Service: Research, writing, production, distribution	00,000
Printed Literature: Brochures, folders, leaflets, posters, calendars	00,000
Sponsorships: Bursaries, prizes, awards	00,000
Trade or Technical Conferences, Seminars: All materials, catering, hiring, expenses	00,000
Feature Articles: Research, negotiation, writing	00,000
Photography: Shooting, prints, captions	00,000
Stationery: Letterheadings, news release headings, photo caption headings, envelopes	00,000
Facility Visits: Transportation, accommodation, catering, hiring, materials, expenses	00,000
Exhibition Material: Display panels, models	00,000
Postages:	00,000
Telephone:	00,000
Travelling Expenses: Car allowances, fares, hotel bills, hospitality	00,000
Contingency Fund: Say 10%	00,000
Total (£'s, $, etc.)	000,000

6. Evaluation of Results

At the regular progress meetings, work undertaken and planned can be judged and checked against the budget. Running assessments will be possible of short-term jobs such as press receptions, accumulative assessments of, say, film presentations or news coverage, and overall assessments of completed long-term tasks or of the PR operation in general.

The methods of evaluation will differ between exercises but the following are examples:
1. The number and value of enquiries received.
2. The readership figures of journals carrying stories, or the audience figures for TV programmes in which the organization has featured.
3. The shift of opinion, or establishment of an image, as measured by an opinion survey.
4. Improved dealer attitudes as reported by field sales staff.
5. Greater success of advertising campaign following educational PR work.
6. Contracts gained as a result of film showings demonstrating previous contracts.
7. Improved knowledge of product, gained from field survey.
8. More understanding, sympathetic press following facility visit(s).
9. Reader interest of house journal as shown by response to questionnaire card.
10. Improved attitudes of previously hostile critics.
11. Feedback of information useful to research and development.
12. Feedback of product, service, staff or distribution criticism, or reduction in feedback of complaints.

The above are ones of interest to marketing but they do not take into consideration the much broader aspects of PR in fields such as community relations, staff recruitment, factory relocation, job satisfaction, or financial relations. Moreover, the list above may look rather vague and generalized until given meaning in the shape of practical examples. Many have been quoted in the course of this book, and others will be found in the case studies that follow.

CHAPTER 14

Ten Case Studies

British Air Ferries and Toyota (GB) Ltd

Although this is partly another motor-car study, it is very different from the press preview of the Citroen described on page 225 which was aimed at the entire European motoring press. Basically, this is a joint PR exercise organized by a lively consultancy for British Air Ferries and Toyota (GB) Ltd and supported by the Swiss National Tourist Office and Polaroid (UK) Ltd. The exercise, run by ex-motoring journalists Mike Mepham and Mike Casale of the MAP consultancy, co-ordinated BAF's inaugural flight from Stansted to Basle with a preview of the 2-litre Toyota Corona due to be launched in Britain on 1 July 1972. The flight was 29 July, returning next day.

In this study there are two continuing PR operations which coincided with the Basle trip, and first it will be useful to consider each in turn.

There are three sides to the BAF business: cargo, passengers and cars. BAF had run a Southend–Basle service. When taken over by Transmeridian Air Cargo, who use Stansted Airport, it was decided to open up the route again. They were already operating ferry services from Southend to Rotterdam, Ostend and Le Touquet, and from both Coventry and Bournemouth to the Channel Isles. But they attracted little interest from the travel trade and freight press, except in times of crisis. It was therefore necessary to make BAF more generally newsworthy, and for BAF to meet the trade. We will return to the trade relations aspect later.

The joint exercise with Toyota came about like this. The consultants reasoned that if a journalist was going to spend a day out of his office it was not enough just to fly him to Switzerland and give him lunch. Yet gimmicks and junkets were a worse and extreme alternative. The story to be told to the press was the convenience of the new route for passengers and for those taking their cars to Switzerland. The way to make this really relevant was to fly over some interesting new cars which the journalists could then drive round in Switzerland. MAP also handled the Toyota account. These cars from the world's third largest car manufacturer were very newsworthy, and in 1971 the 1600 Celica coupé had arrived in Britain on the day of the International Car Test at Silverstone where it had stolen the show. From an initial sale of 45 cars in Britain in 1965, sales had shot up to 1265 in 1970, 5000 in 1971 and 14,000 in 1972.

The Toyota 2-litre Corona was about to be launched in Britain. If the car could be imported in time, and run in, it could be flown out on the BAF's inaugural flight to Basle, and the opportunity to drive it would take journalists out of their offices for a day. The plan was discussed with Mike Caridia, sales manager of Toyota (GB) Ltd, and the first two Toyota Coronas to arrive in Britain were designated for the flight. Toyota's two highest mileage representatives were put in charge of the cars.

On 15 June Mike Casale of MAP went to Switzerland and checked the details, having now got the support of the Swiss National Tourist Office and also Polaroid. In addition to the two new cars, a Crown Estate and a Corolla coupé were also to be flown out and Toyota Switzerland agreed to lend the party two extra cars for organizational use.

Fifteen journalists accepted the invitation, including representatives from the *Evening News*, *Evening Standard*, *Sun*, *The Times*, *Sunday Times*, *Sunday Mirror*, *Autocar*, *Motor*, *Motoring News*, *Good Motoring*, *BBC TV* and *Thames TV*. The rest of the party included Mike Keegan, chairman of BAF, Mike Caridia, sales manager of Toyota, Albert Kunz of the Swiss National Tourist Office, Mike Mepham and Mike Casale, two drivers and two BAF executives. The Canadair CL44 took off from Stansted at 9 pm and a meal was served during the 1½-hour flight. A coach took them from Basle Airport to the Hotel Schweizhof where an informal evening and a late meal was enjoyed. In Basle they were assisted by Dr. Gotswiller of the Basle Tourist Office.

Next morning at 9 am the journalists were allotted to the four cars. They were given road maps but were not obliged to follow a given route.

In one of the cars loaned by Toyota Switzerland and bringing up the rear rode a mechanic and the Toyota sales manager. The journalists were invited to take it in turns to drive the cars, but to add to the interest Polaroid (who also gave the guests free sunglasses) lent the party seven cameras and the Swiss National Tourist Office offered prizes for a photo contest conducted during the visit. Their destination at the end of the morning test drive was Engelberg, eighty miles from Basle, where they were due to meet at 1 pm to take the funicular railway and cable car up to Titlis, 3239 metres above sea level, for lunch at the famous mountain restaurant.

As it turned out, none of the journalists had experienced a cable car ride before, so this added to the novelty of the trip. At the lunch Mike Caridia addressed the guests who were presented with electric cigar lighters. One of the guests had to file a story for a Sunday newspaper, and telephoned London from the top of the mountain. There were also Telex facilities laid on at the Basle hotel. Then they returned in the cable car to Engelberg and drove back to Basle in a change of car. At the hotel, rooms had been reserved for freshening up before dinner and the return flight that night to England. At Stansted everyone had cars for their homeward journey, but two journalists took over the new 2-litre Coronas for road testing.

Since the flight, PR has continued—maintaining the quality theme of the Toyota "collection" in TV and press advertising—with the Motor Show in October, the introduction of the motorized caravan, and a sponsored race at Kempton Park on Easter Monday, 1973.

Meanwhile, on behalf of BAF, MAP ran a press luncheon at Brown's Hotel, London, on 14 December 1972.

Then MAP ran a dealer relations programme for BAF in January 1973, consisting of conferences in Coventry and Bournemouth. Morning conferences were followed by lunch and a visit to the aircraft at the local airport; evening conferences were followed by dinner and the aircraft was demonstrated by means of a mock-up interior. In mid-January a dinner party was held in London at Quaglinos for the heads of tour operators and their wives. Thus, the marketing/PR programme combined a demonstration flight and a luncheon for the press, and personal confrontation trade seminars to take the ferries to the freight and travel trade, and a function for tourism chiefs.

Chemical Bank

These quotes from the *New York Times* give some idea of the role of a street banker in the Chemical Bank's progressive urban affairs programme:

> "I was the only white person in a group of ex-addicts. There were about 30 of them. I spent a lot of time getting to know the streets, getting to know the people, getting to know the language, and I guess the biggest final acceptance I got was when people in the program said:
>
> " 'It doesn't make any difference really, finally, what color you are'—and these guys were militant. 'If you're for real, you're for real, and there're people bulling on both sides. But if you are for real, then we got a thing.'
>
> "I've run the gamut of all kinds of responses up there. There're certain kinds of people in the community who are convinced that the banks are the bastards, and no matter what you say you don't convince them any different.
>
> "There're other people up there who say you not only have to talk and talk, you have to walk the walk, and they look at what you've done....
>
> "Hell, I'm not doing this to show banks are good guys—people will find out if you're doing the job—but to show people there's a way to do it."

The article, *Street Banker in Harlem*, was based on a tape-recorded interview by reporter John M. Lee with Douglas Ades, an assistant vice-president and director of urban affairs for the Chemical Bank.

When Chemical Bank's urban affairs unit was set up in 1970, the Bank's objective was "to take leadership position in attempting to solve certain social and economic problems existing in New York City, with emphasis in the black and Puerto Rican neighbourhoods". Just as this section has two contrasting motor-car PR studies, so it has this one which contrasts so strikingly with the Midland Bank's campaign addressed to the well-to-do young horse riders and admirers of Princess Anne.

Every department of the American bank is expected to contribute to its growth and profits. Chemical do not think their two goals are contradictory because its prosperity and future are inextricably tied up with New York City. If New York prospers, so does Chemical. If poverty-blighted areas of the city are revitalized, the Bank wins new customers and earns more money. Once again we see the association between ethics and economics that makes PR a matter of human relations in business. "The hard fact is that we cannot afford *not* to have an Urban Affairs program", says the Bank in a brochure that describes how the unit is organized and what it does and is in itself part of the PR exercise.

Street bankers don't sit at desks and wait for custom. Their main function is to serve as a link between the community and the Chemical Bank, but in so doing they frequently become the community's link with other organizations and institutions. They have helped people through the maze of city government, directed social bodies to specific needs in Harlem, and evaluated Harlem programmes for other corporations.

A few examples will demonstrate what Chemical's street bankers have done. They helped arrange financing for the first McDonald store franchise in Harlem, and provided the start-up loan for an electronics manufacturing plant. In-depth counselling, on the spot, was given to help potential borrowers assemble the necessary financial background information. Street bankers have introduced applicants to free consultant agencies like the Interracial Council for Business Opportunity and Capital Formation. They work with positive action groups such as the Community Thing Drug Program and the financing of day care centres as when interim loans have been helpful to groups awaiting permanent government or foundation funding. Chemical helped to keep the Successful Ex-Narcotics Users organization alive, provided loans for construction and rehabilitation projects, and became the leading bank in financing a new concept in low income housing/multi-service centre in East Harlem.

The urban affairs scheme began as a long-term investment, yet picked up immediate business benefits because, through the initiative of face-to-face confrontation with street bankers people who had been rebuffed by banks in the past were able to try again and obtain the loans they needed. In collaboration with the Community Business Resources Loan Unit, Chemical have pioneered new banking techniques with start-up loans, the need for which would never have been known but for the street bankers moving about in the community. These street bankers have found, for instance, that bookkeeping and accounting is a serious problem in an impacted community, but bank electronic record-keeping and payroll systems are a logical answer. The new accounts opened range from fairly substantial deposits to the checking and savings accounts of young people who otherwise spent their money as soon as they got it.

Director of urban affairs is Douglas Ades, from whose interview-article quotations were given at the beginning of this study. He was a former minister and narcotics rehabilitation street worker, neither a bank official nor a PRO. He has a staff of two officers and four street bankers, three operating in Harlem and one from the Bedford-Stuyvesant office. Urban affairs comes under the control of the public and urban affairs department directed by vice-president James P. Murphy. The department administers the Bank's government relations programme, urban and social responsibilities activities, and corporate contributions programme. There is an urban affairs advisory committee made up of senior officers from metropolitan, personnel, operations, marketing and credit departments.

The street banking exercise has attracted the attention of the media and has been the subject of many newspaper articles and television interviews.

Citroen and the Bord Failte — Irish Tourist Board

This is a joint study showing how a Continental car manufacturer and a national agency in another country co-operated to organize a complex press event under security precautions.

First, there was Citroen of Paris, the French motor-car manufacturer, who wished to provide test-ride facilities for motoring correspondents attached to the press of Europe.

Second, there was the Bord Failte—Irish Tourist Board, charged with the task of promoting conventions, incentive travel and allied business in the Irish Republic. The Board operates in association with Aer Lingus-Irish, B + I Motorway Division, CIE (Irish transport company), Irish Hotels Federation, Irish Transport and General

Workers Union, regional tourist organizations, and Shannon Free Airport Development Company. But as the study shows, the Board was able to extend its influence to secure British co-operation across the border in Northern Ireland.

For the press preview of the Citroen GS in July–August 1970, a new location was sought and Citroen's head of public relations asked the Board's Paris office for suggestions. Previously, press previews had been held in Italy, Spain, Morocco and the South of France. Now, Citroen wanted a very different location. The requirement was for a location with a good road network giving a variety of road conditions; modern hotel accommodation including a hotel that could be virtually taken over for a period of six weeks; the availability or possible provision of certain technical facilities of a special nature within the hotel grounds; and proximity to an airport. Quite an assignment!

Working in the strict secrecy demanded by a new car launch, even to the extent of an operational code name, the Board put up a number of suggestions. Of these, Rosapenna in County Donegal, the beautiful Republican county that borders the Northern Ireland county of Londonderry, was chosen by Citroen's PR chief after visiting the suggested locations. It was an excellent choice, quiet, remote, with a mixture of roads as might be expected in a scenic coastal area. The Bureau then found the special requirements stipulated by Citroen and the principals concerned met to work out final details and costs.

The Board obtained the co-operation of the customs authorities to allow the import and re-export of more than twenty-two test vehicles together with spare parts and ancillary equipment. The Irish police co-operated by closing roads for the test runs. The co-operation of the British Department of Trade and Industry in Northern Ireland was sought and obtained to permit test vehicles to be driven through Northern Ireland *en route* for Donegal, and the British Army and the Royal Air Force in Northern Ireland agreed to make available the military airport at Ballykelly for the Citroen private jet which was flown there every day from various points in Europe and whence passengers were lifted by helicopter to the Rosapenna Hotel.

The actual daily operation during the press preview period of six weeks was for a ten-seater Mystere 20 private jet to fly from a different major continental city to the airfield at Ballykelly from which two helicopters took the guests to the Rosapenna Golf Hotel where, after a traditional Irish whiskey and then lunch, a test drive of the car was arranged on a specially closed road. Golf, horse-riding, tennis, fishing or swimming was available after the test run. After dinner there was entertainment at the hotel. For those who wanted to know more about the technicalities of the GS engine, there were experts on hand. Next morning, either extra test runs or photo sessions took place before the party departed by helicopter.

When the test circuits had been decided upon, contact was made with bar and restaurant owners on the chosen roads to provide refreshments free of charge to visiting journalists. The accounts were sent to a central point and paid from there. Maps of the circuits were produced, marked with places of interest. Under strict security, a petrol tanker was kept close by. The comment is worth making here that this was a one-off exercise requiring original arrangements that might never be required again. It was not a ready-made package deal. This called for quick, thorough and intelligent local organization, on which Citroen had to rely, making sure that its wishes and instructions were clearly translated and communicated.

During the six weeks some 450 journalists visited Donegal—many visiting Ireland for the first time—and they came from thirteen European countries. All were motoring correspondents, and the majority laid special emphasis in their articles on the novel Irish location which contrasted so interestingly with the locations of previous years. By its very setting, the operation invited journalists to describe the countryside, the quiet roads and the friendly facilities, and indirectly to enhance reader interest in the car itself. The Board naturally saw to it that the visitors were supplied with tourist literature by the regional office in Donegal.

Citroen presented each journalist with two typical Irish sweaters, one for himself and one to take home to his wife or girl friend. Different size sweaters were foreseen! The Arran sweater was of real utility because the journalists had no idea of their destination when boarding the aircraft, and some thought they were heading for the heat of the South where car launches are commonly held. While the Irish weather was pleasant enough, it was not of course Mediterranean with red-hot pebbles on the beach.

The on-the-spot Citroen organization consisted of four members of the Paris PR department, assisted by eight mechanics. The six-weeks PR operation was directed by J. Wolgensinger, head of public relations for Citroen.

The car received exceptional press coverage in Europe. Citroen spent some £10,000 in the Republic. From the Board's point of view, their costs were about £1000 and they were well pleased with their share of the international press coverage.

One of the best lessons to be learned here is that an unusual and successful event of a complicated nature can be run many miles away in another country when there is a confident organization hosting the event, and an imaginative and resourceful "on-the-spot" native service. More recently, the Irish Tourist Board has created the Convention Bureau of Ireland which has brought large American annual conventions, British sales conferences, European press previews, and other events and people to Ireland.

James Hayes and Sons Ltd

James Hayes & Sons Ltd, part of the J. Lyons Group of Companies, supply Haylin workwear garments and their rental business is one of the largest in the UK. This study describes how the Rome line was launched in Britain during the summer of 1972, with special reference to the services of a marketing-orientated PR consultancy, Winkler Marketing Communications Ltd.

The garment rental industry has been established in the UK since the 1930s and is an expansion of the laundry business. Workwear garments for factory workers ranging from boiler suits to attractive overalls are supplied, laundered, repaired and replaced, leaving management free from control problems and releasing capital that would otherwise be tied up in stock.

A typical service agreement is to supply each employee in a company with three garments, and more if the job specification demands a high number of changes per week. Every member of the staff is measured in order to receive personalized garments which are provided in a choice of colours and styles and, in some cases, are specially designed for the client company.

Hayes work in conjunction with the Italian firm of Klopman International on the production of the material required for their Haylin garments. In 1972 Hayes wished to produce a new workwear range with emphasis on fashion and comfort, and agreement was made that Klopman should supply Hayes with their exclusive Dacron/cotton fabric. This Du Pont polyester and combed cotton material is woven in Klopman's multi-million pound mills at Frosinone near Rome where more than one million yards of material are produced each week.

With this partnership established, Hayes then needed a manufacturer to make the new range of garments and one of the most modern and best equipped in the UK was chosen, Alexandra Overalls Manufacturing Ltd of Bristol. This company was founded in 1952 specifically to design and market what was then a new concept in industrial workwear, fashion overalls. Alexandra co-operated with Hayes in the development of the new range and extended their already rigid quality control system to the Haylin garments.

With all the tie-ups between the three companies completed, a PR exercise was required to support the marketing operation. The new garments were named Rome Line, and international top models were flown to the Eternal City to be photographed and filmed in the overalls, coats, boiler suits, shirts and trousers, and matching jackets and trousers.

News releases and pictures were sent to all journals covering the three industries as well as to management and industrial magazines and fashion editors on womens magazines.

An important part of the PR programme was an 8-page external company newspaper, printed web-offset in full-colour, with front-page emphasis on the Rome Line. *Haylin News*, issue No. 1, Summer 1972, was mailed to 8000 prospects.

Among its illustrations were pictures of the original headquarters of James Hayes, laundry workers, and the horse-drawn delivery vans of the early 1920s. The original company was founded in Lewisham in 1868, then moved to Camberwell in 1908. It was acquired by Lyons in 1926, whose hotel laundering it had long undertaken under contract. Now it is the world's largest laundry. The journal not only launched the Rome Line but did a splendid PR job for Hayes who, among other things, offer dust control systems, and by a series of acquisitions have expanded their laundry services in the London Airport, Wembley, Midlands and North of England areas, and also taken over the well-known Achille Serre linen hire operation. All this was recounted in *Haylin News* so that it was given quite a wide readership interest. This demonstrates the usefulness of the external company magazine described in Chapter Nine.

The three companies combined to produce an attractive laminated wallet which carried a set of full-colour pictures of models wearing the Haylin Rome Line garments, each picture bearing a description on the back. The wallets were used by all three companies for mail shots, salesmen's aids and as general sales literature.

As a result of this combined promotion, the Rome Line range was successfully established within food factories, drug companies and other clean working environments.

Hope Technical Developments Ltd and The British Safety Council

This is the study of a British invention that was marketed at home and abroad almost entirely by PR techniques together with trade exhibitions and sales literature. It also shows how an enterprising voluntary organization can help in a marketing operation.

Motorways and TIR ferries have seen the introduction or greater use of giant six–ten-wheel articulated vehicles such as tankers, bulk carriers, container-trailers and transporters. They are the sort of transports that can jack-knife viciously unless fitted with safety equipment such as the Hope Anti-Jack-Knife device. Fleets belonging to owners such as Lansing Bagnall, Calor Gas, Marley, Tyburn, Waitrose and the oil companies have adopted the Hope device. Fitted with this equipment it is *almost* impossible for an "artic" to lose stability and jack-knife. If the vehicle hits a brick wall, nothing can stop it folding up.

It works on the principle that in a dangerous road situation, such as loss of control and wheel skid following braking, control can be provided at the "hinge" point of the vehicle, the king-pin. There are two components, an air operated multi-disc slipping clutch which is fitted to the upper fifth wheel of any type of semi-trailer operating in conjunction with air-braked, 2-inch SAE coupled trailer units. Mounted on the topside of the rubber plate below the floor of the semi-trailer, it does

TEN CASE STUDIES   231

not occupy load space and weighs only 78 lb (35.5 kg). When the vehicle brakes are applied, the discs are squeezed together and damp out any dangerous or uncontrolled rotation between tractor and trailer.

The "fifth wheel dampener" is the invention of Englishman Fred Hope, a man who had built up a road haulage business of his own and had practical knowledge of the perils of jack-knifing and the need of some safety device to prevent it from happening. He was not an engineer, but he set up Self-Energising Disc Brakes Ltd (now Hope Technical Developments Ltd of Ascot) and designed a better braking system. Then he went on to produce his now famous and more sophisticated Anti-Jack-Knife device which acts as a drag on the coupling and reduces the tendency for the trailer to fold up round the tractor.

Demonstration was the obvious way to promote his invention, and Fred Hope earned the title of "Fearless Fred" when, before invited audiences, he deliberately executed hair-raising jack-knife skids, and then repeated the incident without jack-knifing, thanks to the use of his device. The first model had its drawbacks, being bulky and requiring lubrication, but the perfected version was lighter, more compact, self-adjusting and permanently lubricated within its light alloy casing.

He took his idea to America where the powerful Teamsters Union put on a demonstration before Congressional representatives of the Interstate Commerce Commission and the truck industry at Bolling Air Force Base near Washington, DC. That was in early 1966 and the story was given coast-to-coast TV and newspaper coverage, with a big illustrated feature in the union magazine *Teamster* for June and in other American journals later in the year.

In Britain Fred Hope needed influential support to break down the conservative reluctance to spend about a £100 on making a semi-trailer safer. So he went to see James Tye, controller of the British Safety Council. Tye had been campaigning against a great many unsafe and deadly products and practices long before anyone had ever heard of Ralph Nader, and with great success. He knew exactly what to do, being a PR "natural". He researched the device and produced a report. Then he advised Hope to hire Hendon aerodrome on the eve of the Commercial Motor Show and invite TV, newsreel and press cameramen to attend a demonstration. Hope went through his "Fearless Fred" act, and Fred Davis, chairman of York Trailers was to say afterwards that this anti-jack-knife demonstration gained more news coverage than the whole of the Commercial Motor Show.

Raymond Baxter's presentation of the device on BBC-TV's *Tomorrow's World* in the Spring of 1967 aroused a storm of controversy in *Motor Transport*, both Fred Hope and James Tye publishing letters to refute claims that the TV programme had been alarmist. There were some who found it convenient to underplay the hazard of jack-knifing, but within a year a brake manufacturer was advertising a safer brake, the Road Research Laboratory produced a favourable report on the device, and Transport and General Workers Union officials were speaking up for it. Significantly, drivers were enthusiastic about the device.

The story went round the world, and the cuttings came back from South Africa, New Zealand, South America and of course the USA. It was televised in many countries, and appeared on cinema screens in South Africa which had no TV.

It was a feature of the International Container Services and Equipment Exhibition at Olympia, London, in 1968.

On 19 March 1969 the Watford *Evening Echo* ran a whole-page article about David Chopping who had lost three friends when his car was struck by a jack-knifing lorry, and the article brought out the British Safety Council's recommendation to the Government that "all new articulators should be compulsorily fitted with safety equipment such as the Hope Anti-Jack-Knife device".

Through the late sixties and into the seventies, Fred Hope's fifth wheel dampener continued to be a good story, and greater road safety was pioneered among the big transport builders and operators so that when a "product publicity" PR story appears in the transport trade press about additions to a fleet it is becoming common to read a specification that says: "It is a 10 ft-wheelbase Leyland Super Comet coupled to a Scammell single-axle trailer. ... A Hope anti-jack-knife device is fitted to the trailer king-pin."

And in the Hope Technical Developments four-colour brochure there are testimonials from Hipwood & Grundy Ltd, Hargreaves Transport Ltd, Hoveringham Gravels Ltd, and T. Wall & Sons (Ice Cream) Ltd, while full-colour drawings of vehicles in their self-identifying liveries speak for themselves. The brochure closes with the words "One common denominator of the varied vehicles illustrated is the

Hope Anti-Jack-Knife Device. These operators have proved, to their satisfaction, the value of the investment. Are your artics as safe as they could be?"

"Safety is a negative selling feature" said one of the American motor industry chiefs some years ago. To market something that a lot of people don't really want—no matter how great the need!—requires first-class communications. In this study both Fred Hope and James Tye showed their ability to communicate, and to exploit the media and techniques of communication.

Midland Bank Limited

"Essentially a long-term PR operation" is how Midland Bank regard their sponsorship of the first ever Horse Trials Championships of Great Britain for novice and open horses. This study is therefore a look at a PR activity that began in 1968 and could go on indefinitely, a kind of "Peyton Place of public relations"!

The Midland Bank Group sponsors one-day horse trials throughout the UK because this is a growth sport based on country activities which happen to fit in with the Bank's policy of lending to farmers. This policy "to look upon applications from farmers for help with a sympathetic understanding of their needs" was announced by Lord Monckton in the *Farmer and Stockbreeder* in December 1958, and the story of associated PR exercises is described in the author's *Public Relations in World Marketing*. Not only does horse trial sponsorship follow on the earlier appeal to the farming community, but it generates sufficient publicity to justify its existence.

It also ties in with the decentralization of the Bank so that regional directors, established in all corners of England and Wales, together with local managers, visit the Bank's sponsored events, present prizes in the form of special bank cheques and rosettes, and meet a cross-section of the community they would otherwise not have come into contact with. In this we see how intimately PR and marketing can be associated, and this has been brought out elsewhere in this book with the Banks' sponsorship of Opera "proms" and the *Why Not Uncle Willy* film exercise.

The Midland Bank Horse Trials Championships of Great Britain have attracted national TV coverage and provide a platform for the Bank's top executives to appear in public. One cannot enter for these championships: qualification is by winning or otherwise succeeding in a Midland Bank sponsored one-day or two-day horse trial. The importance of this can be seen against the statistics for these events generally, there being 29 trials and 2169 starters in 1968 and 54 trials and 5096 starters in 1972. The Bank is therefore supporting a growth sport for the young and the Bank's market here is primarily one of young people in the age group 16–30. Riders are relatively wealthy people, and although they are bound to have strong family connections with existing banks there is evidence that sponsorship of the sport is moving these young people towards the Midland. Equally, the presence of senior Midland officials at these events is resulting in increased local contact and in some cases firm business for the Bank.

Developing out of this enterprise has been the book *Riding for the Gold* which was produced within two weeks of the Munich Olympic Games at which Britain won two gold medals in the three-day event. It was announced in equestrian magazines in November 1972 as "this *free* 32 page booklet (with 16 pages in colour)", and also linked with congratulatory advertisements on the Munich result which appeared in the *Financial Times*, *The Times* and the *Daily Telegraph* on the morning following the end of the competition. The print order was 50,000, of which 2000 copies were sent to members of the Combined Training Committee, the governing body of horse trials. At the Bank's championships at Cirencester Park, copies were distributed with programmes. Over 20,000 coupon replies were handled. In April 1973 the book was advertised in the *Radio Times* to coincide with Badminton, taking up the balance of the supply. The unit cost of each book was 13p.

The book *Riding for the Gold* is only one of the PR "products" resulting from the sponsorship of horse trials, and so sending out further ripples of communication. Films of the championships have made it possible to convey the Bank's message to winter evening and other audiences, helping to perpetuate the PR activities of previous years. This is therefore very much an accumulative PR activity and a sponsorship which may have more realistic and direct contact with the market than some of the broader-based sponsorships like those of Wills, Players, Whitbread and Yardley.

Rentokil Ltd

The Rentokil Library is a collection of films, books and wallcharts that has grown into a family of PR efforts since the first films, *The Challenge* and *House For Sale*, were made in 1958 and 1959, and the first sponsored book, Dr. N. E. Hickin's *The Woodworm Problem*, came out in 1963. Today, a very creditable group of documentary films, books and diagrammatic wallcharts are available on industrial and domestic pest control, timber and property preservation and hygiene. They are non-commercial in their presentation, of a high standard of educational interest and the films especially have been made to work for the company and its subsidiaries all over the world. Customer education has been the major PR objective of this fascinating growth company which repeatedly gains feature articles in journals such as *Management Today* and the *Daily Telegraph Colour Magazine*.

The author was PRO to Rentokil from 1959 to 1963, succeeded by Peter Bateman who had worked with him, and with this awareness of the company's marketing and PR activities for more than fifteen years, plus the company's successful use of every PR technique in the book, it is not surprising that the author frequently quotes Rentokil examples. It is a perpetual case study in PR, thanks very largely to a PR-minded top management. In confining this brief study of the Rentokil Library it is none-the-less possible to give glimpses of the greater PR programme. Other references will be found elsewhere in this book.

Documentary films have been a hard-working marketing/PR tool for Rentokil. They have been linked with the training of personnel in public speaking and the organizing of literally hundreds of one-day and half-day schools, evening film-and-talk receptions, film shows and talks to local organizations; they have been included in the weekly shows presented to women's and other organizations by Guild Sound and Vision; placed in national film libraries; and given world distribution through the Central Office of Information. For overseas showings many foreign language versions exist. There is no question about their immense value in bringing home to potential clients the nature of the problems Rentokil offers to solve.

How better can the ravages of rats or dry rot be explained and prospects convinced that eradication is possible if the right scientific skills and materials are applied, than through the visual impact and authenticity of a film? The Rentokil films deliberately omit commercial references—except in the credits—and they speak for themselves, or are complemented by competent technical speakers. As a result, they have won awards, been shown on television, used for general pest control training purposes, adopted by the COI and frequently chosen as examples for demonstration of PR films to students. But these are the bonus showings in addition to being used for their plain purpose of customer education. To some extent this is borne out in the Rentokil Film Unit Report for 1971-2 which states that "during 1971 our films were shown on 2511 occasions in the UK, an increase of 430 (17 per cent) on the previous twelve months and an average of 50 shows per week throughout the year," and later comments on fewer bookings from outside libraries such as the Central Film Library. This tends to support the point made in the chapter on films that controlled or company-organized film showings are preferable or more important than more casual and less identifiable distribution through film libraries.

It is interesting that the first film *The Challenge*, made for the original Disinfestation Ltd (a subsidiary of the original British Ratin Company) and before the adoption of Rentokil as the Group name, remains the favourite. Its subject is rats! That is very significant because it all began when K. G. Anker-Petersen came to England in 1927 to sell the rodenticide Ratin for the Danish import-export agency, Sophus Berendsen.

The Rentokil Film Report shows that *The Challenge* was given 482 showings in Britain in 1971. That film alone has also served the company magnificently in its build-up of more than forty overseas subsidiaries, one marketing-PR venture being world tours by directors who gave film shows and talks in many cities in all continents, often with the co-operation of the Board of Trade or the Department of Trade and Industry. Perhaps the culmination of this was the award of the OBE to the then Joint Managing Director W. H. Westphal in 1972 "for services to exports".

Most of Rentokil's films have been made comparatively inexpensively by the Rentokil Film Unit, headed by Robert Farmer, yet they have been of professional and international award-winning standard and have measured up to the quality demands of the COI and television. One in particular, *The Intruders*, is remarkable for its photography of cockroaches, creatures that shun the light, with sequences showing the opening of the egg case and the hatching of the nymphs. Such technical excellence obviously enhances the company's image of scientific expertise.

In 1972 the Film Unit produced four new films of which *No Place Like Home* was directly related to an entirely new marketing operation, the selling of Rentokil services to property owners claiming home improvement grants. It deals with the need to renovate older properties and was made for use in conjunction with local authorities to publicize the Housing Improvements Grant Scheme.

"There are still lots of people", says the commentator, "who don't understand grants and loans, and many simply think they cannot afford their share of the cost." The film demonstrates how modernization with grant aid can rescue thousands of homes from decay and save them from demolition with the consequent uprooting of communities and separation of friends and relatives. The 22-minute 16 mm colour sound film is thus aimed at landlords, tenants and occupiers of "twilight houses", and of course the underlying implication is that Rentokil timber preservation, damp proofing and insulation services can help with the process of repair, although the film makes no specific commercial references.

The Rentokil book library is impressive, and never before have such titles by eminent scientists appeared in the list of a famous publisher, in this case Hutchinson-Benham. Beginning with Dr. Hickin's *The Woodworm Problem*, there have been no fewer than seven books from his pen. Dr. P. B. Cornwell has produced the two-volume work on cockroaches, and three other authors have contributed to the thirteen titles produced since 1962.

Rentokil agree all production costs on approval of estimates and a net selling price is agreed. They pay the production costs and at six monthly intervals receive from Hutchinson 60 per cent of their receipts from trade sales. An alternative form of sponsorship would be to guarantee to purchase an agreed number of copies at a discount (usually $33\frac{1}{3}$ per cent) and accept a lower royalty on book trade sales.

Copies are often presented to students of technical colleges, they are in public and college libraries, and on the shelves of architects, surveyors, public health inspectors, housing managers, building inspectors, solicitors, estate agents, building society officials, bank managers and many others. They are doing a permanent PR job for Rentokil.

When the books come out they are well reviewed, and also announced by news release. The release on Dr. Hickin's *Termites—A World Problem* in November 1971 resulted in the COI using it in *Book News From Britain* and a column by Michael Lake in the *Guardian* was syndicated across the USA by the *Los Angeles Times/Washington Post* Services. Overseas cuttings were received from the USA, India, Australia and elsewhere.

A. C. Farrington, Rentokil's marketing director, says of the Rentokil Library series. "It is an effective marketing aid and a form of instruction and reference for clients, potential clients and staff. It is tangible evidence of Rentokil's knowledge and experience."

A new addition to the Rentokil Library is the series of 20 in × 16 in full-colour wallcharts explaining the biology and habits of pests and timber diseases such as woodworm, rats, cockroaches and dry rot.

The Library is presented very simply in a neatly house-styled series of synopsis leaflets contained in a small wallet obtainable from The Rentokil Library, 16 Dover Street, London, W1X 4DJ, where the company has its attractively displayed exhibition and information centre in the West End of London.

W. H. Smith Ltd

Very closely related to marketing is the programme of "merchandise information" illustrated news releases which W. H. Smith's marketing department sends out to the national press. It is all part of the development from Smith's historic "railway bookstall" image to that of large modern stores selling books, newspapers, magazines, stationery, records, greeting cards and fancy goods. Their releases are quite different from the usual run of news stories, the exception that successfully breaks the rule perhaps. They might be better described as pictorial newsletters for women's page journalists.

They are reproduced in black on buff-yellow paper with a brown heading. The illustrated products bear single-spaced caption stories, and prints of the pictures are available on request.

A marketing programme is set out for the year, with fifteen Friday to Thursday cycles when new products are offered or a particular seasonal range is promoted. Usually, four or five items are included in each cycle.

The press relations programme is divided into national and regional mailings. Releases for the national newspapers and women's magazines are less frequent than for the regional press, having to be sent out further in advance for the women's press, and sometimes being accompanied by samples. With 200 major shops in the UK, the regional campaign has mailings about every three weeks, and the co-operation of branch managers is sought, care being taken to avoid overlapping if the same newspaper covers more than one branch area. The managers actually despatch the releases to their own local papers, adding their own names and addresses as the source for further information. Samples are at the discretion of local managers.

A typical issue of the pictorial newsletter release describes a floral art paper flowers kit; Easter egg containers, novelties, egg cups and children's gifts; and the W. H. Smith annual Win-a-Pony Competition. This product publicity service is useful to women's page writers seeking new ideas, and being illustrated the release quickly shows exactly what the products look like. Thus the compromise is achieved between the needless expense of mailing out hundreds of prints every few weeks with the offer of a choice of stories and pictures. This seems to be a very sensible marketing oriented press relations exercise for a retailer with a national chain of stores and many lines but a planned programme of special purchases and promotions. Noticeably, the merchandise consists of items other than the books or branded goods publicized by publishers and manufacturers. In this way, the products help to sell the store, especially when they are own-name or bargain buys.

Thomson Holidays Ltd

A weekend in Moscow for only £29 is something very newsworthy, and this provided Thomson Holidays' PR Department with a vigorous and rewarding press relations exercise which proved to be a forerunner for a repeat performance later on for a weekend in Leningrad.

The addition to the Thomson Holidays Winter 1972/73 programme of a first-ever series of three- and four-night holidays in Moscow was announced at an 11 am press conference in a London hotel on Tuesday 22 February 1972. The conference had a Russian flavour, from tourist posters on the walls to a member of the THL staff dressed in a hired Cossack outfit who dispensed Russian wine provided by Intourist. The press were offered beef stroganoff as part of the buffet lunch.

All the national and many regional dailies carried the story on 23 February. The enthusiasm of the press, and its pleasure at being able to report something with real news content, is shown by some of the following opening paragraphs:

"Have you ever thought of a weekend in Moscow? Just to see what it is like? Next winter, Thomson Skytours are offering a winter weekend in Moscow—Thursday to Sunday—from £29" (*Evening News*, London).

"A winter weekend in Moscow—with a city tour and a trip to the Kremlin thrown in—for just £29 inclusive" (*Daily Record*, Glasgow).

"A winter weekend in Moscow is an exciting new holiday offer announced by Thomson Holidays in London today" (*Evening Chronicle*, Newcastle).

"British holidaymakers will be offered a new type of holiday this year—a winter week-end in Moscow for £29. The plans for the three-to-four-day holiday were yesterday announced by Thomson Holidays" (*Western Morning News*, Plymouth).

"A winter weekend in Moscow is the latest offer announced by Thomson Holidays in London today" (*Reading Evening Post*).

These selections are quoted—there were many more—because they demonstrate how valuable press coverage can be gained *when there is a good story*. Moreover, the main point of the story is summarized in the first paragraph, an object lesson to any news release writer.

Even the *Sunday Times* managed to print: "Russia may seem an unlikely destination for a short winter break. But Thomson Holidays are hoping to persuade people next winter that a long weekend in sub-zero Moscow from £29 can be just as rewarding as an out-of-season holiday in the Mediterranean...." The *Financial Times* was able to report a month later: "The £29 short tours to Moscow organised by Thomson Holidays for next winter have outsold initial supply. Thomson has now dropped plans to use Boeing 737 aircraft and is switching to much bigger 707s to handle the rush."

As a result of the initial announcement Lionel Steinberg, Thomson's director of external relations, was interviewed on BBC-TV's *Nationwide* on 23 February. The Moscow weekends for £29 story was featured in travel articles in all media throughout 1972.

In early March the *Evening Standard* offered one of the Moscow weekends as a prize in a contest headed *Your chance to win a free trip to Moscow*, and the *Watford Evening Echo* and the *Luton Evening Post* reserved fifty places on the 2 November flight and made exclusive but full-price offers to their readers.

The 5200 Moscow holidays were sold in just over a week. Britannia Airways negotiated with the Russians to operate the larger Boeing 707 aircraft instead of the 737. An extra 2360 seats went on sale on 27 March, backed only by trade press publicity in the form of a short news release. All seats were sold in four hours.

In early April, by arrangement with Intourist, Bryan Llewellyn (chief executive of Thomson Travel Holdings), with two marketing executives of Thomson Holidays, led a selected group of journalists to Moscow. The journalists were columnists Jilly Cooper (*Sunday Times*), Ann Sharpley (*Evening Standard*), Arthur Sandles (*Financial Times*), Victor Chapple (*The Sun*) and Tom Savage (BBC-TV).

See the Kremlin—and over-eat was the headline to Anne Sharpley's three-column piece in the *Evening Standard*, and her concluding remarks were: "So much to see, so much to ponder. As you stagger back on the aeroplane filled with vodka, caviar, anger, goodwill, liking, loathing, contradictory impressions, unanswered questions, admiration and relief to be going home, you'll never be quite the same again. And after a few hundred thousand more of our lot have been there neither, I think, will Russia."

Writing in the *FT*, Arthur Sandles (with a nice heading that summed it all up) had this to say: "The pretty English girl wandered off the Moscow pavement into the square. Immediately the Russian policeman stepped forward. Jaywalking is discouraged in Moscow. There was a brief debate and the policeman sternly demanded his two rouble fine (about £1). With a winsome smile the girl looked up and kissed him. In the confusion and amusement of onlookers the fine was forgotten."

In the *Sunday Times* Jilly Cooper wrote a somewhat hilarious article, commenting for instance on the customs delaration which said: "Do you have any unworked scrap, raw products of animal origin or slaughtered fowl", and an official handout which forbade the import of clichés. Commenting on the visit to Lenin's tomb, she wrote: "A soldier started making V-signs at me. I was about to make one back, when I realised he was telling us to walk in twos." Then, according to Jilly Cooper, their female guide announced in the car: "Inside the walls you will find high legislative organs, and in the centre the highest organs in Moscow. To the right is one of the Trade Union Houses which used to house the balls of the noblemen." But "Boris Gudonov itself was out of this world. The theatre is beautiful and the performances staggering." There was also a good deal of poignancy in Jilly Cooper's wealth of three-day observation, and she gave the impression in her bitter-sweet mixture of prejudice and enlightenment that in such a short visit an incredible amount could be learned about Russia and the Russians.

In July, Thomson Holidays staff in the UK and overseas were brought up-to-date on the Moscow developments with front and centre page articles in the staff newspaper, *Holiday Maker*, edited by former PR executive Pam Legate.

Throughout the year, THL's press office was swamped with requests for places on two projected press trips. During the summer, unsuccessful negotiations were held between BBC and ITV production teams and Intourist London and Moscow for permission to report the holidays on film. Due to the duration of these negotiations, final arrangements for the press trips were held over until October.

The first weekend flight to Moscow departed on 2 November. As a number of key journalists and THL staff would be in Vienna that weekend attending the annual ABTA convention, the press trip was held over until 16 November.

THL PR executive Doug Goodman flew to Moscow on the first press visit, with a photographer and Alan Brien of the *Sunday Times*; the last minute breakdown of BBC negotiations with the Russians, and the time required for obtaining visas, precluded the addition of extra journalists on that flight.

Following negotiations with a UK supplier of vodka, a vodka party was arranged for all clients travelling on the 2 November and 16 November flights. Following check-in at Luton Airport, clients were invited to sample chilled vodka in the airport restaurant.

TEN CASE STUDIES   243

As a result of the 2 November trip, articles and references to Thomson's Moscow holidays appeared in Alan Brien's *Sunday Times* column on three successive weeks, and on the *Sunday Times*' Compass travel page. Further coverage was obtained in the Luton area press and *UK Press Gazette*. Brien reported objectively, and more seriously than Jilly Cooper, while *UKPG* carried a picture, and reports also appeared in *Travel Trade Gazette* and *Travel News*. Ray Hankin wrote a long article in *Travel News* that closed with the words "For nothing breeds competition like success."

Photographs taken on this trip were sent by Doug Goodman to UK regional papers throughout the country and an unprecedented number of cuttings resulted, illustrating the news value of local folk visiting Red Square for the weekend!

The main press trip was made on 16 November. As a result of this trip a feature appeared in the *Daily Mail* on 20 November (with three follow-up letters in the correspondence column); Monty Modlyn and Shirley Green both broadcast on BBC Radio on 20 November; articles appeared in successive issues of both *Travel Trade Gazette* and *Travel News* (a total of five, from gossip items to two full-page features); and other articles were published in various regional newspapers.

Moreover, a number of enthusiastic features appeared under the bylines of journalists who took the holiday independently. Several journalists also took up cancellations on future departures. Press comment was consequently continuous.

The Moscow weekends produced a wealth of publicity not only for the new holiday but for Thomson Holidays generally. More than that, Thomsons welcomed the goodwill that these Russian holidays produced and on the 16 November flight this was transmitted by the clients to the journalists who travelled with them.

United Glass Ltd

This is a complete and compact promotional campaign which demonstrates the use of market research, trade press advertising, external house journal, direct mail, press relations and a trade exhibition with press relations support in the marketing of a new glass container to meet the increased demand for fruit juices. It is therefore in many respects a model campaign.

United Glass Ltd of Staines, Middlesex, with eight bottle factories, supplies one-third of the glass bottles and jars used in the UK. Despite the introduction of new packaging materials, the market for glass containers continues to grow on an average of about 3 per cent per annum. Although the company is a secondary supplier, it has a very positive market orientation. Its marketing department researches precisely what is happening in its customers' present markets and probes for new market potential.

At the beginning of 1972 it was decided to examine the market for natural fruit juices (generally known as breakfast juice, although 50 per cent of them are drunk at other times of the day) and Mass Observation were commissioned to carry out a consumer study.

When the results of the survey were nearing completion, the UG publicity department was asked to prepare a campaign with the objective of persuading UK bottlers that the market for fruit juices had reached an explosive point and that UG were the people who could give them all the information they needed on this market.

The market research department carried out desk research into the situation on the Continent where it is known that fruit juices are mainly packed in glass, and details of the American market were obtained from the Florida Citrus Commission through UG's associate company Owens-Illinois, Toledo. When all this information was collated, the following campaign was mounted:

In September 1972 whole-page advertisements headed *Who squeezed all the facts out of the fruit juice market*? were placed in *Packaging News, Packaging Review, Packaging, Soft Drink Trades Journal, Food Manufacturer* and other journals, centering on the consumer study which enquirers were offered at £25 a copy. The report covered purchasing habits, usage of containers, consumption of fruit juices, and attitudes. The report was also featured in the series of institutional advertisements that UG were running in the wine, spirit and brewery trade press.

The external company magazine *Packaging Forum* had a special issue devoted to the fruit juices report with articles on *World Demand Shoots Ahead, A Time For Change in the UK Market, What is the Consumer Profile?, Sources of Fruit Juices for UK Bottlers, What About Shipping and Processing*? and *Existing and "Pipeline" Legislation for Consumer Packs*. Three thousand copies were mailed to all customers in the foods and drinks markets plus advertising agencies and design companies. This was a piece of prime market education, and the magazine has already been mentioned in the chapter on external house magazines.

The "special report" edition of *Packaging Forum* was also sent to trade press editors, accompanied by a news release. The press relations effort also included a two-page exclusive feature article in *The Grocer* of 2 September. In the double-column measure introduction to the article was the following statement:

"One company concerned in the development is United Glass which has just completed a comprehensive research study of the fruit juice market in Britain as well as several other countries. The study includes consumer attitudes towards this kind of product as well as analysing the state of the market and its future potential.

"The findings will be published shortly and the full study is available at a cost of £25 per copy."

All this led up to the International Packaging Exhibition at Olympia, London, in October 1972 where fruit juice was featured as one of the displays on the UG stand.

Coinciding with the exhibition was the *Financial Times* Packaging Survey IV on 5 October in which John Buck's article *New Markets For Glass Containers* surveyed the scene and had this to say about United Glass:

"One indication of long-term confidence in the performance of the industry comes from the fact that Owens-Illinois, America's largest glass container concern, took up its option in June to increase its stake in United Glass to 50 per cent. . . .

"Other promising areas of development include the packaging of pet foods, fruit juices and pasteurised fruits and vegetables. Of these the fast-growing fruit juice market appears to offer the most exciting prospects in the immediate future.

"Until recently, most fruit juice was imported ready-packed in cans, and to a lesser extent in bottles and jars. But now, bottlers in the UK are beginning to import frozen concentrated juices in bulk for reconstitution and bottling in this country. Obviously this is creating a new and potentially large market for British-made bottles—so much so that United Glass have just issued an in-depth consumer research report on the fruit juice market in the UK."

The two brief excerpts from the detailed articles in *The Grocer* and the *FT* indicate what can be achieved with feature articles, the first being supplied by UG and the second being based on information gleaned from UG and other sources. Both fit nicely into this two months campaign.

The impact of this carefully planned and executed campaign is shown by the number of companies who contacted UG by letter or telephone. A first copy or additional copies of the "special report" company magazine were requested by 34 companies, and during the following two months 38 copies of the consumer study were purchased at the price of £25. New product launching of a secondary product to manufacturers who have to plan their own production and marketing strategies is a lengthy business, so this initial response was most satisfying.

Appendix I

Bibliography

(in addition to books listed at the end of Chapter 3 and mentioned on page 77)

Books

BOLT, GORDON J., *Communicating with EEC Markets*, Kegan Page, London, 1973.
BOLT, GORDON J, *Marketing in the EEC*, Kegan Page, London, 1973.
CHAPMAN, R. W., *Marketing Today*, 2nd ed., Intertext, London, 1973.
CRISFORD, JOHN N., *Public Relations Advances*, Business Books, London, 1973.
DESCHAMPSNEUFS, H., *Marketing Overseas*, Pergamon Press, Oxford, 1967.
FISHER, LAWRENCE, *Industrial Marketing*, Business Books, London, 1969.
HART, NORMAN, *Industrial Publicity*, Cassell/ABP, London, 1973.
KOTLER, PHILIP, *Marketing Management*, Prentice Hall, Englewood Cliffs, N.J., USA, 1972.
JENKINS, JOHN R. G., *Marketing and Customer Behaviour*, Pergamon Press, Oxford, 1972.
JEFKINS, FRANK, *Dictionary of Marketing and Communication*, Intertext, London, 1973.
JEFKINS, FRANK, *Press Relations Practice*, Intertext, London, 1968.
JEFKINS, FRANK, *Planned Public Relations*, Intertext, London, 1969.
LOWNDES, DOUGLAS, *Marketing and the Uses of Advertising*, Pergamon Press, Oxford, 1969.
MAY, LESLIE H. (Ed.), *Printing Reproduction Pocket Pal*, Advertising Agency Production Association, London, 1969.

RODGER, LESLIE W. (Ed.), *Marketing Concepts and Strategies in the Next Decade*, Cassell/ABP, London, 1973.
WATTS, REGINALD, *Reaching The Consumer*, Business Books, 1970.
WILLS, GORDON, *Marketing Through Research*, Pergamon Press, Oxford, 1967.

UK Journals

Adweek, 110, Fleet Street, London EC4 (Weekly).
Campaign, Gillow House, 5 Winsley Street, London W1A 2HG.
Marketing. Gillow House, 5 Winsley Street, London W1A 2HG.
Marketing Forum, Institute of Marketing, Moor Hall, Cookham, Berks.
Marketing and Advertising News, Competition House, Telford Way, Kettering, Northants.
Public Relations, Institute of Public Relations, 1 Great James Street, London WC1.
UK Press Gazette, 2–3 Salisbury Court, Fleet Street, London EC4Y 8AB.

Appendix II

Professional and Vocational Examining Bodies

THE following run examinations in the UK and invigilation can usually be arranged for students who wish to sit for the examinations. The regulations and syllabus should be obtained before enrolling for a course of study at a college or correspondence school.

British Association of Industrial Editors, 2a Elm Bank Gardens, Barnes, London SW13 (House journal editing).
Communication Advertising and Marketing Education Foundation, 1, Bell Yard, London WC2A 2JX (incorporating the examinations of the AA, IPA and IPR for the CAM Certificate and CAM Diploma).
Institute of Marketing, Moor Hall, Cookham, Berks. (Certificate and Diploma examinations in Marketing).
Institute of Public Relations, 1 Great James Street, London WC1N 3DA (IPR Course Certificate for those not qualified to take the CAM exam in PR).
London Chamber of Commerce and Industry, Commercial Education Scheme, Marlowe House, 109 Station Road, Sidcup, Kent, DA15 7BJ (Higher Certificate in Advertising, Marketing and Salesmanship).

Appendix III

The Institute of Public Relations Code of Professional Conduct

1. *Standards of Professional Conduct*

A member, in the conduct of his professional activities, shall respect the public interest and the dignity of the individual. It is his personal responsibility at all times to deal fairly and honestly with his client or employer, past or present, with his fellow members, with the media of communication and with the public.

2. *Dissemination of Information*

A member shall not knowingly or recklessly disseminate false or misleading information, and shall use proper care to avoid doing so inadvertently. He has a positive duty to maintain integrity and accuracy.

3. *Media of Communication*

A member shall not engage in any practice which tends to corrupt the integrity of the media of communication.

4. *Undisclosed Interests*

A member shall not be a party to any activity which deliberately seeks to dissemble or mislead by promoting a disguised or undisclosed interest whilst appearing to further another. It is his duty to ensure that the actual interest of any organization with which he may be professionally concerned is adequately declared.

5. Confidential Information

A member shall not disclose (except upon the order of a court of competent jurisdiction) or make use of information given or obtained in confidence from his employer or client, past or present, for personal gain or otherwise, without express consent.

6. Conflict of Interests

A member shall not represent conflicting or competing interests without the express consent of the parties concerned after full disclosure of the facts.

7. Sources of Payment

A member, in the course of his professional services to his employer or client, shall not accept payment either in cash or kind in connection with those services from any other source without the express consent of his employer or client.

8. Disclosure of Financial Interests

A member having a financial interest in an organization shall not recommend the use of that organization, nor make use of its services on behalf of his client or employer, without declaring his interest.

9. Payment Contingent upon Achievements

A member shall not negotiate or agree terms with a prospective employer or client on the basis of payment contingent upon specific future public relations achievements.

10. Supplanting Another Member

A member seeking employment or new business by direct and individual approach to a potential employer or client shall take all reasonable steps to ascertain whether that employment or business is already carried out by another member. If so, it shall be his duty to advise the other member in advance of any approach he proposes to make to the employer or client concerned. (Nothing in this clause shall be taken as inhibiting a member from the general advertisement of his services.)

11. *Rewards to Holders of Public Office*

A member shall not, with intent to further his interests (or those of his client or employer), offer or give any reward to a person holding public office if such action is inconsistent with the public interest.

12. *Employment of Members of Parliament*

A member who employs a Member of Parliament, of either House, in connection with Parliamentary matters, whether in a consultative or executive capacity, shall disclose this fact, and also the object of the employment to the General Secretary of the Institute, who shall enter it in a register kept for the purpose. A member of the Institute who is himself a Member of Parliament shall be directly responsible for disclosing or causing to be disclosed to the General Secretary any such information as may relate to himself. (The register referred to in this clause shall be open to public inspection at the offices of the Institute during office hours.)

13. *Injury to Other Members*

A member shall not maliciously injure the professional reputation or practice of another member.

14. *Instruction of Others*

A member who knowingly causes or permits another person or organization to act in a manner inconsistent with this Code or is party to such action shall himself be deemed to be in breach of it.

15. *Reputation of the Profession*

A member shall not conduct himself in any manner detrimental to the reputation of the Institute or the profession of public relations.

16. *Upholding the Code*

A member shall uphold this Code, shall co-operate with fellow members in so doing and in enforcing decisions on any matter arising from its application. If a member has reason to believe that another member has been engaged in practices which may be in breach of this Code, it shall be his duty to inform the Institute. It is the duty of all members to assist the Institute to implement this code, and the Institute will support any member so doing.

17.

A member shall, when acting for a client or employer who belongs to a profession, respect the code of ethics of that other profession and shall not knowingly be party to any breach of such a code.

Index

Acts of Parliament
  Education Act, 1870 47
  Fair Trading Act, 1973 10
  Industrial Relations Act, 1972 42
  Television Act, 1955 101
  Trade Descriptions Act, 1968–72 10, 12, 31
Ades, Douglas 223–5
Advertisement
  manager 73
  revenue 60
Advertiser's Annual 47, 65, 192
Advertising 4, 6, 8, 15, 18, 21, 25, 26, 30–32, 41, 74, 86–87, 96, 101, 103, 109, 151, 198, 201, 202, 206, 222, 243, 244, 249
  agencies 4, 20, 30, 33, 68, 101, 179, 198, 200, 215
  below-the-line 151
  radio 94, 95, 100, 103
  sports arena 109
  television 94, 95, 96, 100, 101, 151, 207
Advertising Association vi, 20, 249
Advertising Standards Authority 32
Adweek 57, 248
Aer-Lingus-Irish 225
African Development 58
After-sales service 38–40
Air ferry 220–2
Airlines 20, 107, 166, 220–2, 225
Air time 96, 101, 123
Alcoholics Anonymous 20
Alexandra Overalls Manufacturing Ltd. 229
Algerian Pipeline 115, 118
All India Radio/TV 94, 95–96
Anglo-Japanese links 140
Anker-Petersen, K.G. 236
Anne, Princess 4, 223
Annigoni 195

Annual general meetings, reports 114, 116, 117, 190–1
Anook of the North 110
Anti-jack-knife device 230–3
Anti-smoking campaign, smoking ban 150, 207
Anti-theft car lock 97
Appointment, promotion stories 82–83
Archers, The 102
Articles, exclusive signed feature 85, 88, 203, 235
  associated advertising 86–87
  cost of producing 87
  features, supplements 86, 245
  how to obtain publication 86
  syndicated 88
  value of 87–88
Articulated lorries 230–3
Arup Designers 150
Aspro 22
Asset stripping 205
Association of British Travel Agents 242
Association of Specialized Film Producers 131
Audi NSU 29
Australia 49, 62, 65, 68, 106, 108, 114, 134, 140, 146, 238
Automobile Association 20

Baltimore Sun 48
Bangladesh 95–96
Banks, banking 114, 115, 120–1, 122, 123, 128, 137, 147, 148, 154, 166, 171, 184, 190, 223–5, 233–4
Bankside Globe Theatre 147
Barker, Ronnie 105
Barnum and Bailey's circus 199
Basle Tourist Office 221
Bata Shoe Company 38

INDEX

Bateman, Peter 235
BBC Handbook 97, 99
BBDO 20
BEA 107
Beanstalk 12
Beaver, Sir Hugh 137
Beer, brewers 18, 20, 22, 100, 133, 142, 148, 169
Belgium 59, 63, 155, 166, 176, 220
Below-the-line advertising 151
Bernays, Ernest 33
Better Business Bureau 30
Bicycle 19
Bild Zeitung 48, 62
Birth control 126
Bisto 34
Blanket, bulk mailing 53, 55
Blythe, Chay 141
BOC 20
BOCM 20
Bolt, Gordon 211, 247
Bookstall sales 56
Boots 20
Bottles
  glass 243–6
  non-returnable 24, 206
Bovis Fee Construction 128, 150
Bowden, Lord 37
BP 3, 115, 123, 128, 140, 158, 160
Brainwashing 201
Brand leader 26
Brand loyalty 32–5
Brand manager 32
Branding, brand names 18, 37, 69, 73, 144
Brandt, Willy 104
Brasso 20
Breakfast cereals 32
Bribery 30, 33, 61, 68, 183, 250, 252
Brien, Alan 243
British Air Ferries 220–2
British Airways 107, 166
British Association of Industrial Editors 164, 249
  House Journals '73 Survey 164–5
British Broadcasting Corporation 94, 108, 146, 241
  Alexandra Palace 159
  External Services 96, 97
  50th Anniversary 96
  Handbook 97, 99
British Code of Advertising Practice 30, 101
British Export Marketing Centre, Tokyo vii
British Federation of Master Printers 196
British Industrial & Scientific Film Association, Festival 121, 131
British Leyland 28, 42, 177, 232
British Oxygen 20, 31
British Printing Industries Federation 196
British publications overseas 63–64
British Rate and Data 50, 52, 65, 77
British Ratin Co Ltd 20, 236
British Safety Council 231, 232
Brother typewriter 25
Brooke Bond Oxo 25
  PG Tips 111, 112–13
Brown, Lord George 104
Brown Constructors, John 115, 118
Buck, John 245
Buffer stocks 54
Buitoni 34
Burglar alarms 90
Burnley Building Society 149
Bush 38

CAM Certificate, Diploma 7, 212
CAM Education Foundation 37, 249
CAM Society 72
Campaign 57, 248
Campbell, Donald 134
Canada 49, 59, 65, 68, 114, 128, 142, 143, 144, 145, 147, 148, 198
Candida 50
Capital letters 69, 73
CAP Committee 31
Capitol Radio 94
Caption story, extended 74
Caridia, Mike 221–2
Car Test, International 221
Carry-home packs 22
Casale, Mike 220, 222
Celebrity marketing 203
Central Film Library 131, 235, 236
Central heating 38, 42, 154

INDEX   257

Central Office of Information   89, 96, 98–99, 121, 124, 132, 235, 236, 238
Ceylon Tea Centre   157
Challenge, The   235–6
Chaplin, Charlie   105
Chapman, R. W.   247
Chataway, Christopher   100
Chemical Bank   115, 223–5
Chemicals   64, 114, 122
Cherry picker   32
Chichester Ltd, Francis   137
Children's competitions, exhibitions   22
China   vii, 45, 108, 177
Chittock, John   81, 131
Chopping, David   232
Chrysler 180, 29
Churchill, Sir Winston   105, 198
Churchman cigars   117
CIE   225
Cigarettes   26, 109, 133, 137, 141–8
Cinema, silent   105
Circulation   33, 46, 54, 60–61, 62, 63, 68, 176
    area   49, 53–55
    controlled   56, 63–64
Circus   viii, 199
Citroen GS   220, 225–8
City editor, page   36–37
Civil engineering   115, 118, 160, 171, 172
Clichés   67, 76, 118
Clocks, alarm   40
Close-up toothpaste   25
Closed circuit TV   94, 128
Closing Circle, The   24
Coca-Cola   4, 95
Cockroaches   118, 236
Codes of ethics   250–3
Cognitive dissonance   201
Collins, Mary   73
Colmer, Mike   80
Colour magazines, supplements, weekend   18, 50, 145, 194, 235
Colours, product   22–23
Comet Warehouses   26
Commoner, Barry   24
Common Market, EEC   33, 37, 45, 58, 60, 96, 126, 128, 140, 175–6, 192, 211–12

Communicating with EEC Markets   211, 247
Community Business Resources Loan Unit   224
Community relations   148–9
Community Thing Drug Program   224
Comparisons   30
Complaints   10–11, 16, 28
Computers   19, 20, 42, 112, 181, 186
Confectionery   10, 22
Conferences   130, 179–86
    car parking   181
    date   182
    guest list   180
    hospitality   182–4
    programme   183
    residential courses   181
    time   182
    venue   181
Confidence   40
Conversation, conservationists   24, 115, 205, 206
Conservation Year   115
Conservative Government, Party   22, 207
Consumer choice   16
    sovereignty   16
    panel   17
Consumerism   9, 24, 205
Container Services and Equipment Exhibition, International   232
Containers, glass   243–6
Contests   22, 23, 160
Contacts, press   4, 51, 68, 91
Contra-suggestion   31, 33
Controlled circulation   56, 63–64
Cook's, Thomas   198
Cooper, Jilly   241
Cooper, McDougall   114
Copy date   49, 51
Copywriters, copywriting   21, 77
Corbett, Ronnie   105
Cornwell, Dr. P. B.   237
Corporate advertising   198
    identification   198
    image   19, 30, 36–38
    public relations   36–38, 115, 198, 202
Corona soft drinks   23
Coronation Street   106

258 INDEX

Corporation for Public Broadcasting, USA 101
Cosmopolitan 50
Coventry Cathedral 115, 124, 125
Crane Ltd 38
Craven Foundation 148
Crisford, John 247
Crosse & Blackwell Maggi Soups 35
 alphabetti spaghetti 36
Crossroads 106
Cruises 12, 88, 122, 123
Cuprinol 19
Customer relations 11, 23, 24, 27–29, 32, 137
Cutlip, Professor S. M. 67

Daf 20, 42, 108
Daily Express 36, 46, 56, 73, 77
Daily Mail 47, 56, 243
Daily Mirror 46, 50, 56, 82
Daily Telegraph 36, 46, 50, 56, 234, 235
Daily Times (Lagos) 48, 61, 62, 63
Danish Bacon/Cheese Boards 157
Datsun 23, 39, 141, 177
David, Fred 231–2
Dealer relations 9, 11–12, 23, 35, 41, 108, 129–30, 168
Definitions
 advertising 4
 documentary film 110
 metamarketing 197, 198–9, 202
 news 72
 propaganda 198
 public relations 8, 15, 31, 33
 publics 215
Denigration 30
Denmark 107, 131, 157, 236
Dennis & Robinson 25, 185
Deodorant 20, 27
Deschampsneufs, H. 247
Detergents 20
Dictionary of Marketing and Communication 77, 199, 247
Discount houses, firms, price lists 26, 40
Disinfestation Ltd 20, 236
Disneyland 158

Distribution
 adequate 25, 72
 channels of 24–26
 inadequate 25, 54
 of newspapers, magazines 49, 55–58
Do-it-yourself products 11, 167, 189–90
Domestic appliances 28, 184
Double pricing 22
Driver Behaviour Congress, International 207
Drug addiction 115, 123, 224–5
Du Maurier Council for the Performing Arts 147
Du Pont polyester 229
Dunn & Co 23
Dunn, Elizabeth 17, 30, 74
Dutch Dairy Bureau 157

Early adopters 29
Easiclene 20
Edelman, Daniel J. 135
Eden, Sir John 100
Editorial policy 49–51
Edsel car 23
Education Act, 1870 47
Egypt, Arab Republic of 59, 115
EIBIS 79, 89, 124
Eidophor screen 130
Electricity Board
 showrooms 25, 28
 undertakings 122
Electronic Product News 63, 176
Electronic products 18, 20, 23, 64, 119, 142, 190
Electron's Tale, The 119
Elsevier, IPC Europe BV 63
Emballages 64
EMI Special Film Unit 128
 Music For Pleasure 146
"Envelope, The" 61
European air bus 123
Evening Echo, Watford 232, 241
Evening News 75, 221, 240
Evening Standard 198, 221, 241
Evoluon Exhibition 22
Examining bodies 7, 15, 37, 69, 72, 75, 162, 164, 203, 204, 212, 249

Exchange relation 200
Exhibition practice
  attendance at 155, 161
  BBC External Services 97
  buses 154
  date 162
  in-store 157
  international, press links 64
  invitations to 161, 162
  models 156, 158
  mobile 154
  motorized vehicle 154
  mutual display 156
  outdoor 160
  overseas trade fairs 98
  permanent 158–9
  portable 155–6
  press kits 90–92, 152, 191
  press officers, offices 74–75, 92–93, 153
  PR support for 153
  publicity for 153
  ship 155
  sponsored 139
  time of day 163
  trade centres vii, 157–60
  train 154–5
  VCR 131
  venue 157–160
  window 156
Exhibitions (named)
  British Weeks 157
  Business Equipment 139
  Commercial Motor Show 139, 231–2
  Container Services & Equipment, International 232
  Do-it-Yourself 139
  Evoluon (Eindhoven) 22, 159–60
  French Fortnights 157
  Hotelympia 18, 29, 139
  IBA Television Gallery 159
  Ideal Home 139
  Japan Floating Fair 155
  Joint Ventures 98, 152
  Motor Show 138, 222
  Packaging, International 245
Exploitation of the Industrial Sponsored Film 131
Exporters and Broadcasting 97

Export PR 58–66, 97–99, 121, 127, 131, 172, 175–8
External affairs 205

Fair Trading Act, 1973 10
Farmer, Robert 236
Farrington, A. C. 238
Fashion goods 23
Favours 68
Feedback 16, 205, 219
Feel Free deodorant 27, 145
Fees, consultancy 72, 213–14
Ferry services 11, 154, 155, 176, 220–2
Fiat 20
Field sales force 28
Fifth wheel dampener 231–2
Fillers 73
Film Producers Guild 122, 131
Films
  actors 118–9, 124
  advertising 110, 111
  animation 119
  audiences 117, 120–2
  awards 115, 118, 121, 124, 148, 185, 236
  bookings 117
  cartoon 119
  characteristics 111–2
  charity 116, 148
  colour 111, 117, 128
  commentator 118–19, 119, 123
  cost 112, 125
  credits 110
  critics 124, 131
  definition 110
  distribution 110, 112, 120–4, 132
  documentary / industrial / sponsored 95, 102, 107–8, 110–32, 148, 154, 158, 217, 235–8
  dubbing 112, 119, 123
  Dutch 112
  festivals 121, 148
  Financial Times 108, 131
  free loan 120, 123, 131
  Grierson, John 110
  Indian 177
  information about 131
  international appeal, use 112, 125–7

INDEX

Films—*cont.*
  joint production 108, 112
  length 117
  libraries 117, 120, 123, 131–2, 235, 236
  library shots 101, 107, 108, 121
  life of 111
  locations 118
  mime 112, 125
  mobile cinema shows 122, 126
  music 119
  on TV 97
  playback 112
  première 124
  prerecorded 129
  prints 123
  production 110, 117–20
  public cinema 116
  purpose 110, 111–17, 179, 182–4
  roadshows 122, 126
  scriptwriter 118
  silent 104, 105, 112
  sound 119
  stills 118, 124
  stock 119
  stop action 119
  sub-titling 125
  synopsis leaflets 121, 124
  test cards 108, 123
  users of 114–15, 118, 119, 123
  Westerns 107
Films For Industry 131
Finance in Europe 128
Financial Times 36, 46, 55, 57, 63, 82, 108, 234, 240, 241
  Architectural Award 150
  Clipper yacht race 63, 145–6
  Industrial Photography Awards 80
  industrial film reviews 131, 151
  marketing scene 57
  packaging survey 245
  technical page 77
Fish fingers 20, 21
Fleet Street 4, 47, 61, 68, 69, 80
Floor covering, tile 29, 30
Florida Citrus Commission 244
Food products 29, 34, 35–36, 37, 122, 149, 190, 243–6
Footwear 10–11, 146

Ford Cortina 23
Ford Motor Company 20, 23, 94, 129
Fourth estate 45
France, French 33, 39, 48, 60, 61, 64, 65, 95, 96, 140, 143, 155, 158, 178, 189, 220, 226–8
Franchiser 168–9
Frankfurter Allgemeine Zeitung 48, 62
Fraser, Sir Hugh vii–viii, 151
Free advertisement, publicity, puff vii, 4, 73, 108
Free gifts 23, 25
  on TV 108
Free sheet 56, 57–58
Freelance writer 86
Frequency of publication 49, 51
Friends of the Earth 24, 201
Frost, David 106
Fruit juices 244–6
Fumigation Services Ltd 20
Furniture polish 26

Garden products 114, 122, 149, 154, 160, 189–90
Gardener's Question Time 102
Garment rental 228–30
Gas fire 19
Gas showroom 28
Gas undertaking 122
Geddes, Lord 125
Germany, German 10, 39, 48, 60, 61, 63, 95, 96, 140, 145, 155, 157, 158, 176, 181
Ghana vii, 37, 60
Gibbs dentifrice 116
Gift catalogues 26
Gift coupons 26
Gift houses 26
Gillette Company, The 6, 16, 20, 27, 134–5, 145
  products 135
  sponsorships 134–5, 145
Giuseppina 123
Glossies 52, 194
Golden Wonder potato crisps 34
Goodman, Douglas 242, 243
Grapevine 6
Green, Benny 4

Green, Shirley   243
Greene, Nancy   143
Grierson, John   110
Grocer, The   246
Grub Street   47
Guarantee   38
Guarantee card   17
Guardian, The   17, 30, 46, 62, 74, 238
  Young Businessman of the Year   vii, 151
Guernsey, Guernsey tomatoes   103
Guild Sound & Vision Ltd   122, 232, 235
Guinness   18, 20, 100, 137, 158, 177

Halo effect   25, 130, 135
Hankin, Ray   243
Hare, Alan   145
Harlem   223–5
Harmonizing   37
Harrods   viii, 25
Hart, Norman   247
Hartogh Relations Publiques   174
Harvey's sherry   25
Hawaii Five-O   107
Hayes and Sons, James   14, 166, 228–30
Haywards pickles   25
Heaphy, Bernard   128
Heath, Edward   101, 104, 201
Heijn, Albert   138
Heineken   169
Heinz beans   25
Hendon aerodrome   231
Hennessy, James Pope   148
Herculon   21
Nerio-Watt University   205
Hickin, Dr. N. E.   235
Hidden Persuaders, The   33, 170
Hi-fi equipment   18, 103, 108
Hillary, Sir Edmund   271
Hitler, Adolf   105
Holland, Dutch   8, 22, 42, 60, 62, 63, 64, 127, 138, 145, 149, 155, 157, 158, 159–60, 169, 174, 176, 181, 188, 199
Hollis Press & Public Relations Annual   68, 77, 90
Hollywood   197

Home delivery   56
Hong Kong   18, 64, 107
Hope, Fred   231–3
  anti-jack-knife device   16, 230–3
  Technical Developments Ltd.   231–2
Horse Trials Championship of Great Britain   233–4
Hosting   4
Hotelympia   18, 29
House for Sale   235
House journal
  external   56, 61, 164–78, 217, 229–30, 243–5
  internal   164, 242
  prestige   113
  promotional   171
House journal publishers:
  American Express   166
  British Airways   166
  British Railway Hotels   166
  Brown-Boveri   172
  Duckhams Oils   166
  Dr. Pepper   169
  Foyles   166
  GEC   172, 174
  Gibbons, Stanley   166
  Hayes, James   166
  ICI   172, 173, 175
  Ingersoll-Rand   168
  International Nickel   173, 175
  Heineken   169
  Kodak   166, 169–70
  National & Vulcan Insurance   174
  Pan-American Airways   166
  Phonogram   167
  Roberts Construction   171
  Sabena   166
  Sheraton Heathrow   166
  Smit Internationale   174
  Standard Bank   166
  Swissair   166
  Tandberg   169
  Toyota   166
  Travelers Insurance   168
  United Glass   166–7, 170, 244–5
House of Fraser   viii, 151
House style   31, 187
Housing Improvement Grant Scheme   237

262 INDEX

Hoveringham Gravels 207, 232
Howard, Elizabeth Jane 148
HP Sauce 34
Hungary 65
Hutchinson-Benham 237-8
Hygena 20
Hypermarkets 26

IBM 19, 20, 112, 181
ICI 31, 128
  Holland BV 188
  Pathfinders 111
  Plastics Today 172, 173, 175, 176
Image 8-9, 10, 211
  corporate 19, 31, 214
  politicians 104
  product 104
  study 214
Imballagio 64
Independent Broadcasting Authority 94, 95, 99-100
  Television Gallery 159
India, Indian vii, 48-9, 60, 62, 94, 95-96, 97, 103, 107, 108, 126, 127, 157, 176, 177, 238
Indian Engineering Export Promotion Council 157
Indian Tea Centre 157
Induction courses 123
Industrial Relations Act, 1972 42
Industrial trade unionism 30
Industrial Verpakken 64
Insecta Laboratories 20
Institute of Directors 130
Institute of Marketing 37, 249
Institute of Practitioners in Advertising 31, 73, 198, 249
Institute of Public Relations 15, 69, 72, 75, 162, 203, 204, 249
  Code of Professional Conduct 162, 250-3
  Course Certificate 249
  Register of MPs 252
Insurance 144, 168, 178, 184
Interests
  conflicting 251
  financial 251
  undisclosed 250

International Business Press Associates 64, 89
Interracial Council for Business Opportunity and Capital Formation 224
Intourist 240, 241, 242
Intruders, The 118, 236
Invitations to press events 92
IPC 63-64, 139, 175
Irish Hotels Federation 225
Irish Republic 94, 95, 96, 157, 158, 181, 225, 228
  Convention Bureau of 181, 228
Irish Tourist Board 225-8
Irish Transport and General Workers Union 225-6
Israel 59, 64
Italy 33, 45, 64, 65, 127, 145, 157, 166, 176, 198, 229

Jack-knifing 230-3
Jam 22, 122
Japan, Japanese vii, 18, 23, 25, 39, 48, 64, 96, 108, 140, 143, 155, 166, 173, 176, 177, 220-2
Japan Industry Floating Fair Association 155
Japan Trade Centre 157
Jenkins, John R. G. 247
JICNARS 55
Job numbers 213
Journalists 23, 45-46, 47, 48-49, 54, 61, 67, 69, 91

Kennedy, John 104
Kent, Duke of vii
Kenya 94, 95, 108
Keukenhof Gardens 149
KLM Royal Dutch Airlines 20
Kipling, Mr 20
Kitchen furniture 20, 25, 154, 185
Klopman International 166, 229
Knocking copy 30
Koradin-Verlag 64
Kotler, Philip 197-204, 207, 247

Labour Government, Party 207

INDEX

Lagos University
  Institute of Mass Communications 38
Lagos bus service 45
Laing, John 112, 115, 124, 125
Lake, Michael 238
Languages, foreign 58–60, 62, 63, 64, 96, 112, 125, 137, 140, 172–4, 176, 190
Legate, Pam 242
Library
  film 117
  music 119
  shots 101, 107, 108, 121
Librium 19
Life cycle, product 17, 18–19, 23
Life Insurance Advertisers' Association (USA) 144
Lineage 60–61
Lippincott & Marguilles 14, 198
Livery, vehicle 31, 232
Llewellyn, Bryan 241
Lloyds 158
London, Port of 114, 158, 199
London Chamber of Commerce and Industry, Commercial Education 249
London Hospital 29
London Philharmonic Orchestra 146
London Symphony Orchestra 146
Los Angeles Times 48, 238
Loss leader 25
Lost literacy 60, 62
Lowndes, Douglas 247
Lucy, Geoffrey 97
Lyon Group Ltd 164
Lyons Group, J 166, 228

Maggi soups 35
Mailings, mailing lists 50, 51, 52, 54, 67, 70–71, 72, 78–79, 99, 245
Malaysia vii, 49, 60, 126
Management communication 205
Management Today 235
Manchester, University of, Institute of Science and Technology 37
MAP Consultancy 220
Marcus, Norman 204–7

Margarine 25, 30
Market education 29–30
Market research 21, 22, 23, 214, 244
Market segment 21, 23
Marketing 55, 57, 69, 71, 248
Marketing
  applied to PR 70–79
  horizontal 18
  mix 15–42
  vertical 18
Marketing and Advertising News 131, 248
Marketing Concepts and Strategies in the Next Decade 205
Marketing Forum 27, 55, 57, 248
Marketing Management 197
Marks and Spencer 11, 20
Mass Observation 244
Maximizing cost effectiveness 211
Maximizing press coverage 198
Maximizing profits 201, 205
May, Leslie H. 247
Mazda 39, 177
Media
  cinema newsreel 98, 110
  documentary, industrial, sponsored films 95, 102, 107–8, 110–32, 148, 154, 158, 217, 235–8
  electronic 94–109, 110–32
  evaluation of 216–7
  exhibitions *see* Exhibitions
  house journals 54, 61, 113, 164–78, 217, 229–30, 243–5
  posters 108, 147, 189, 196
  press *see* Press
  printed literature 187–96, 235–7
  radio
    local BBC 72, 99
    commercial ILR 94, 96, 100, 101, 103
  television *see* Television
Melbourne Age 49
Melinex polyester film 188
Member of Parliament, employment of 252
Menswear 18
Mepham, Mike 220–6
Meraklon 21
Mercedes-Benz 10

INDEX

Merchandising 5, 23, 32–36, 135
Metamarketing 197–207
Metropolitan Police 114, 160
Mexico 66, 109
Midland Bank 114, 120–1, 123, 148, 223, 233–4
Midland Bank Executive and Trustee Company 120–1, 186
Milk bottles 22
Mississippi showboats 199
Mobil oil 36, 137
Mobile cinemas, shows 122, 126
Modlyn, Monty 243
Monckton, Lord 233
Monsanto Chemicals 31
Montreal Gazette 49
Morris Marina 39
Moscow 239–43
Motor cars 10, 20, 23, 25, 28, 29, 38–39, 148, 166, 178, 184 190, 221–2, 225–8
Motor Transport 232
Motoring and the Motorist 102
Mullard 119
Munich Olympics 95, 144, 234
Murphy Chemicals 114
Murphy, James P. 225
Music, library 119
Myer, Kenneth 131

McDonald Store 224
McLuhan, Marshall 105
McWhirter, Norris and Ross 137

Nabarro, Sir Gerald 105
NABS 116
Nader, Ralph 10, 28, 201, 231
Name plugging 133, 142, 144
Naming 19–21, 31
Narcotics 113, 115, 123, 224–5
National Coal Board 206
National Geographic 57
Nationwide 241
NatWest 128
Necchi sewing machines 16–17, 23, 25, 54, 108, 127
Nestlé 35

Neue Verpacking 64
New Internationalist 58
New York 223–4
New York Herald Tribune 143
New York Times 48, 223
New Zealand Meat Producers Board 96
News 72–73, 97, 98–99, 101, 102–3, 105–6, 124, 153, 240
News agencies 72, 74
News at Ten 100, 159
Newsline 99
Newspaper Press Directory 47, 50, 55, 65, 71, 77, 79
Newsreel 98, 110
News release
 bad 67, 69–70
 blanket mailing 53, 55
 criteria 68, 206
 four kinds 74
 length 74
 mailing 50, 51, 52–54
 opening paragraph 240
 overseas 59
 presentation 69, 73
 processing 78–79
 product publicity viii, 211, 233
 rejection 49, 69, 73
 rejection, twelve reasons for 70–79
 seven point formula 76
 subject of 69, 74–75, 240
 superfluity of 78
 timing of 71
News value 33, 240
Nigeria vii, 25, 37–38, 45, 48, 58, 60, 61, 63, 94, 95, 123, 126, 127, 134, 146, 176, 177, 181
Nigerian Broadcasting Corporation 94, 95
Nixon, Richard 104
Non-business products 197, 203, 207
Non-returnable bottles 206
No Place Like Home 237
Norden, Denis 117
Northern Ireland 226–7
Northwestern University 197
Norway 169
Nudes 188
Nuffield Trust 113

INDEX 265

Observer, The 4, 29
Obsolescence, induced 17
Oil rig model 160
Olympics
  Mexican 109
  Munich 95, 144, 234
Omega 109
Omo 20
Opel 30
Open ended questions 17
Open University 105–7, 130
Opinion leaders 173, 215
Opinion research 211
Oughton, Hubert 31
Over-exposure 201
Overseas press directories 50, 65–66
Owens-Illinois Company 244–5
Oxo 19

P & O 88, 123, 124
Pacifica Foundation 101
Pack 64
Package tour operator 12, 32, 239–43
Packaging 23–24, 64, 243–5
Packaging Engineering 64
Packaging Exhibition, International 245
Packaging Forum 245
Packaging in Britain 24
Packard, Vance 33
Paint 11, 22–23
Pakistan 60, 96
Palmer, Arnold 143
Pan-American Airways 107, 166, 187
Payment
  by results 241
  sources of 72, 213–14
  methods of 72, 213–14
Pepper, Dr 20
Personnel management 42
Persuasion 33, 201–2
Pest control 20, 157–8, 184, 235–8
Petrol 36
Petters engines 118, 148
Peyton Place 106, 233
Pharmaceuticals 19, 40–41, 149, 202
Philips 18, 22, 128, 129, 149, 159–60, 167

M.M.P.—K

Pictures, photographs
  Awards, *FT* Industrial Photography 131, 151
  captions 84–85, 152
  colour 83
  composition 83
  cropping 84
  dolly girls, cheesecake 80–81
  editors 80
  glazed, glossy, matt prints 84
  progress 115
  size of prints 84
  size of subject 84
  specialist photographers 81
  10 common faults 81–82
  10 rules for PR pictures 83–84
  working with the photographer 83
  writing captions 85
Piggybacking 214
Pirelli 187–8
Planned Public Relations 216, 247
Plans board 30
Plastic containers 24
Player, Gary 143
Player, John & Sons 109, 133, 141, 143, 147
BAIE House Journals 73 Survey 164
Bankside Globe 147
Horizon factory project 150
Information Bureau 144–5
Plumbs chair covers 25
PM Reports 102
Point-of-sale 12
Polaroid (UK) Ltd 220–2
Police
  Metropolitan 114
  San Francisco 115
Political news 68
Politicians 104, 198, 200–1, 253
Pollution 24, 115, 205, 206
Portugal, Portuguese 60
Post Office films 116
Post Office landline 128
Postal subscription sales 56–57
Potterton 38
Powell, Enoch 105
PR Planner 50, 65, 71, 77, 79
PRADS 78–79, 90

266 INDEX

Pravda 96
Premium offers 26, 32–36
President, making of the 68, 104–5, 198, 199, 200
Press agencies 72
 agentry 197, 203
 Association 72
 Australian 49, 65
 British 33, 45–58, 221, 232, 240–3
 Canadian 49, 65
 Chinese 45
 conferences 52, 61, 91, 102, 239
 contacts 4, 51, 68, 91
 cuttings 15, 75, 90, 91, 232, 238
 Dutch 64
 facility visits 53, 92, 123
 French 33, 48, 61, 64, 65
 German 45, 48, 61, 62, 64
 Hungarian 65
 Indian 49–50, 62
 information, sources of 65–66
 international 59–63
 Italian 33, 45, 64, 65
 kits, packs 90–92, 152, 191
 Japanese 58, 65
 Malaysian 49
 Mexican 66
 motoring 221–2, 225–8, 232
 national 47–48, 52, 53, 54, 62
 Nigerian 45, 48, 58, 60, 61, 62, 63
 regional 48, 88
 relations 4, 7, 14, 27, 33, 41, 45–46, 67–93, 221, 225–8, 232, 235, 239, 239–43
 relations, rules of good 68–69
 Russian 45
 Scandinavian 20, 39, 42, 60, 63, 64, 66
 Singapore 49
 Sunday 48, 52, 62, 221, 240
 Swedish 63
 trade, technical, professional 48, 56, 61, 232, 244–5
 venality of 45, 60–61
 women's *see* Women's press
Press Relations Practice 76, 77, 247
Price consciousness 40
Price cutting 25–26
Pricing 21–22, 40

Print Buyer 193
Print for PR
 annual reports 190–1
 calendars 187–9
 diaries 136, 187
 folders, booklets 189–90
 guides 137, 187
 handy aids 190
 house journals 172, 187, 195
 instructions 190
 maps 137
 postage stamps, FDC's 191
 posters 189
 press kits 191
 recipes 190
 sponsored books 136–9
Printing processes 49, 52–53, 187
 glossies 52, 194
 halftone screen 193, 194, 195
 letterpress 52, 71, 192–4
 offset-lithography 52, 72, 108, 191–9
 photogravure 52, 71, 192, 194
 silk screen 192, 196
 stereos, electros 193
 typesetting 192
 web-offset-litho 72, 194, 195, 196
Printing Reproduction Pocket Pal 77, 196
Prizes, TV 108
PRO: basic qualities of 51
Product colours 22–23
Product flavours 23
Product group 19
Product image 19
Product life, life expectancy 39, 40
Product life cycle 17, 18–19, 23
Product name 19–21
Product proliferation 22
Product shelf life 40
Product size 22–23
Promotional PR 6
Propaganda 6, 33, 198, 201
Properties, studio 101, 107
Proprietary medicines 13, 40–41
Public affairs, director viii, 42, 205
Publicity
 free vii
 product viii, 211, 233
 stunts 33, 203

INDEX

Public office, rewards to holders of 252
Public Relations 57, 131, 248
Public relations
 American 33
 budgeting 213–14, 216, 218
 campaign planning 211–19
 community 148–9
 consultant 7, 13, 16, 20, 36, 68, 72, 86, 147, 213, 220–2, 228
 corporate 36–38, 41, 178, 202
 customer 11, 23, 24, 27–29, 32, 137
 dealer 9, 11–12, 23, 35, 41, 108, 129–30, 168
 defined 8, 15, 31, 33
 external affairs 205
 fees, costs 72, 213–14
 financial 36–37, 41
 Institute of *see* Institute of Public Relations
 management function viii, 42, 205
 objectives 15, 88, 211, 215
 public affairs viii, 42, 205
 publics viii, 5, 21, 215–6
 results 15, 211, 219, 251
 six point campaign planning formula 212–13
 tangibility of 15, 88, 211–12
 urban affairs 22–23
Public Relations Consultants Association 72
Public Relations in World Marketing 233
Public Relations Society of America 203
Public service broadcasting 94
Public speaking 235
Publics viii, 5, 21, 215–6
Publishing 49–66
Puerto Rican neighbourhood 223
Puff, puffery, puffing viii, 73
 legitimate 206

Quaker Oats 20
Queen Elizabeth II 96, 125, 195

Racing Information Bureau 142
Radio 60, 72, 94–100, 102–3, 105, 111

 advertising 100, 103
 audiences 103
 BBC Local 72, 99
 BBC External Services 96, 97, 99
 BBC facility unit 102
 Box 103
 Fiftieth Anniversary, BBC 96
 IBA independent local 94, 96, 99, 100, 101, 103
 Luxembourg 95
 overseas 94, 95, 115
 PR material for 102–3
 programmes 97, 99, 102
 White Paper on 100
 World Service 97
Radio Times 195, 234
Rank, Hovis and McDougall 20, 122, 164
Rate card 52
value 4
Razor blades 134
Reader enquiry service 63
Reader's Digest 97, 193
Reader's letters 18
Readership 18, 55, 165, 166–7
 profile 49, 55
 survey 55, 56, 166–7
Reading and noting survey 36
Recommended prices 22
Records, gramophone 22, 146
Recruitment, staff 114, 160
Rediffusion 101, 103
Rentokil Ltd 20, 31, 114, 118, 127, 156, 157–8, 185, 235–8
 film unit 236–7
 Film Report 236
 Library 235–8
Resale price maintenance 22, 40
Ridgway, John 141
Riding for the Gold 234
Right-hand driving 39, 126, 177
Rinso 20
Road Research Laboratory 232
Roberts Construction Group 171
Robertsons jams 122
Roche Products 19
Rodger, Leslie W. 205, 207, 248
Roget's Thesaurus 77
Rolls-Royce 38

268 INDEX

Rome Line, The 229
Roosevelt, Franklin Delano 105
Rosapenna Hotel 225–8
Rosetti, Antonio 188
Rotary Clubs 122
Rothmans of Pall Mall Ltd 137, 141–2
 South Africa 142
 Canada 145, 148
Rothschilds 128
Royal National Lifeboat Institute 116, 118, 123, 148
Royal Opera House 147
Run Away to Sea 123
Russia vii, 45, 95, 239–43

SAAB 141
Safety 102, 231–3
Saint, The 107
Sakura Maru 155
Sales conference 115–16
Sales literature 31
Sales operation 27
Sales promotion 32–6
Sales targets 115
Salesmanship 27, 115, 185, 202, 203
Sample mailings 22
San Francisco Chronicle 48
San Francisco Police Department 115
Sanderson, F. 128
Sandles, Arthur 241
Satisficing 205
Savile, Jimmy 207
Scandinavia 20, 39, 42, 60, 63, 64, 66, 107, 115, 169, 176
Schools 102, 122–3, 189, 235, 237
 one-day 179, 184
Scientex Ltd 20
Sedgwick, A. R. M. 27
Segment, market 21, 23
Self liquidating offers 137
Semantic differential scale 216
Seminars 131, 156, 199, 222
 car parking 181
 date 182
 guest list 180
 hospitality 182–4
 programme 184
 venue 181

Service, after-sales viii, 9, 38–40
Sewing machines 16, 17, 23, 25, 38, 108, 122, 149, 185
Seychelles 108
Shannon Free Airport Development Company 226
Sharpley, Ann 241
Shell 123, 158
Silent film, screen 104, 105, 112
Simca 29
Simon, H. A. 205
Singapore vii, 49
Singer sewing machines 25
Size, product 22–3
Sleeves, photogravure 52
Slogans 31
Smith Internationale 113, 127, 174
Smith & Sons (England) Ltd, S. 20, 21
Smith, Ian 104
Smith, W. H. & Son, Ltd 20, 238–9
Smiths Industries Ltd 20, 22, 158
Smoke Rings 117
Social awareness, social marketing 204–7
Social cost 206
Social grades 21
Soft drinks 22, 23, 26, 196, 206
Soft selling 185
Sony 108, 129
Sophus-Berendsen 236
South Africa 59, 95, 142, 146, 148, 171, 232
Spain 64, 66, 176
Spares 38–39
Spectator Books 136
Sponsored
 art 147–8
 beauty contest 132, 149
 books 136–9, 235–8
 causes, charities 148
 culture 147–8
 drama 147, 151
 education, research 134, 139, 140
 exhibitions 139 *see also* sponsors of
 expeditions, adventures 141
 films 142, 144, 148, 150
 local events 148–9
 music (opera, orchestras, bands, festivals) 146–7, 151, 233

Sponsored—*cont.*
professional awards   150–51
sports
  air racing and flying   133, 144, 150
  athletics   144
  basketball   146
  cricket   134
  curling   143
  cycling   144
  football, Soccer   109, 142
  football, Rugby   141, 144
  golf   109, 112, 122, 133, 143, 144, 151
  horse racing   133, 142, 144
  land speed   134
  motor racing   109, 141, 142
  motor rallying   141
  Olympics   95, 109
  powerboat racing   144
  rally cross   144
  show jumping   133, 135, 223–4
  skiing   143
  snooker   144
  speedway   144
  swimming, life saving   144, 148
  table tennis   144
  tennis   109, 142, 144, 145
  water speed   134
  yacht racing   63, 141, 145–6
TV awards   135
Sponsors
  Advance Electronics   139
  Alcan   143, 151
  Alpine Double Glazing   135
  Ampol Group   134, 140
  Bank of Montreal   143
  Bata Shoes   146
  Benson & Hedges   133
  BOC   140
  Booksellers Association   148
  BP   140
  Castle Beer   142
  Caterer & Hotelkeeper   139
  Champion   145
  Clarks Shoes   146
  Clows Garages   142
  Coca Cola   144
  Daily Mail   133, 138, 139
  Daily Telegraph   133

Daks   143
Do-it-Yourself   139
Dunlop   133, 143
Evening News   141–2
Elna   149
Financial Times   63, 80, 131, 145–6
FMC   138
Ford Motor   142, 146
Gillette   134–5, 145
Goodyear   145
Gulf Oil   145
Guinness   136, 140
Heijn, Albert   138
Hitachi   142
Imperial Tobacco   143–4
John Dewar   145
John Player & Sons   109, 143, 144–5, 147, 234
Joseph Seagram   143–4
Labbatt's   142
Lancome   143
Leica   136
Mackeson's   133
Martini   142–3
Michelin   137
Mitsui   140
Midland Bank   133, 138, 233–4
Norwich Union   144
Pears Soap   136
Peter Jackson   143–4
Philips   149
Piccadilly   137, 143
Pioneer Concrete   134
Prudential Insurance of America   144
Rand Daily Mail   142
Rembrandt Group   148
Rentokil   136
Ronson   136
Rothmans   137, 141, 142, 145, 148
SA Breweries   142
Schweppes   133
Senior Service   143
Shell   137
Smiths   141
SMMT   139
Sun   135
Sunbeam Electric   143
Sunday Times   136
TWA   146

270 INDEX

Sponsors—*cont.*
  United Africa Company 134
  United Tobacco 140, 148
  Whitbread 133, 148, 234
  W. H. & D. O. Wills 144, 145, 146–7, 148, 150, 234
  Yardleys 133, 141, 145, 234
Sponsorship 109, 133–51
Sports arena advertising 109
Staines dishwashers 29, 83
Stalin, Joseph 105
Stansted Airport 220–2
Standard Bank Review 58, 166, 177
Stainberg, Lionel 240
Sterling Products 31
Stockists lists 54–55, 73
Stokes, Lord 28
Store promotion 25
Store status 25
Stork challenge 30
Stork margarine 25
Straits Times 49
Street Banker in Harlem 223
Successful Ex-Narcotics Users 224
Sud-Aviation 114
Sun 46, 56, 221, 241
Sunday Mirror 221
Sunday Times 136, 221, 240, 241–2, 243
Supercalendered 52
Supermarket 26, 36, 138
Swan Vestas 19
Swarfega 19
Sweden, Swedish 20, 39, 42, 60, 64, 91, 142, 155
Swiss Centre 157
Swiss National Tourist Office 220–2
Switzerland 59, 67, 157, 166, 172, 176, 207, 220–2
Sydney Morning Herald 49
Sydney Opera House 134
Symbols 31, 187
Syndication, syndicated articles 48, 62, 88, 89

Tabloid 64
Taiwan 18
Tanaka, Prime Minister 140
Tan-Zam Railway 59, 177
Tanzania vii, 37, 59, 95, 108
Tanzania Radio 59
Tea 18, 111
Teamster 231
Teamsters Union 231
Teasers 162
Television
  Act, 1955 101
  advertising 94, 95, 96, 100, 101, 151, 207
  air time 95, 96, 101, 123
  audience figures 212
  BBC 99, 101, 103, 108, 109, 221, 232
  cable 100–1
  CBS-TV 115
  closed circuit 94
  colour 96, 117, 159
  commercial 26, 31, 94, 108–9, 159
  community 101
  films, clips, on 95, 102, 108–9, 236
  give-away prizes, shows 108
  history of 96, 159
  IBA 94, 95, 99–100
  interviews 103–4, 106
  ITN 99–100
  ITV companies 94, 99, 100, 221
  library shots 101, 107, 108
  licensed operators 94
  making of the President 68, 104–5, 198, 199, 200
  News at Ten 100, 139
  news readers 119
  overseas 94–95
  politicians 104–5
  prerecorded casettes 129–31
  presenters 3, 207
  PR material for 101–2, 236
  programme staff 33
  programmes, series 106, 123, 241
  sponsored 94, 95
  telecine 119
  Telmar Programme Service 130
  test card films
Tesco Stores 25
Test marketing 6, 16, 26–27
Third World 58, 122, 126, 175, 177–8, 201
Thomson Holidays 239–43

Thoresen car ferry   155
Tide   20
Tide of Traffic   115
Timber preservation   235–8
Times of India   49
Times Educational Supplement   122
Times, The   36, 46, 82, 142, 221, 234
Timing, news releases   52–53
Titlis   222
Today   102
Togo   vii
Toiletries   27, 133, 134, 145
Tomorrow's World   123, 232
Toronto Globe and Mail   49
Tourism   11, 12, 32, 88, 108, 112, 122, 123, 157, 158, 198, 199, 222, 239–43
Townswomen's Guilds   122
Toyota   29, 39, 166, 173, 177, 220–2
Trade and Industry, Department of   vii, 152, 182, 236
Trade Descriptions Act, 1968–72   10, 12, 31
Trade
  dealer, distributor relations   9, 11–12, 23, 27–29, 35, 41, 108, 129–30, 168
  technical, professional press   48, 56, 61, 232, 244–5
Trading stamp operators   26
Traffic management   64
Translations   79, 89, 124, 191–2
Transmeridian Air Cargo   230
Transport and General Workers Union   232
Transworld Airlines   107
Travel agents   11, 198, 225
  trade press   243
Traveler's Insurance Companies   168
Tree Top soft drinks   23
Trevino, Lee   143
Trierische Landeszeitung   48
Tube Investments   31
Tug services   113, 127
TV Times   25, 195
Tye, James   231, 233
Typography   31, 187

UK Press Gazette   243, 248
Underlining   69, 73

Undisclosed interests   250
Unique selling proposition   198, 201
Unit sizes   22
Unit trust   36
United Africa Company, UAC   38, 134, 177
United Glass   166, 243–6
United States Trade Centres   157
Universal News Service   72
Universities
  American   140, 197
  Australian National   140
  Birmingham   139
  Heriot-Watt   205
  Ibadan   134
  Kejo   140
  Lagos   38
  libraries   173
  Mitsui   140
  Northwestern   197
  Open   106
  social marketing   207
  support from sponsors   149
Unsubstantiated claims   77
Upper Volta   vii
Urban affairs   223–5
USA   3, 7, 25, 26, 33, 37, 45, 47, 48, 60, 61, 62, 64, 65, 68, 94, 101, 106, 115, 127, 134, 137, 139, 140, 143, 144, 146, 157, 158, 168, 169, 172, 181, 194, 196, 197, 198, 203, 204, 223–5, 238, 244–5

Valium   19
Van den Berghs   30
VAT   22
Venice International Industrial Film Festival   121
Vickers-Crabtree   119
Video tape   116, 120, 121, 128, 154
  Cartrivision   129
  cassette recorder (VCR)   129
  disc   128, 131
  Philips VCR   129, 130
  Philips video disc   131
  prerecorded material   129–30
  RCA Magtape   129
  recorder, electronic (EVR)   129

Video tape—*cont.*
  Telefunken-Decca (TED) 131
  Telmar Programme Service 130
  Telscan Television Inv. 131
Voice of Kenya Radio/TV 94, 95
Volkswagen 25, 149
  Beetle 30
Voluntary group system 42
Volvo 20, 42, 107, 108

Walker, Peter vii
Wanamaker, Sam 147
Warburgs 128
Warnes, Martin 198
Washington Post 48, 238
Watches 22, 109, 141
Watts, Reginald 248
Weekend colour magazines, supplements 18, 50, 145, 194, 235
West Africa 58
Westphal, W. H. 236
Which magazine 9, 30
White, Sally 142
Whitewashing 6
Why Not Uncle Willy? 120–1, 123, 233
Wild Life Trust 148
Willings Press Guide 65
Wills Embassy Series 146
Wills, Gordon 248
Wills, W. D. & H. O. 116, 123, 124, 150
Wilson, Harold 101

Win-a-Pony competition 239
Wining and dining 3, 6, 68, 91
Winkler Marketing Communication Ltd 14, 166, 228
Winner Marketing Communications Ltd, Paul 14
Wolgensinger, J. 228
Woman 55, 194, 195
Woman's Day 50
Woman's Hour 102
Woman's Own 195
Woman's Realm 19, 21
Woman's Weekly 50
Women's Institutes 122, 235
Women's Lib 201
Women's press 18, 19, 21, 50, 52, 55, 61, 102, 195, 238–9
Woodworm and Dry Rot Centres 157
Woodworm Problem, The 235
Worker participation 30
World PR Congress, 1973 67
Worldwide Export Publicity 98
Wyatt, Woodrow 196

York Trailers 231
You and Yours 102
Young Farmers Clubs 122
Young Scientists and Inventors Contest 160

Zambia 177